MUSIC MATTERS

The Performer and the American Federation of Musicians

by
GEORGE SELTZER

The Scarecrow Press, Inc.
Metuchen, N.J., & London
1989

British Library Cataloguing-in-Publication data available

Library of Congress Cataloging-in-Publication Data

Seltzer, George, 1924–
    Music matters.

        Bibliography: p.
        Includes index.
        1. American Federation of Musicians.   2. Trade-
    unions—Musicians—United States.   3. Music—Eco-
    nomic aspects—United States.   I. Title.
    ML3795.S36   1989   331.88′1178   88-33671
    ISBN 0-8108-2176-1

For my mother, Rose,
    my wife, Millie, and
        our children (in alphabetical order)
            Jay, Judy, Lisa, Rob, and Sarah

Contents

Preface

THIS PROJECT DID NOT begin as a labor of love. It began as a labor of curiosity. As a performing musician, I have been interested for many years in the multiple relationships that exist among the individual performer, the American Federation of Musicians, and the profession itself. In this highly diversified field of endeavor, has the AFM been of value to the musician? What is its potential to serve musicians in the future? What has the profession been like, and what are its prospects in the twenty-first century? What has been the professional life of the performer and what is it likely to be?

The largest of entertainment unions, the American Federation of Musicians is a unique organization. It represents the incorporated studio musician and the drummer who plays the VFW hall Saturday nights, the New York Philharmonic soloist and the clarinetist in a Southern municipal band, the second trumpet player in a pit orchestra for a Broadway musical and the combo playing for a wedding reception in St. Louis, the touring Country and Western star and a violist in the Denver Symphony.

By following the development of the Federation from its beginnings in the nineteenth century, it is possible to view in a new way the inseparable development of musical performance and performers in the United States and Canada. Of special interest is the dichotomy between music as an art and as a business as well as the treatment of minorities and women, the American Symphony Orchestra League, music education in public schools and the university, and the specific threat and challenge of automation.

This project owes a debt to an earlier, more narrowly focused, history of the AFM, *The Musicians and Petrillo* by Robert D. Leiter (1953), and unpublished research by Guy A. Scola, a former Federation staff employee.

Another debt is owed to the many individuals—national leaders of the AFM, local officials, union and non-union performers from all strata of the profession, booking agents, orchestra managers and other purchasers of music—who agreed to be interviewed. Since the great majority desired anonymity, I have identified no one except International President Emeritus James C. Petrillo and then International President Victor W. Fuentealba, who specifically agreed to be quoted.

My early investigations of this topic were also aided by a research leave granted in 1984 by Miami University. This enabled me to attend local, regional and national/international AFM meetings. It also allowed me to visit libraries in various parts of the country and the international headquarters of the Federation in New York and provided the opportunity to conduct interviews.

Because, in many cases, Federation documents (both at the national and local levels) are incomplete, I am very grateful for the insightful comments freely given over many months by my knowledgeable friend Eugene V. Frey, member of the AFM International Executive Board and President of Local 1 in Cincinnati.

Dick Roberts and Rita Line, respectively president and secretary of Local 31, Hamilton, Ohio, also graciously shared their knowledge and experience both as performers and as Local union officers. Additionally, I am indebted to the many dedicated, helpful, courteous professionals who staff the libraries of Miami University. They made my task a pleasure. Special thanks for special favors also are due to Sarah Barr, Karen Clift, Annemarie Woletz Franco, Jon Hendricks, Janice McLaughlin, Ruth Miller, and Mary Sohngen. And, of course, these words would have never reached the publisher without the word-processing skills and knowledge of Joan G. McLaughlin, who has earned my profound thanks.

GEORGE SELTZER
Oxford, Ohio
August 1987

Chapter I
Roots: The Beginnings of Unions
of Performers in the U.S. and Canada—
Affiliation with the American
Federation of Labor

THE PRECARIOUS ECONOMIC plight of performing musicians on this continent has been documented
repeatedly since the mid-eighteenth century. In writing
about the musicians of the colonial era, Gilbert Chase says,
"Few of them could earn a living solely by music, even with
dancing and fencing as more remunerative sidelines. Some
of them were obliged to become Jack-of-all-trades."[1]
"Music meant nothing to the majority of people unless it
combined a freak stunt."[2]

Even more indicative of social (and economic) status is
a letter written by Thomas Jefferson in 1778 to a friend in
France. He inquired about retaining a gardener, a weaver,
a cabinetmaker and a stone cutter who could also perform
on the French horn, clarinet, oboe, and bassoon.[3] These
same comments could as easily have been made by any
member of the landed gentry in England, Germany or
Austria. Clearly, the "Age of Patronage" existed both in
Europe and in the New World.

The Jack-of-all-trades musician, when he functioned
at all, was a part-time violinist and shoemaker, or a
clarinetist/carpenter, or a drummer/salesclerk—an occu-
pation pattern still dominant today.

The Jefferson era denied social prestige and eco-

1

nomic reward to the performing musician. Nor was this a propitious time for the development of labor unions. In 1806, unions were judged criminal conspiracies,[4] and one judge said "united action by skilled artisans ... is 'pregnant with public mischief and private injury'...."[5] The so-called mutual aid societies of the time appeared to be less concerned with setting wages and enforcing a closed shop than "... with providing death benefits, assisting members who were ill or unemployed, offering loans and credits, maintaining libraries, perpetuating high standards of craftsmanship and settling disputes among members."[6]

One solution to the musicians' economic difficulties led to the founding of the New York Philharmonic as a cooperative venture in 1842. This endeavor entailed mutual responsibility for all management funtions including choosing personnel, engaging conductors and soloists, and setting programs.[7] At best, this was still part-time work. Between Philharmonic performances, those musicians who could played at dances, parties, parades, and whatever else was available. Some occupied themselves with other trades and played not at all between orchestra commitments. By necessity, employment and earning a living came before artistic performance.

Musicians' "unions" reported in both Baltimore and Chicago as early as 1857[8] were probably akin to the mutual aid societies. And before that, there were the Musical Fund Society of Philadelphia and the American Musical Fund Society founded respectively in 1820 and 1849.[9] Not until 1860[10] do we find an organization of musicians "that could legitimately be classified a trade union"[11]—the Aschenbroedel Club of New York City. This club's membership at first was limited to those who spoke German,[12] a solid indication of the ethnic origins of the founders of this and other societies in St. Louis and Cincinnati. By 1864 (the year of its incorporation in New York State) it defined its purposes to be "... the cultivation of the art of music in all its branches, and the promotion of good feeling and friendly intercourse among the members of the profession, and relief of such of their members as shall be unfortunate...."[13]

The Aschenbroedel Club—now renamed the Musical Mutual Protective Union—soon discovered that social accord was not enough. An 1878 amendment to its charter provided for the fixing of uniform rates and the ability to enforce compliance by fines or expulsion from the Union. Two years before the mandatory minimum scales were set, H. W. Schwartz reports there were several fees: "... first class ball, $9.00; ordinary ball, $7.00; regimental parade, $7.00; company parade, $6.00; concert, $7.00. On holidays musicians received $2.00 extra. The leader always received double the musician fee."[14]

Following the example in New York, St. Louis formed its own Aschenbroedel Club in 1864 which became the St. Louis Musicians' Mutual Benefit Association in 1865.[15] Other mutual benefit organizations of musicians with similar objectives appeared in the East and Midwest at about this time. In 1871, the Philadelphia Musical Association (which began in 1863) attempted to bring several local groups together as the Musicians' National Protective Association. Although it lasted less than a decade, it was the first effort towards national affiliation.[16]

By the 1880s, small towns as well as large cities had their own local musicians' organization. Under a variety of different names (for instance, The Stove Moulders' Musical Union was formed in 1896 in Joliet, Illinois [17]), the local societies attempted to provide a fraternal framework with mutual aids and a fund for death benefits. They also had a scale of minimum prices and a code which forbade members to play with nonmembers.

The Cincinnati Musicians' Protective Union was founded in 1881 by a group of about fifty musicians. Their Constitution and Price List (printed in both English and German) proclaimed, "The object of this Union is to unite the Instrumental portion of the Profession of Music, the elevation of the social standing of its members as musicians, the regulated prices, below which it shall not permit performance; To tender pecuniary aid, irrespective of cause of death, to the family or relatives of deceased members and the promotion of the best interests of members of the Association generally."[18] Many years later, the Cincinnati Local (Number 1, AFM) periodical, *Overtones*, concluded, "The normal $165.00 death benefit, financed by means of a 50 cent per member assessment, ... was an attractive inducement for obtaining members."[19]

The 1885 price list in Cincinnati included: Operas, 6 performances and one matinee weekly, $35.00; Theatres, 6 evening performances and one matinee weekly, $14.00; German theatres, each performance with one rehearsal, $3.00 (without rehearsal, $2.50); First Class Balls, $5.00; Ordinary Balls, $4.00; Parades in city until 12 PM, $8.00; Parades until 7 PM, $6.00; and other job description and prices continuing for nine pages.

Portsmouth, Ohio, is typical of the many small towns whose band was the nucleus of the musicians' union. The Preamble to the Constitution and By-Laws of the Portsmouth Brass and Reed Band (dated January 1, 1886) reads: "This organization shall be known as the Portsmouth Brass and Reed Band. The object of the same shall be to cultivate a good musical taste. Also to furnish suitable music for Parades, Processions and other occasions that are suitable for Brass and Reed Music." The original initiation fee was one dollar and the dues were 50 cents per month. To no one's surprise, the leader of the band was also the president of the organization. Still earlier—in 1877—Professor Jacob Breinig and his Ringgold Band of

Terre Haute, Indiana, were instrumental in beginning a musicians' union in that city.[20]

The growth of independent local unions focused attention on competition between local musicians and musicians from adjacent cities and traveling road shows. Local unions also faced the common problems of competition from military bands and the importation of foreign musicians. To combat these difficulties, Charles M. Currier, president of the Cincinnati union, advocated the formation of another national organization. Currier's objectives were to centralize legislative power and secure congressional action to prevent competition from military bands and foreign contract labor. Another goal was "... the protection of musicians against dishonest, unscrupulous, impecunious operatic and theatrical landsharks and managerial swordfishes of concert companies."[21] In December 1885, after approval by the Cincinnati musicians, this call for national unity was circulated to many other unions in larger cities.[22]

As a result, in March 1886, fifteen delegates from musical societies in New York, Boston, Philadelphia, Cincinnati, Chicago, Detroit, and Milwaukee met in New York to form The National League of Musicians of the United States.[23] Currier was elected president of the new organization—a position he held through its first three years.

In common with other national leaders who followed him, Currier had an active, varied and well-traveled career as a performing musician. He was musical director of a minstrel show in New Orleans, a member of the famous Gilmore Band in Boston, and conductor of the Lowell, Massachusetts, Brigade Band and the Haydn Choral and Orchestral Society. In 1863, he moved to Cincinnati and led Currier's Suberb Band, achieving "notoriety" in that city and in New Orleans. 1887 found him in Chicago where he concluded his performing career as conductor of the First Regiment Band, Illinois National Guard.[24]

The NLM grew rapidly, and by 1896 there were 101 affiliated locals throughout the country.[25] The League did make complaints to the immigration authorities about the importation of foreign musicians[26] and to the War and Navy Departments about competition from military bands. In 1887, its convention also appointed (and funded) a committee to lobby Congress for legislation prohibiting competition from military bands and unfair importation of contract labor and foreign bands. The committee had some success. The House of Representatives passed legislation restricting military bands from competing for civilian jobs, and there were further assurances of favorable consideration for changes in the alien labor law. Unfortunately, the committee's funding was depleted before their job was completed. The locals refused to unanimously continue support, and partial success became failure.[27]

Because "... it had no power to prescribe rules binding upon the locals, and they retained complete authority to ... enforce their own policies on membership, prices [and] benefit plans...,"[28] the League was doomed. This strong emphasis on local autonomy also made transfer of membership difficult and forced hardship on traveling bands. Attempts by individual unions to limit the job market exclusively to their own members did not work. Good musicians were employable beyond the jurisdiction of their home local, and the jobs they accepted away from home undermined the integrity of the NLM.

But the greatest problem the League faced was that of identity. Were the musicians who composed the organization artists or laborers? A resolution published after the founding convention in 1886 recommended "... a rigid examination of applicants for membership ... [to prevent] imposters and impecunious musical quacks from practicing their knavish arts and infirm capacity in public...."[29]

This strong statement on the side of an "organization of artists" excluded many supposedly less skilled players who became rivals in the job market at a cut wage. Obviously, the resolution was not favored by all locals.

Both the Knights of Labor (founded in Philadelphia in 1869) and the American Federation of Labor (founded in Columbus in 1886) invited affiliation beginning in 1887 and were regularly denied at annual conventions of the League. Generally, the eastern locals believed their members were artists and avoided identification as laborers. The midwestern and western locals argued that "an organization that funtioned like a trade union, was a trade union."[30] And the disagreement became more pronounced and divisive through the years. During the 1891 convention in Milwaukee, William Wolsieffer (or Wolseifer) from Philadelphia, the League's president, reported that "... those for and against [affiliation with the AFL] appear to be about evenly divided...."[31] But it was Mr. Wolseifer who ruled out-of-order a motion for AFL affiliation because of conflict with NLM standing resolution 8 which said, "... this League cannot become subordinate to any other, or join any organization wherein it might become so subordinate." The argument that affiliation would create an equal alliance with the AFL was in vain.[32]

Confronted by continual rejections, both the Knights of Labor and the American Federation of Labor organized their own competing locals throughout the country and "by 1896 there were over 15 musicians' unions in New York City alone."[33] As early as 1892, the *Musical Courier* reported that "Members of the Musical Mutual Protective Union [New York] have been complaining for a long time that leaders in certain theatres did not pay the union price— $2.50 for each performance, with the exception of operas and operettas which command $3.00 a performance."[34] Clearly, competition between unions had its effect.

This calamitous situation caused Alexander Bremer, the League's president in 1896, to send letters to both the president of the AFL and the Master Workman of the Knights of Labor, protesting "... against the continued practice of your organization issuing charters to so-called Musicians Unions and Assemblies not affiliated with the National League of Musicians."[35] It was to no avail.

Finally, after the 1896 Convention of the NLM failed to resolve the conflict, a post-convention meeting of those delegates approving affiliation formed a temporary organization (i.e., The Federation of Musicians of America), which sent a committee of three—H. D. Beissenherz, C. F. Hahn and Otto Ostendorf—to Indianapolis to request a national charter from the Executive Council of the AFL and its president, Samuel Gompers.

Gompers' response was favorable. He said, "It is understood that all musicians' unions now affiliated with the AF of L shall be granted charters by and attached to the Federation of Musicians. That where more than one local union of musicians exist, an amalgamation upon a fair basis shall be secured. That this office, with your cooperation, shall call the convention for the formation of the Federation of Musicians of the United States or the said organization though it may select another name."[36]

On October 19, 1896, the American Federation of Labor invited all musical societies to meet in Indianapolis in Parlor 36 of the Hotel English. Thirty-one musicians representing twenty-one locals and a representative of the National League of Musicians attended.[37] Once the Executive Council of the American Federation of Labor confirmed that affiliated national organizations are guaranteed autonomy in controlling membership, the American Federation of Musicians was formed, representing approximately 3,000 musicians nationally. (Although 4,000 musicians were originally represented, delegates from Chicago, Louisville, Toledo, and Cripple Creek, Colorado, withdrew.[38]) Their "... premise was that 'all men and women playing musical instruments and receiving pay therefore from the public must, in order to get just wages and decent working conditions, form a labor organization'."[39] Owen Miller, a leader of the faction urging affiliation and a former president of the National League of Musicians, was elected the first president of the new organization.

As early as 1885, Miller had helped form the first St. Louis musicians' union and had been active in Missouri state politics. He served as president of the AFM until 1900, when he decided to assume the office of AFM secretary and editor of the Federation's new monthly magazine, *The International Musician*. Financial considerations undoubtedly played a part in his decision—the position of secretary paid $750 annually, compared to the yearly salary of $100 for president.[40]

The National League of Musicians reacted to the formation of the new organization by attempting to expel all locals that joined the AFM.[41] This action proved to be disastrous. Within five months, 48 of their 101 locals joined the new federation, and by 1902 only three locals were left to represent the League. In 1903, these locals joined the AFM. The New York local, The Musicians' Mutual Protective Union representing approximately 4,000 musicians, became Local 310 after assurances of some autonomy. The League's organizations in Philadelphia and Baltimore became locals in the AFM later the same year.

The demise of the National League of Musicians and the ascendancy of the American Federation of Musicians apparently held no immediate financial advantage—at least for members of the New York local. Their 1904 *Price List* called for: "Balls at all Theaters or Opera Houses ... $8.00. Private balls were worth $7.00. Circuses, Menageries, Museums, Riding Academies, Skating Rinks, etc. for 6 evening performances a week, $15.00. Symphony musicians for 6 concerts a week, $36.00 plus rehearsal fees".[42] Compared to the price list of 1876 in New York (given earlier in this chapter), musicians' fees remained the same or decreased slightly over the intervening 28 years.

With the beginning of the twentieth century, the American Federation of Musicians assumed its international character with the addition of Canadian musicians. In 1897 the AFM invited the Montreal Musicians' Protective Union and the Toronto Orchestral Association to join. The Montreal musicians joined immediately as Local 62 but survived only a few short years.[43] (Today's Musicians' Guild of Montreal, Local 406, was chartered in 1905.) In 1901, the invitation to Toronto was accepted and a charter was issued. Apparently, working conditions for musicians were not better north of the border. A contract for the Summer Opera Season on Toronto Island in 1888 called for "... nine performances per week—$12.00".[44]

By the first decade of the twentieth century, the economic status of individual musicians was not noticeably enhanced, but the organizational skills of the AFM were evident. Writing in 1906, Commons says "... the new organization has 424 locals and 45,000 members. It has brought in practically all instrumental musicians in the United States and Canada who play for a living, either as leaders or as members of orchestras and bands, including all traveling musicians...."[45]

Chapter II
The Pre-Petrillo Years—The Presidency
of Joseph N. Weber

T HE STRONG DESIRE FOR communication among the
musicians of the semi-isolated locals of the new AFM
was readily apparent. This compulsion to share common
aspirations and problems, this need to belong to a larger
community, was realized with the publication of a monthly
magazine under contract to the Federation.
The *American Musician*, privately owned, was published in Cincinnati by editor-publisher Stephen S.
Bonbright,[1] a member of local 31 in Hamilton, Ohio. Its
associate editors included Owen Miller and Jacob J.
Schmalz (respectively president and secretary of the AFM)
as well as other Federation officers. The periodical's first
issue was February 1897— less than four months after the
founding of the union. It stated its function as the "official
organ of the American Federation of Musicians" and
promised to publish all the official news of the union but
would "… not allow its columns to be degraded by purely
sensational matter. No serials, continued stories or long-
winded articles printed."[2] Each local received a free copy,
and other organizations and individuals could subscribe
for fifty cents annually.
These close ties between the hierarchy of the AFM and
American Musician continued until Owen Miller decided to
exchange his job as president of the Federation for the
position of secretary. Because Bonbright and the new AFM

president, Joseph N. Weber, were political opponents, it was clear that the offical status of *American Musician* would not long continue. And, in fact, within a year, the new administration suspended the publication and expelled the editor from the union.[3]

The *American Musician* was succeeded by the *International Musician*, a monthly periodical owned and operated by the AFM. It has been published continuously since July 1901, and its first editor was the Federation's secretary, Owen Miller. Like the *American Musician*, the *International Musician* publishes all the official news of the Federation including minutes of the Executive Board meetings, proceedings of the conventions, and statements of the president and other national officers. Other news of interest includes articles of educational and political significance, advertisements for job vacancies, lists of employers who have defaulted in their union obligations, lists of contracted booking agencies, information about national contracts, and so forth. Each Federation member pays for an individual subscription as part of his or her annual dues.

Who were these musicians who worked with Owen Miller in the beginnings of the Federation and were important in its transition to the administration of Joseph N. Weber? Of the many active musician/union leaders, a few influenced the changing times more than others.

George Nachman, the first First Vice President of the AFM, was important because of his abilities, experience— and because he represented Baltimore in the stronghold of the National League of Musicians. Born and trained in Germany, he emigrated to Baltimore and immediately began his new world professional career in the Front Street Theater. He then traveled the country with minstrel and opera companies before returning to his home city and the Odeon Theater. Once back in Baltimore, he held the

Odeon Theater position for twenty-six years. Now, as a local musician, Nachman became a charter member of Local 17 of the NLM and eventually assumed various national offices in that organization. He fought hard for the establishment of the new Federation and in 1896 brought part of the NLM Baltimore local into the AFM. In 1897, he assumed his national office with the Federation.[4]

Christian Ahbe, the first Second Vice President of the AFM, was also born in Germany. He received expert training first as a violinist and then as a cornetist. But in his fifteenth year, "... being a practical boy and seeing that there was not much money in music, he decided to learn a profession...."[5] For better or worse, the study of surgery lost out to the study of music, and Ahbe left Germany for the United States in 1866. He became a member of Voss' First Regiment Band in Newark, New Jersey, as first cornetist—a position he held for almost twenty-five years. He was also an officer of the Musicians' Mutual Protective Union in that city since its formation and was instrumental in bringing that local into the AFM. As one of the associate editors of the *American Musician*, Ahbe was influential in forming national policy and bringing NLM members into the new Federation.[6]

Charles F. Hahn, an early vice president, was born in Indianapolis where he started his performing career. By 1885 he had moved to Chicago via St. Louis. And it was in Chicago that Hahn began his union career. In 1892, he was elected President of the Chicago Musical Society, representing his local in the NLM during the years of controversy about joining the American Federation of Labor. He brought his Chicago Musical Society into the AFM and into the Chicago Federation of Labor. (Hahn then became a vice president of the AFM and continued his influence under both Miller and Weber.[7])

Jacob J. Schmalz, the first Secretary of the AFM, was

born in Switzerland. He emigrated in 1870 and settled in Cincinnati. As one of the founders of the National League of Musicians, he held national offices in that organization and, in Cincinnati, he was a recognized performer and composer as well as Corresponding and Recording Secretary of the Cincinnati Musicians' Protective Association. In his capacity as an officer in both the NLM and the Cincinnati Union, his actions were important in the movement to form the AFM. Schmalz was well known and respected by his musician peers; his election to Federation national office was easily achieved.[8]

Joseph N. Weber, who became International President of the AFM in 1900, served the Federation in that office until 1940.[9] Like Owen Miller and other musician/politicians, Weber was a performing musician before becoming a union official. In 1890, after playing in many different areas, he formed a union in Denver and attended a National League of Musicians' convention as a delegate. He later continued his travels, becoming vice president of the local in San Francisco and eventually president of the Cincinnati Musicians' Protective Union, where he worked with Jacob Schmalz. In 1899, he was a delegate to the AFM convention and a year later became its International President.

During his tenure, the Federation became a strongly integrated national and international organization with representation in nearly every city in the United States and Canada. Dual unionism virtually had disappeared, and the AFM grew to be the largest union of performers in the world.[10]

This substantial growth of the Federation probably was achieved by successful compromises, skillful organizers, and less than ideal working conditions. But its appeal to many musicians also stemmed from the fraternal qualities emphasized by the tenets of the old mutual aid societies: do not play with non-members or defaulters; do not play for free or for less than scale wages; try to solve problems within the organization.[11]

In 1896, however, musicians who founded the American Federation of Musicians inherited more than fraternal ideals. Two major problems faced by the National League of Musicians—competition from both foreign musicians and military bands of the armed forces—were also part of the legacy.

Mueller says, "The greatest source of competition for orchestra jobs in our undeveloped country up to the time of the first World War were ... players from Germany... France and other European countries."[12] Examples of foreign player importation for orchestras in the United States probably go back to the St. Cecilia Society in Charleston in 1762.[13] But the second half of the nineteenth century brought imported musicians from Europe into direct competition with established players in this country. One of the earliest examples involved the New York orchestra of Theodore Thomas in 1885. The Belgian oboist whom Thomas wanted became a member of the orchestra over the protests of the New York local. Although the union continued its objections over the years, many other players and organizations continued to be imported. Finally, in 1893, Alexander Bremer (president of the Musical Mutual Protective Union in New York) wrote to President Cleveland "on behalf of the musical profession of America" protesting the importation of full orchestras and bands.[14] He did not receive an encouraging response.

The National League of Musicians' protest against Walter Damrosch's importation of a Danish cellist (Anton Hegner) in the same year had more substantial results.

When Hegner appeared on stage, the orchestra refused to perform—probably the first strike by an American orchestra.[15] The conductor was fined, and this helped establish the integrity of the NLM.[16]

The *Musical Courier*[17] reported that when Damrosch appeared before the union to protest the fine, he was met with sufficient hostility to cause his resignation. One member said, "Art be damned, we are playing for money." The *Courier* concluded that "the musician is practicing his profession for the purpose of earning a livelihood," and that if there are duties levied upon goods manufactured in Europe to protect "Mr. Carnegie," then there should be no objections to similar restrictions on imported musicians.

Damrosch then challenged the importation restrictions of the "new" AFM in 1905 and was fined again. This time the charge was that Damrosch had imported five French musicians without advertising for American musicians. Although the conductor's defense was heard by the AFM convention, his $1,000 fine was sustained.[18]

Of much greater concern to the majority of AFM members were the tours of European bands that "descended upon the American scene like an invasion of locusts."[19] American booking agencies enjoyed sponsoring these bands because they were less expensive to hire than American organizations and were attractive to the public. But once in this country, many of these foreign players left their organizations and competed for jobs in American cities.

The AFM sought protection under the Alien Contract Labor Law of 1885 but was continually unsuccessful (as was the NLM earlier) because of the "exception for artists."[20] Even in 1927, President Weber's complaint to the U.S. Department of Labor about the full orchestra imported by the Carlton Hotel in Washington was denied.[21] Because the AFM argument that performing musicians were laborers (rather than artists) was not convincing, other defenses had to be found.

As early as 1882, the New York union (then the Musical Mutual Protective Union) required that foreigners must reside in this country at least six months before becoming eligible for membership.[22] This six-month rule, combined with a prohibition "... to accept as a member a musician who was imported ... by an agent, musical director or employer ... "[23] by the AFM, were the only controls available until fifty years later, when Congress responded to union pressure[24] and bleak depression employment prospects. The Congressional revisions of 1932 more narrowly defined an alien musical "artist," effectively meeting the Federation's criteria for more equitable employment practice.

Competition from military bands was the second major problem common to both the NLM and the AFM. Although the *American Musician* cites a Letter Carriers Band of San Francisco that was encouraged to compete with civilian musicians in 1897[25] and Leiter reports another U. S. Post Office Band that received a city contract for park concerts in 1915 in Omaha[26] and the *Official Proceedings of the Ohio, Kentucky, West Virginia Musicians' Association* (1934)[27] contains six resolutions aimed at the continuing unfair competition from school bands, the AFM considered the threat of military bands most damaging.

The musicians of the Federation believed that military personnel who were fed, clothed, housed, and paid by the government should not be allowed to compete for civilian musical jobs—either as military units or as individuals. A letter from the AFM Executive Board to Secretary of War Russell A. Alger expressed the union's view in very few words. The letter, written in March 1897, said, "... We hold that it is not part of the function of government to allow its enlisted men to enter the field of labor of any character in competition for a livelihood with tax-paying civilians...."[28] The response from Washington merely reiterated the government's position since 1885, which said in part, "... Regimental and other bands and the musicians composing the same may, with the consent of the proper military authority, engage to play for other parties at prices not disproportionately lower than the prices charged by other bands or musicians for similar services...."[29] A 1909 request to President Theodore Roosevelt to restrain the Marine Band from competing with civilian musicians also met with official indifference.[30] Finally, when it became apparent that complaints to the Federal Government were ineffective, the union forbade its members to perform functions with military bands or to play with individual military personnel.[31]

While these prohibitions were in effect, the AFM continued its efforts for legislative change. Eventually, in 1916, the Congress gave specific instructions for both military personnel and military bands to avoid competition with civilian musicians.[32]

There were no substantial complaints from the Federation on this topic through 1945. It was common practice during World War II for the service bands stationed in Washington to broadcast weekly over national radio networks. It was also customary for individual servicemen to play weekend "gigs" (frequently with AFM members) in U.S. and Canadian cities close to military bases during the war years.

For the next fifteen years, the competition from military bands and military personnel for civilian jobs in music continued while the AFM gradually increased its opposition. In 1953, James C. Petrillo, then International President, complained to the Pentagon about the 187

service bands (five in Washington alone) and suggested
they "... cut the thing down to a hundred...."[33]

The Department of Defense ultimately reacted to
numerous expressions of dissatisfaction in 1961: "No enlisted member of the D.O.D. on active duty may be ordered
or permitted to leave his post to engage in a civilian
pursuit or business, or a performance in civil life, for
emolument, hire, or otherwise, if the pursuit, business or
performance interferes with the customary or regular
employment of local civilians in their art, trade or profession."[34] Today there is minimal competition from military
bands with civilian organizations and, except for those few
cities close to large military installations, the individual
serviceman-musician does not greatly disturb the music
job market. To help erase this small threat of non-union
competition, the 1978 AFM Convention allowed service
personnel to become Federation members.

The competition for civilian jobs in music in Canada
was never as severe as in the United States. Canadian
military personnel have been members of the union since
1961 and are expected to be part of the job market when
official duties do not conflict.

A glaring weakness in the loose confederation of
unions that formed the National League of Musicians was
the autonomy allowed individual locals to set membership
qualifications. Each union tried to save the job market for
its own members and did not welcome musicians from
other localities. On the other hand, the NLM member
arriving in a new city was not readily inclined to pay
initiation charges and dues in both new and old locals—
especially since his travels might continue.

The AFM's plan to solve this difficulty was a compromise between local and national authority. In 1902, rules
were formulated allowing an AFM member to apply for a

"transfer card" in another local, pay only current quarterly dues, accept a limited performance status, and be eligible for full membership in the new local in six months.[35]

The "transfer system"—an adaptation of the 1882 New York local's six-month rule for making foreigners eligible for membership—was one of the principal mechanisms for the rapid increase in numbers of Federation locals and members in the first decade of the century. It encouraged "… thousands of traveling musicians, who had remained outside the Federation as long as it confined its benefits to those seeking a livelihood within their own jurisdictions …"[36] to join the union. It also partially reassured locals that there would be some protection for the "home town boys".

By the 1920s, however, it became clear to most locals that they needed still more job protection—this time from traveling bands. The first protectionist move approved by the AFM convention was a thirty-percent surcharge above local wage scales to be charged by all traveling bands. This surcharge was deposited with the local and returned to the musicians when the gig was completed. Because there were faults in this system—somehow many promoters and agents managed to keep for themselves the surcharge, and neither the player, the local, nor the Federation retained any monies—the 1934 AFM Convention made some changes.

The 1934 changes included a reduction of the thirty-percent surcharge to a ten-percent surcharge/dues to be divided among the International, the local, and the traveling musician. At first the dues allocation was four percent to the local, three percent to the national, and three percent to be returned to the musician at the conclusion of the engagement.[37] Later the division became four percent, four percent, and two percent, respectively.[38]

This new way of raising money not only allowed local

talent to "play for less" but also enriched the national and local treasuries, all at the expense of the traveling musician. The inequities were great. While the system allowed some locals to keep their own dues structures unrealistically low and the national offices depended inordinately on this tax source, the traveling musician continued to be mistreated and to complain. The abuse of the surcharge/dues "money machine" (in 1963, this "tax" produced approximately sixty-three percent of all revenues collected nationally[39]) continued until change was inevitable after passage of the Taft-Hartley Act.

The continuing disagreement between those who felt the AFM represented musical "artists" and the trade unionists who wanted to include all working musicians in the job market is evident in the solution to the problem of entrance auditions versus open membership for all who "play for pay." As was common practice in the old NLM, attempts to set musical standards for applicants for membership can be used to exclude some players and lessen competition—at least within the union. But this practice enhances competition overall and encourages nonunion performances "below scale." It also causes disgruntled reactions from accomplished musicians who are forced to audition for "some union hacks."[40]

The other argument states the AFM is interested in representing as many musicians as possible in order to control wages and working conditions—the trade unionist point of view. The compromise between these conflicting concepts is that, "... locals may appoint or elect an Examination Board to pass upon the eligibility of applicants for membership,"[41] but "... All performers on musical instruments of any kind and vocalists, or other individuals who render musical service of any kind for pay, are classed as professional musicians and are eligible for membership...."[42] As a practical matter, the statement made in 1904 by AFM President Joseph N. Weber is still valid: "The A.F. of M. is a unique organization; it does not only represent those that follow Music exclusively for a livelihood, but it represents also those who do not even in a major part depend upon Music for their maintenance. It follows, therefore, that every Instrument Performer receiving remuneration for his services is eligible for membership."[43]

The growth of AFM membership is evident when figures supplied by John R. Commons in 1906 and 1913 are compared. According to Commons, the AFM represented 45,000 members in 424 locals in 1906,[44] by 1913, the union represented 64,000 members in 636 locals.[45]

Commons also compared numbers of AFM members and numbers of jobs and wages in St. Louis in 1906 and 1913. In 1906, there were 600 members, of whom 100 were employed steadily;[46] in 1913, there were 975 members, but still only 100 were employed steadily.[47] In 1906, the theater scale was $21.25 a week for nine performances; in 1913, the scale was $23 a week for nine performances. Apparently scale wages for dances ($4 until 2A.M.), parades ($4 for four hours on Sunday and $3 for four hours on weekdays), and funerals ($3–$4 if to a cemetary and $5 with marching on leaving the cemetary) were the same in both years.[48] Unfortunately, corresponding increases in wages and numbers of jobs had not yet accompanied the growth in the number of professional musicians.

One more conflict needed to be resolved within the Federation before the relationship between the national organization and the local unions was finally established. In 1920, a series of disagreements arose between Local 310 in New York (then, as now, New York City had the largest local of the AFM) and the national administration. These arguments culminated in the suspension of the local in 1921 for violations of national bylaws (i.e., refusal to accept transfers).[49] This gave the national officers an opportunity to charter another local (Number 802) to represent the Federation in New York. To prevent further conflicts between the largest local and the national organization, the International Executive Board insisted that the executive board of the new Local 802 be appointed by the national officers. This went too far. After fourteen years of constant agitation, the Federation finally surrendered and agreed to allow Local 802 the same autonomy as all other locals.[50]

Before 1930, two other significant events further changed the direction and momentum of the AFM. The first of these was political: the adoption of the Eighteenth Amendment to the Constitution (the national prohibition amendment) and the Volstead Act (to enforce it) in 1920.

Although Canadian members of the Federation were not adversely affected—in fact, they may have gained some employment in border cities—musicians in the United States lost jobs in taverns, hotels, cafes, and restaurants.

Following what by now had become longstanding policy, the AFM and the American Federation of Labor joined other groups (hotel and restaurant interests as well as brewers and distillers) in concerted action to preserve and increase job opportunities. Their efforts succeeded with the enactment of the Twenty-First Amendment (the repeal of prohibition) in 1933. Unfortunately, the end of the prohibition era corresponded with the Great Depression of the 1930s. Although prohibition repeal brought back some job opportunities to U.S. musicians, the arrival of the jukebox and the general weakness of the economy were not conducive to better living standards for musicians—or the growth of unions.

The second important development before 1930 was a mechanical-electrical technology which literally changed basic concepts of the musicians' union: the sound movie.

After the release of the first "talkie," *The Jazz Singer*, in 1927, it took only a few years before motion picture houses nationwide were equipped for sound, and 22,000 theater musicians were unemployed.[51] Worst of all, in the trade union view, these musicians lost the best jobs in the profession. Although theater work lacked the gratification of playing classical music or jazz, it was steady, did not require travel, and paid well.

The vaudeville theaters were also adversely affected by the new technology. Live acts (and live musicians) could not compete economically with the flood of Hollywood productions. By 1930, large city theaters could show double (even triple) features for an admission charge of only 25 cents to 50 cents. A living wage for live performers was out of the question.

Technological unemployment was not a new problem for unions. And for musicians, the sound movie was only the first of many forms of musical automation developed during the twentieth century. What makes these "music machines" different from other forms of automation is that the machine does not make music—the musician makes music and makes the technological device that puts the musician out of work. The function of the musician remains unchanged—he still makes music. The music machines merely preserve and disseminate. This is a problem unique to the field of music,[52] and the attempts by the AFM to "preserve the job market" as it confronts each new form of automation makes the union itself unique.

The Federation was not prepared to face this first major[53] threat of technological unemployment. In 1927, President Weber said, "... a general danger to employment will not develop as from present observation it appears that the public accepts the Vitaphone [the music machine] merely as a novelty."[54] This statement was followed in 1929 by another incorrect assumption: "... It is the opinion of the Federation leadership, based upon exhaustive study, that mechanical music ... will fail eventually to give satisfaction in any theater as a substitute for the appearance of artists in person."[55]

To substantiate this opinion, AFM conventions in 1928 and 1929 authorized an extensive advertising campaign "... to expose the sound movie as an 'anti-cultural' development"[56] Although these efforts helped create a favorable image of the Federation in the national press, they did not convince the public that canned music was undesirable.

The only direct gain for Federation members to balance the loss of 22,000 theater jobs were a few more musicians hired in Hollywood to add to the 200-odd "mood music" players employed to help actors in silent movies. The increase was small. In an assessment made in 1969, Senator Howard Cannon said, "... 20 years after the introduction of the movie sound track, only 339 musicians were permanently employed on the movie lots in place of thousands who had worked previously in the picture theaters."[57]

Other movie theater jobs were saved in Rochester and Indianapolis by converting at least a nucleus of the theatre orchestra into the beginnings of symphony orchestras.[58]

Opportunities for more radio employment also helped the jobless musicians. The founding of the major networks (NBC in 1926 and CBS in 1928) and the newly found ability to sell commercial time for both local and network broadcasting helped convince radio management that "talent was worth paying for." First in Chicago (in 1922) and later in Kansas City (in 1924),[59] AFM locals demanded pay for performance. And although the Depression helped make radio a primary source of entertainment for impoverished America, "radio employment [fell] far short of the lost employment in movie houses...."[60]

Still other aids for the unemployed musician were the

opportunities presented by the Works Progress Administration. Although this agency of the Federal government (created by executive order of President Roosevelt in 1935) is best remembered for its engineering and public works construction programs, the Art Program was also of great importance.

This first major venture by the United States government into subsidy of the arts produced paintings, drawings, sculpture, and thousands of murals for public buildings. Writers prepared guidebooks, and theater people developed new dramatic techniques and entertaining plays. In addition, many kinds of musical groups were subsidized to give thousands of performances across the country. Symphony orchestras, jazz groups, and chamber music ensembles were heard live and on radio through the late 1930s and early 1940s.

As an important side effect, WPA orchestras were the immediate predecessors of the professional symphony orchestras in Buffalo, Oklahoma City, Springfield, and Salt Lake City. Robert Whitney, the first conductor of the Louisville Philharmonic, was an apprentice conductor with a WPA orchestra in Chicago under Frederick Stock. Even the National Youth Administration (supervised by the WPA) supported concerts and recitals by young musicians during these years.

For the unemployed performer, the minimal support system of the WPA was welcome assistance. (As of September 1939, 8,000 musicians had been employed by WPA.[61]) In a very real way, WPA helped keep the arts in America alive during the dismal years of economic depression.

The 1930s brought a precipitous drop in AFM membership. The combined effect of the 20-percent Cabaret Tax (a continuing World War I "luxury tax" levied on admissions to establishments offering live entertainment), the sound motion picture, prohibition, the jukebox, and the Depression brought AFM membership down from a peak of over 146,000 in 1929 to a low of about 100,000 in 1934.[62] Competition from amateurs (i.e., school bands and orchestras), radio broadcasts (and rebroadcasts), and especially from recorded music was growing rapidly, but the Federation's responses did not come until the 1940s. Under the new forceful and combative administration of James C. Petrillo, the AFM would make some of its most positive and controversial decisions.

Chapter III
The Days of James C. Petrillo

L ONG BEFORE HIS ELECTION in 1940 as International President of the American Federation of Musicians, James C. Petrillo was a powerful union leader. His professional life was the stuff from which legends are born—not all of them good.

Chicago was Petrillo's arena. After a short, not-too-successful career as a trumpet player, he moved into union politics and became president of the independent American Musicians Union in 1915. After three years in this position, "... he saw that the little independent union wouldn't take him far ... in 1918 he joined the powerful Local 10 of the AFM."[1] He became vice president of the local in 1919 and its president in 1922—a position he held for forty years.[2] As Petrillo said many times, "If I was a good trumpet player, I wouldn't be here. I got desperate. I hadda look for a job. I went in the union business."[3] Petrillo probably was not a good trumpet player, but throughout his career he managed to add enough humor to his comments to soften the sting of his more caustic remarks.

A lack of formal education and the hard life of the Chicago ghettos were no detriment to Petrillo. Accustomed to violence and the rough, brutal experience of the gang-dominated times, he successfully forced the organization of the Chinese restaurants and, for the first time, insisted that radio stations pay musicians. Performers had previously played on radio for publicity only—but times were changing.[4] Those days were recalled by a now-retired Chicago musician. He remembers playing in a string trio for a half-hour radio show in 1924. The scale wage for all three players was $35 (including rehearsals)—a real financial windfall.[5]

Organizing the theater orchestras in 1927 started one of the biggest strikes in AFM history and caused the local—and Petrillo—to face court injunctions and mob violence. It also brought two of the twentieth century's most famous lawyers—Clarence Darrow and David Lilienthal—to the defense of the Federation. And with their expertise, the union won.

In 1933, it was rumored that Petrillo had been kidnapped by one of Chicago's better known mobs for a ransom of $50,000—and that Local 10 had paid the ransom.[6] Union politics forced an audit of union funds only days before an election of officers. Evidently the union paid no ransom, but the local increased the number of bodyguards for their president (Petrillo had had two Chicago detectives assigned to protect him for some years) and purchased an armored car for his use.[7] In those days, Al Capone and others viewed Local 10 as a ripe plum to be picked. The smell of the cash generated by the union was almost irresistible.

Over the years, there have been allegations of wrongdoing by Petrillo in those early years in Chicago—not one has been proved.[8] In contrast, Westbrook Pegler (no friend of unions or Petrillo) was able to write in 1943, "... Petrillo ... is, to my almost certain knowledge and to my strong conviction, not a crook."[9]

Petrillo fought consistently for more job opportunities for "his boys." If this battle caused conflict with powerful political figures, it bothered him not at all. Chicago mayor Anton J. Cermak, who wanted to use a school band for his inauguration, U.S. Vice President Charles G. Dawes, who wanted an imported Hungarian band to play in a Chicago hotel, both Republican and Democratic parties, which wanted to use recorded music from sound trucks, and even the American Federation of Labor, which owed $2,800 to Local 10, all lost to "The Chief."[10] ("The Chief," one of Petrillo's nicknames, was used early in his career and continued to his last years.) An organizing battle Petrillo did not win was his attempt to unionize church organists—Mrs. Petrillo objected.[11]

These were hard times in Chicago. Prohibition had closed thousands of saloons, making thousands of musicians unemployed. The movie theaters, as they adapted to sound films, added more musicians to the unemployment lines. The Depression made everything worse: union scale was only "what the traffic will bear"—not a living wage. And yet, in 1930, Local 10 included "… well over 90% of the professional instrumental musicians in Chicago."[12]

In those days, and throughout his career, Petrillo was known to be sentimental and humorous as well as hard, tough, crude, and shrewd. "An animal," one opponent called him.[13] "But if he makes a promise," one purchaser of music said, "you don't need it in writing."[14] He was also a clever, farsighted labor leader who "had real vision and guts to do something about it."[15]

The legends persist, some undoubtedly apocryphal. One story tells of slingshots used against the windows of Chinese restaurants while Petrillo was inside, trying to convince the owners that they needed union musicians. The owners eventually asked, "What is it you want, Mr. Petrillo?" Another story is about the twelve-hour conversation between Petrillo and Clarence Darrow regarding the defense of Local 10 while the executive board lost interest and retired to sleep in the next room. Still another tale is about the union bodyguards hired to watch the Chicago detectives who guarded Petrillo. Another legend is about the drunken party in an Italian restaurant with pasta and lots of wine that ended with Petrillo taking each of his protectors to their homes. Then there is the story of Petrillo's trumpet performance, at the age of eight, at Hull House for Jane Addams. And there are many tales of gang-style threats on his life and the firebombing of his home. Another details the negotiations for a Grant Park Orchestra contract during which Petrillo reminded the Chicago Park Board, "You feed the monkeys but you won't pay the musicians." (Fittingly, the band/orchestra shell in Grant Park now carries Petrillo's name.)

Some legends are undoubtedly true. Local 10 is head-quartered in a building built in 1933 for and by Petrillo (and named in his honor in 1984). It has bulletproof glass throughout, and the staircase leading to the president's office on the third floor has positions on each landing for bodyguards. The positions were protected by bulletproof glass. The president's office, a complete suite "in case the chief can't get home overnight," contained "the largest desk Marshall Field's had," a gun in a desk drawer, and a bulletproof door. Petrillo's phobia about germs compelled him to offer only his little finger for a handshake, to order lecterns covered with sterile towels, and to cover hotel room floors with fresh newspaper.

By 1932, Petrillo had won election to the international executive board and began to present his strong views about the future of the union in this larger arena. As early as 1929, he had stated his position on the dangers of music performance reproduction. The argument was that by making recordings, "the musician was destroying him-self"[16]—an argument opposed by President Weber and adapted by the AFM only after Petrillo became Interna-tional President in 1940.

The earliest attempts to control unrestricted record-ings were not directly linked to the Federation. In 1932, aring and his incorporated orchestra and (in 1934) /hiteman and his orchestra tried to establish a legitimate claim for royalties (i.e., performance rights for performers) on the sale and/or broadcast of their recordings. They instigated a series of appeals to the courts based in part upon a legend on each record specifying "for noncommercial use."[17] The litigation was unsuccessful. The opposition included the broadcasters and jukebox operators, the record companies (who thought they should hold the copyright), and ASCAP and BMI, representing the composers and publishers who already owned the copyright on the printed music and thought too many other claims would decrease sales and dilute their share of the profits.

Although President Weber voiced support for efforts to amend the copyright laws,[18] the AFM was not in the midst of the battle. This is understandable. The Federation's main concern at that time was the unemployment of its members caused by recorded music. To further enhance the remuneration of the relatively few musicians whose skill and talent were responsible for producing the records was not an important priority. The trade unionist principle of "the most for the many" ruled the day.

Meanwhile, in Chicago in 1936, Petrillo faced a challenge from his old independent union, The American Musicians Union. John L. Lewis of the United Mine Workers and head of the Congress of Industrial Organizations CIO, invited the AMU to join the CIO as its musicians' union. Petrillo immediately dropped the $100 initiation fee for Local 10, thus attracting almost all of the rival union's members and effectively stopping dual unionism in musical affairs until the mid-1950s.

Another battle won in 1936 over John L. Lewis again concerned the CIO. William Green, president of the AFL, expelled all unions of the CIO from the AFL—including his own union, the United Mine Workers. So that Green would not become a "member without a union," Petrillo made him a member of the AFM.[19]

Disturbed by the menace of recordings and discouraged by the inaction of the international union, Petrillo took action in his own backyard—Chicago. In 1937, Local 10 banned the making of records in its jurisdiction. This was no "shot in the dark." Everyone realized that Chicago musicians would lose employment as other locals continued to allow recording and the record companies would be relatively little inconvenienced.[20] Petrillo obviously hoped some locals would follow his lead and that the international leadership would have to take a similar position. This did not occur.

What did occur was the not surprising antipathy of a small minority of Local 10 members who had played for recordings and an open clash between Petrillo and President Weber.[21] Weber, now over seventy years old, gradually lost the political war and retired honorably with a substantial pension in 1940. James C. Petrillo was elected International President of the American Federation of Musicians at the age of forty-eight.

THE RECORDING BAN:
PREPARATION-RESOLUTION

Although no long-range plan of action was announced, the new international leadership set to work with what now seems a logical step-by-step preparation for battle against "canned music," The agenda included (in chronological order) the capture of soloists and conductors from another AFL union, the American Guild of

Musical Artists (AGMA); the unionization of the Boston Symphony Orchestra; and, finally, the ban on all recordings.

Until Petrillo became International President, the AFM seemed uninterested in organizing the instrumental soloists, conductors, and accompanists who regularly appeared with the unionized symphony and opera orchestras. These musicians (approximately 200) had formed their own union in 1936 (along with many singers, choreographers, and ballet dancers), the American Guild of Musical Artists (AGMA). In 1937, under the leadership of prominent performers such as Albert Spalding and Lawrence Tibbett, AGMA became affiliated with the Associated Actors and Artistes of America, a full-fledged member of the American Federation of Labor.

Petrillo's basic argument against the Guild was that this separate organization should not be allowed to exist because it would lead to other guilds of orchestra players, pianists, jazz players, and others which would eventually destroy the ability of the AFM to bargain effectively.[22] His prediction was only partially correct. Other guilds or associations were formed within the AFM in the second half of the century, but they did not hamper the basic functions of the organization.

A more compelling reason to bring these "guild musicians" into the AFM was the necessity to present a unified organization of all instrumental performers in the upcoming attempts to unionize the Boston Symphony and strike the record companies.

Petrillo notified the Guild that AFM members would not perform with accompanists, instrumental soloists, or conductors who did not belong to the Federation—under a deadline of only one month.[23] This direct, blunt ultimatum was typical of Petrillo's confrontational style. Although the action was justified on jurisdictional grounds, it caused affront and unnecessary antagonism. Because of the national and international status of the artists in AGMA, the press was intrigued and generally took sides with the soloists. Petrillo's remark, as quoted by *The New York Times*, did not help: "Since when is there any difference between Heifetz playing a fiddle and the fiddler in a tavern? They are both musicians."[24]

The controversy grew. An antitrust investigation was threatened by the Department of Justice,[25] and an unsuccessful court case was instigated by the Guild. Finally, a compromise was reached which gave the AFM what it wanted: all conductors, instrumental soloists and accompanists were required to join the Federation.

The stage was now set to bring about the unionization of the Boston Symphony Orchestra. In contrast to the New York Philharmonic, which began as a cooperative venture by musicians, the orchestra in Boston originated with the paternalistic support of Henry L. Higginson. In 1881, Mr. Higginson, a Boston financier, hired the original orchestra and conductor on a contractual basis and promised to pay any deficits of the orchestra's operation.[26] This attempt to adopt paternalistic government support, long practiced in Europe, to paternalistic capitalism in the United States was successful. The Boston Symphony Orchestra became the country's first permanent orchestra, and its pattern of financial support served as a model for other orchestras for the next half century.[27]

As the principal benefactor of the orchestra, Higginson's conservative views in musical programming and in politics were evident.[28] He met any attempt for concerted action by the orchestral musicians with the threat of complete withdrawal of financial support. It was not until 1920 (a year after Higginson's death), that a serious effort was made to obtain higher wages and better working conditions.

Squeezed by post-World War I inflation and supported by the Boston local of the AFM and the temporary
shortage of fine musicians (European "imports" were few,
and new orchestras further to the west required personnel), members of the orchestra requested wage increases.
The board of directors, also troubled by inflation and
acting on the principle of avoiding collective bargaining,
refused the request. Although not directly affected by the
wage demands, the orchestra's concertmaster, Frederic
Fradkin, sympathized with the musicians, joined the
union, and argued openly with the conductor before a
concert. During the concert, as a sign of protest, Fradkin
refused the conductor's request to rise and acknowledge
the applause of the audience. He was fired for insubor-
dination, and "thirty six other members of the orchestra
failed to appear for the [next] concert."[29]

The revolt continued with picketing and the short-
lived formation of a union-sponsored rival orchestra. But
newspapers opposed the musicians, the public seemed
uninterested, and within weeks the strike was broken,
"...even though 90 percent of the orchestra ... had joined
the AFM."[30] As a result, the orchestra lost more than one
third of its members. The union lost this battle because of
the unyielding position of management and the Federation's inability to bring outside pressure to bear.

Within less than a year, the orchestra was rebuilt by
hiring a combination of new members from the United
States and Europe and rehiring some former members.
By 1924, when Serge Koussevitsky became Musical Director, the audition pattern for new musicians changed.
Koussevitsky believed in the superiority of American-
trained performers, and although the AFM "... blacklisted
the members of the Boston Symphony and fined union
members for playing at Koussevitsky's auditions,"[31] by the

late 1930s the majority of the orchestra was native born and trained.

There is no evidence that management of the Boston Symphony Orchestra had changed their opinion about collective bargaining—they were opposed. But Koussevitsky was obviously more sympathetic to the plight of the orchestral player.[32] He had belonged to musicians' unions in Europe before coming to Boston and generally attempted to intervene on behalf of the players in disputes with the board of trustees.

Wages and working conditions were not as good in Boston as they were in the other major symphony orchestras, by now all unionized. But the pressure from within for collective bargaining was insufficient to cause change. The combination of satisfaction in performing in a prestigious orchestra, the sympathetic attitude of the conductor, and the memories of the broken strike probably were responsible for the retention of the status quo.

The Petrillo administration, now in control of conductors, soloists, and accompanists (from AGMA), and in preparation for a recording ban, was ready to unionize this last major group of non-union instrumentalists. The campaign involved a boycott using the Union's power to destroy the Boston Symphony Orchestra's earning potential by eliminating radio broadcast income and recording income, by preventing union soloists and conductors from appearing with the orchestra and conversely preventing non-union conductors (i.e., Koussevitsky) from appearing with union orchestras, and by preventing the orchestra from using concert halls in other cities in the United States or Canada.

The Weber administration succeeded in stopping radio broadcasting by the Boston Symphony Orchestra in 1939 by threatening "... to pull out its own musicians from radio programs if the broadcasters permitted the nonu-

nion group to go on the air."[33] RCA Victor, which exclusively recorded the Boston Symphony, did not renew
the contract in 1940, because to do so meant the loss of all
union musicians for the remainder of their catalog. Major
conductors and soloists such as Bruno Walter, Carlos
Chavez, Howard Hanson, Efrem Zimbalist, Joseph Szigeti,
and Rudolph Serkin[34] were instructed not to perform with
the orchestra. Finally, the annual tour of the orchestra was
curtailed by AFM pressure on concert halls in Rochester
and New York.

The Federation's efforts were successful. After protracted negotiations between President Petrillo and the
orchestra's management, an agreement was signed in
December 1942 bringing all the members and conductors
of the Boston Symphony Orchestra into the AFM.

The agreement did entail a modification of the
Federation's bylaws. Until this time, symphony musicians
could accept an orchestral position outside their local's
jurisdiction only with the permission of the new local.
Although this procedure was not rigidly enforced, the
Boston Symphony Orchestra management felt it to be too
restrictive. By using his powers under Article I, Section 1 of
the AFM Bylaws, Petrillo, after consulting with those locals
that might be affected by a change, revised the ruling to
allow the Boston Symphony to hire from anywhere in the
United States or Canada.

This bylaw preceded the Petrillo administration by
twenty-nine years. In 1911, in response to President
Weber's request, a bylaw was added to the constitution of
the AFM allowing the president to make " ... executive
orders binding upon all members and the Locals if, in his
opinion, the enforcement of the Constitution and By-Laws
and Standing Resolutions of the Federation make such
course necessary."[35] This bylaw was again amended in 1930
to allow the president to "annul and set aside" the constitu-

tion, bylaws, and standing resolutions "and substitute therefor other and different provisions of his own making" whenever in his opinion such action is necessary "... to conserve and safeguard the interests of the Federation, the Locals and/or members."[36]

Despite the longevity of this ruling, as an example of the "bad press" that hounded Petrillo during this period, Wellington Roe has Petrillo revising the AFM constitution in the 1940s by adding the provisions of Article I, Section 1 so that his "...power would be absolute."[37] Petrillo's middle name, Caesar, suggested much to Roe and others who chose to emphasize "dictatorial powers" in their reports on the Federation.

Both Weber and Petrillo used sparingly the power granted by this bylaw. Earlier in 1942, Petrillo using Article I, Section 1, had changed a bylaw to allow AFM members who joined the military to retain AFM membership without payment of dues while on active service. Despite this innocuous usage, advocates of union democracy cited Article I, Section 1 as evidence of dictatorial governance. Petrillo tried unsuccessfully to have the bylaw removed at the 1957 AFM Convention.[38] In 1958, however, upon the request of President Elect Herman Kenin (and again with the support of Petrillo), the bylaw was eliminated.[39]

The year 1942 was an eventful one for the American Federation of Musicians. While the extended bargaining sessions were proceeding with the Boston Symphony Orchestra, Petrillo, obviously anticipating ultimate victory, continued toward the goal of achieving a recording ban.

The 1941 and 1942 AFM conventions had approved research and then action against continued recorded performances because of the inroads that had been made on employment opportunities for Federation members. Accordingly, in June 1942 notification was sent to all recording and transcription companies that "... on or after August 1, 1942 ... our members would not render service."[40]

Petrillo felt strongly about the debilitating effects of commercial recording upon the Federation. The following quote is typical of his views repeated in many speeches and interviews:

> Nowhere else in this mechanical age does the workman create the machine which destroys him, but that's what happens to the musician when he plays for a recording. The iceman didn't create the refrigerator the coachman didn't build the automobile. But the musician plays his music into a recorder and a short time later the radio station manager comes around and says, "Sorry, Joe, we've got all your stuff on records, so we don't need you any more." And Joe's out of a job.[41]

The recording ban, coming during the first full year of World War II anguish, caused immediate, and hostile, reaction in the press and many areas of government. It was no surprise that the National Association of Broadcasters issued statements strongly opposed to the Federation's action. After all, RCA Victor and CBS not only were broadcasters but also were the two largest manufacturers of records. Nor was the press reticent in its disapproval. They seemed generally to take the position of Elmer Davis, Director of War Information, that a recording ban was detrimental to the war effort by eventually causing small radio stations to fail (and thereby hurting the flow of vital information) and causing undue hardship for defense workers and military personnel who needed the recreation supplied by jukeboxes in restaurants and cafes.[42] To these moderate objections, journalists added more inflammatory comment on "Petrillo, Boss of U.S. Music," "Little Caesar," "musical Hitler," and "music czar."[43]

The recording ban of course had no effect on recordings already made or the continuing production of these records. Because the record companies had anticipated the union's action, there was a large supply of recent recordings ready for sale. It is fair to assume that the classical catalog of recordings was in good supply; the only immediate effect of the ban was upon new "pop" tunes and musical commercials. Mary Austin believes, "... the recording companies made more money than they would have without the ban because they were able to clean out their inventory of unsold records."[44]

In response to the public clamor and the perceived threat to morale, and therefore the war effort, the Department of Justice brought action under the antitrust laws. Although the suit was denied in Federal District Court in October 1942 (and this decision was upheld by the Supreme Court in February 1943), the Federation was forced to defend its action before a subcommittee of the Senate Interstate Commerce Committee, making the AFM the first labor organization to be investigated by Congress.[45] In January 1943, Petrillo appeared before the committee and indicated the Federation's willingness to negotiate with the recording industry.[46]

Within a month, "the AFM offered to terminate the recording ban ... if the recording and transcription companies would agree to pay fixed royalties to the Federation for each record and transcription made ...."[47] These funds were to be used to reduce musicians' unemployment by supplying "free, live music to the public."[48]

This was the essence of Petrillo's innovative strategy. For the first time in labor-management relations, those who used automated devices were asked to share responsibility for the resulting unemployment. And, as a bonus, the public would hear live music for free. There was no request for higher salaries or royalties to be paid to the musicians, members of the AFM, who actually made the recording. Instead, the royalties were to supply "the most for the many"—the trade union principle.

The recording companies rejected the union's offer. "They refused to contribute to a fund to be spent at 'the union's uncontrolled discretion' and they rejected the 'dangerous fallacy' that a 'specific industry owes a special obligation to persons not wholly employed by it.' "[49]

Leiter suggests another reason why the record companies were not eager to reach a settlement with the AFM.[50] In these war years, there was an acute shortage of virgin shellac (from India) vital for producing good records. This shortage of raw material, along with the backlog of records made prior to the ban, gave the producers "breathing room" to consider at length any union offer.

After months of fruitless negotiations, the record companies took the dispute to the War Labor Board (WLB). Before a three-member committee that would report later to the full board, hearings were held in New York City.

While those hearings were in progress and after several meetings with the International Executive Board, Decca Records (the third largest record maker) broke ranks with the other companies and signed an agreement with the Federation for the resumption of record production. The contract met all the essential demands of the union.

The Decca contract was made in September 1943—thirteen months after the start of the recording ban. By the beginning of 1944, almost one hundred more smaller record and transcription manufacturers had agreed to similar arrangements. The two largest record makers—RCA Victor and Columbia[51]—continued their complaint before the WLB.

In March 1944, the committee recommended to the full board that the recording ban be lifted. The War Labor Board directed that the recording ban be lifted in June

1944—six months after all but the largest two record makers were producing recordings. The International Executive Board of the AFM "... voted not to comply with the order."[52]

Although the WLB accepted the principle of a royalty fund, it had ordered the union to negotiate the amount of contribution with RCA and Columbia. The union's rejection was predictable. With standard terms set now with over one hundred producers, why settle for less from the holdouts?

The controversy continued with the WLB referring the case to Director of Economic Stabilization Fred M. Vinson and in turn to James F. Byrnes, Director of War Mobilization. In October 1944, Petrillo and the International Executive Board (IEB) met with Vinson and Byrnes. As the meeting concluded, Justice Byrnes said he "would take the matter under consideration."[53]

On October 4, 1944, President Franklin D. Roosevelt wired Petrillo, appealing to his patriotism and good citizenship. He asked the AFM to comply voluntarily with the WLB directive "... in the interest of orderly Government."[54] The wire was sent despite the ruling of Director Vinson that the recording ban would not impede or delay the war effort.

Before agreements were reached with any record makers, Petrillo had agreed to lift the ban if Roosevelt requested him to do so.[55] Now the situation was different. With one hundred and five signatories to its recording contract and with recordings being produced for over a year under this contract, the IEB and Petrillo felt no patriotic principle would be served by allowing RCA and Columbia to gain more favorable terms. Roosevelt's request was respectfully declined.[56]

RCA and Columbia finally agreed to the AFM recording contract when it became clear that other record com-

panies were gaining larger shares of the market with their
new products under AFM contract. Jascha Heifetz's decision to switch from RCA Victor to Decca indicated that
"more of the same" might be in store from other musical
stars.[57] On November 11, 1944, contracts were signed with
the Federation, effectively bringing recording to full production. The ban had lasted for more than twenty-seven
months.

The Recording and Transcription Fund created by
the AFM contract with the record makers (eventually
numbering approximately 600 companies) was controlled
by the Federation. Fees paid by the record makers varied
from ¼ cents to 5 cents for records selling up to two
dollars. For all records selling above two dollars, the fee
was two and a half percent of the sale price. No fee was
charged for commercial transcriptions for single broadcasts, but the fee for library transcriptions was three
percent of their gross revenues. All payments were separately administered, kept free of other Federation accounts, and were not used to pay salaries of administrators.[58]

Disbursement of the fund began in 1947 by providing
free live music in parks, schools, hospitals, homes for the
aged, and other similar places. Musicians were paid no
more than union scale wages directly from the fund.

Allocations of the fund were made on the basis of
$10.43 to each local for each member in good standing,
except for the three largest locals—New York, Los Angeles, and Chicago. In these locals, the allocation was
$10.43 for each of their first 5,000 members in good
standing, and $2 for each additional member in good
standing.

The Recording and Transcription Fund collected approximately $4,500,000 through 1947 (the original con-
tract with all record companies ran until December 31,

1947). These funds paid for almost 19,000 performances with 45,000 individual paychecks.[59]

PETRILLO'S FIGHT FOR MORE RADIO JOBS
PLUS THE INTERLOCHEN INCIDENT
EQUALS THE LEA ACT

Petrillo's constant preoccupation with more job opportunities for musicians was a logical continuation of Federation policy. He saw the recording ban as only one aspect of this greater problem.

Radio employment for AFM members began with the profitability of the networks and local stations. But continued and increased employment was hampered by network shows (when one union band served many stations nationwide), the use of recordings, and competition from amateurs such as school bands and orchestras. The recording ban was only one approach to this problem—it attempted to control recordings at the source. The commercial use of records on radio presented an opportunity to control recordings at "point of use."

While preparations were being made for the strike against the record companies, Petrillo began a direct approach with the radio stations to increase employment. Beginning in his first year as International President (1940), he demanded that a set number of musicians be hired under contract for each station and network—essentially a quota system based upon AFM estimates of profitability.

The many objections from network-affiliated stations to this policy were answered with the response that the quota merely balanced the "free" music supplied to them by the network.

The networks themselves were most vulnerable to

union pressure. Name performers or name bands could become unavailable, the network studio musicians could be removed, or ultimately, a strike could be called (which other unions would honor) and close the network completely. To avoid these unpleasant alternatives, the networks many times argued the AFM's case with their own affiliates.

Union pressure was least effective upon the unaffiliated stations that refused to hire their "quota." If arguments extolling the benefits of live music failed, the stations simply continued to use recordings. There were few instances of work stoppages during these war years, but typical of Petrillo's general disregard of public opinion, a strike was called against a station in St. Paul contrary to a non-strike pledge by labor for "the duration." Although the strike was criticized by William Green, President of the AFL,[60] and Petrillo's arrest was ordered by a Minnesota court,[61] the union won the battle with the station and lost the war to public opinion.

Despite AFM policy, many radio stations never hired a single musician—all their musical air time was filled with recordings and transcriptions. This was a pervasive problem for the Federation. A comprehensive survey of radio use of recordings was made by the Federal Communications Commission (FCC) in 1942. "It was found that of the average station's total broadcast time 42.6 percent was devoted to recorded music and 33.7 percent to 'live' music. These figures showed that of the total time devoted to music, 55.9 percent was taken by recorded music. A further breakdown revealed that of the non-network stations, 91.3 percent broadcast recorded music more than 60 percent of the total music time. Of 298 stations in that category, 232 used recorded music between 80 and 100 percent of the music time."[62]

Petrillo had long believed that school band and orchestra radio broadcasts reduced the opportunity for employment of professional musicians. In 1928, as President of Local 10 in Chicago, Petrillo demanded (and received) standby fees before he would allow an NBC broadcast of the National High School Orchestra at the convention of the Music Educators National Conference. The request was made two days before the scheduled broadcast.[63]

In 1941, as International President, Petrillo "... was successful in forcing the cancellation ... of broadcasts ... by school bands in Chicago, Cleveland, Washington, Milwaukee, St. Louis and San Francisco, among other cities ...."[64] Although a broadcast by the student orchestra of the Eastman School of Music also was cancelled in 1942, further programs had AFM approval because by then the entire orchestra was unionized.

The National Music Camp at Interlochen, Michigan, a nonprofit educational institution, seemed to have been an important target for Petrillo's battle against amateur radio broadcasts. Since 1930, the music camp had been broadcasting continentwide on Saturdays and Sundays during their eight-week summer session. The camp's band, orchestra, and chorus during that time included high school students from most of the United States and Canada.

In 1941, Petrillo attempted to halt the regular weekly broadcasts over NBC. He relented when told by network officials that plans and commitments for that year had been completed. Evidently, the Federation was convinced that NBC would bring the matter to the union before the 1942 camp season.[65] They did not, and Petrillo forced cancellation of National Music Camp broadcasts one day before they were to begin.[66]

Whether or not NBC violated an agreement with the AFM was immaterial to the young musicians, their friends, and relatives, and the news media around the country.

They knew only of the personal disappointments and the apparent ruthlessness of the union. The public clamor was immediate and sustained. Although there might have been some sympathy in informed quarters for the recording ban, this perceived outrage against children was not forgiven.

On August 25, 1942, the American Institute of Public Opinion conducted a poll concerning the activities of the AFM. The poll showed "... that 75 percent of the persons interviewed commented 'unfavorably' on Petrillo's rulings and that 73 percent approved of the government taking legal action against the union."[67]

Public indignation gradually subsided. Compared to the daily tragedies of World War II, the Interlochen incident paled. The Federation might have won this battle if it had not been for Petrillo's ignorance of or disregard for public opinion.

In early 1944, Petrillo brought the "Interlochen incident" to the attention of the public and the Congress. He said, "However, when all the shooting was over and we came to the summer of 1943, there was no Interlochen high-school student orchestra on the air. Nor was there in the year 1943 any other school band or orchestra on the networks and there never will be without permission of the American Federation of Musicians."[68]

This statement again aroused the interest of Congress. Many congressmen were already resentful of the AFM strike against the St. Paul radio station (and the Federation's broken non-strike pledge). The Lea Act[69] was the congressional response to the Federation's policies in the radio industry. The AFM had the dubious distinction of being the first union to be investigated by the Congress (in 1943) and now it added to that reputation by being the first union to have legislation passed specifically to control its actions. The Lea Act is known, justifiably, as the "Anti-Petrillo Law."

The Lea Act made it a criminal offense for unions to "use coercion ... to win observance of its rules by radio stations [that is: employ more people than needed, pay more money for people, pay money instead of hiring more people, pay more than once for services, pay for services not performed, interfere with noncommercial educational programs]. The law also extended this ban to any compulsion of persons to exact payment for the use of recordings, or to restrict the manufacture and use of recordings or to exact payments for using transcriptions of programs previously broadcast and paid for."[70] By its terms, the Lea Act directly challenged many Federation policies.

After consulting with the International Executive Board and legal counsel, Petrillo decided to test the Act's constitutionality. He chose WAAF in Chicago as the target by demanding that it hire more musicians. When the station insisted that more performers were unnecessary, the AFM called a strike and the test case was on its way through the court system.

Although the U.S. District Court in Chicago ruled in Petrillo's favor, the Supreme Court declared the law constitutional in 1947. Petrillo accepted the verdict. "This is my country and the Supreme Court makes the final rulings on its laws. No one will ever say that Jim Petrillo fought his country or the Supreme Court. I thought that I had the law on my side, and I made the best fight I knew how. The Supreme Court has spoken, and I bow to its dictates."[71]

Petrillo may have become reconciled to obeying the law, but he still felt his actions were proper. Years later, in referring to the "Interlochen incident," he said, "With children you always lose—but I was right. They took jobs away from professional musicians."[72]

The AFM attempted to live with the new restrictions of the law. On September 22, 1947, a Music Code of Ethics was signed with the Music Educators National Conference (MENC) to define the respective rights of amateurs and professionals. This was no Federation innovation. The essence of this code had been presented to the International Executive Board by the then president of MENC, Joseph E. Maddy (also the president of the National Music Camp), in 1936, and action had been deferred to locals.[73] The code has been revised periodically since 1947 with only modest success as a planning guide.

An immediate effect of the Lea Act was the elimination of standby fees. Within a very few years it caused the disappearance of studio orchestras and later the staff musicians. No test was ever made of the Act's provisions that could have adversely affected the Recording and Transcription Fund.

At first, the Lea Act's repeal was proposed and fought for by the AFM. But by the middle 1960s the Federation had decided not to carry the fight further, on the basis that this was "fruitless and nonrewarding so long as the repressive provisions of the Taft-Hartley and Landrum-Griffin Acts remain intact."[74]

By 1973, the Federation acquiesced to membership pressure, changed its policy, and again began the fight for the Act's repeal. The lobbying continued until the Bill to Repeal the Lea Act (Public Law 96-507) was signed by President Carter in December 1980.[75]

THE RECORDING AND TRANSCRIPTION FUND BECOMES THE MUSIC PERFORMANCE TRUST FUND—THE FIRST EFFECT OF TAFT-HARTLEY

In 1946 the time was right for legislation such as the Lea Act. The early postwar years were filled with the economic tension of transition to peace-time life. There were shortages of many kinds of civilian goods, and the public was impatient with perceived featherbedding and other forms of "make work." The policies of the AFM, although not much different from those of other unions in the building trades or railroading, were conspicuous because of the bad public relations engendered, at least in part, by Petrillo's disregard of and apparent disrespect for the public and the news media.

The same attitudes in the electorate and in the Congress that produced the Lea Act were soon at work to again modify labor-management relations. The Labor Management Relations Act of 1947 (the Taft-Hartley Act) was clearly a reaction to the New Deal labor-management legislation of the 1930s. Among many provisions of Taft-Hartley that would eventually affect the AFM, Section 302 caused the most immediate concern.

Section 302 made the Recording and Transcription Fund criminally unlawful by forbidding a union to "... cause or attempt to cause an employer to pay or deliver or agree to pay or deliver any money or other thing of value, in the nature of an extraction for services which are not performed or not to be performed."

While Taft-Hartley legislation was still pending in Congress, the AFM Convention in June 1947 authorized another recording ban to forestall this threat to the Recording and Transcription Fund. Accordingly, upon the passage of Taft-Hartley in August (and evidently after long consultation with legal advisors), a letter was sent to all record and transcription makers telling them their contracts would not be renewed and that "... on and after January 1, 1948, the members of the American Federation of Musicians will no longer perform the services provided for in said contract."[76] As Petrillo said, "After all, there was no law that said a musician had to fiddle if he didn't want to."[77]

Again, the record companies had long warning in

advance of this second recording ban, and a sizable stockpile of records and transcriptions were made in the months immediately prior to January 1948. Although Petrillo threatened "... permanently and completely, to abandon that type of employment,"[78] he was not believed. After all, he had said the same during the first recording ban.

Both sides began a "waiting game." The recording companies needed to be concerned only with the lost market for new "pop" tunes—all else was in good supply. The AFM faced a loss of earnings for only about three percent of its members—those who actually made the recordings.[79] A constraint upon both parties was the gradually increasing supply of recordings arriving in the United States and Canada from Europe and Central and South America.

Negotiations were finally begun in October 1948, and a plan developed by AFM attorney, Milton Diamond, was eventually adopted as a workable compromise.[80] The new plan, The Music Performance Trust Fund (MPTF), kept or slightly modified many of the provisions of the old Recording and Transcription Fund: funds are obtained from the record companies based upon price and volume of sales; the proceeds are distributed throughout the U.S. and Canada on a pro rata basis in geographic areas that coincide with AFM locals; funds must be expended in the year following receipt; funds must be used for live musical performance for the public when no admission is charged and when it will increase appreciation for music; musicians receive no more than union scale payment directly from the fund only for service rendered, and the fund must approve all projects.

The new provisions of the Music Performance Trust Fund made it lawful under the Taft-Hartley Act. The fund is administered by an independent trustee named originally by the record producers and subsequently by the Secretary of Labor, and the fund may employ musicians who are not members of the AFM.[81]

Upon written assurance from the Department of Justice that the MPTF was in compliance with Taft-Hartley, the new agreement became effective on December 14, 1948. The second recording ban had lasted more than eleven months.[82]

The MPTF worked. Diamond had been able to restructure the ingenious ideas that formed the Recording and Transcription Fund into a new format that satisfied the law, the record producers, and the union. For the next few years it seemed to be the answer to all prayers.

Petrillo, who claimed this achievement as the highlight of his career,[83] began to build upon the Trust Fund foundation. In 1951, he negotiated a new contract with the major radio and television networks. He said, "The most important part of this contract is the 5 percent that the networks have agreed to pay to the Music Performance Trust Fund, based on their gross revenues derived from the use of television film."[84] To gain this addition to the MPTF, Petrillo allowed simultaneous broadcast over both AM and FM stations without additional compensation to the musicians. A principle he had supported for almost ten years was surrendered.

By 1952, the MPTF was receiving revenues from four sources: record and transcription companies, producers of theatrical motion pictures (for release of film to television), producers of films for television, and producers of television jingles and spot announcements.[85] The Music Performance Trust Fund was now the Music Performance Trust Fund*s*. And the funds were big business—the largest purchaser of music in the world. "In 1954 it spent some $2,350,000 ... for 16,997 public performances in which nearly 189,000 musicians took part."[86]

MPTF—ALSO THE CAUSE OF DISSENT, REVOLT, AND DUAL-UNIONISM

World War II changed the way North Americans lived. The postwar AFM was different from the pre-war union. Musicians were better trained and, for whatever reasons, music may have appealed to more very talented (and just talented) people as a profession. The membership of the union grew from about 135,000 in 1940 to over 231,000 in 1948.[87] The days were gone when a mediocre player could move from style to style—only the highly talented musician could be versatile and good. The age of specialization was here: it was a rare symphony musician who could play good jazz; few club date musicians could do well in theater jobs; seldom was a Dixieland player also good at Bebop. There was much more competition for jobs and a deeper gulf between the comparative few who succeeded and those who did not. The appeal of the MPTF to the great majority of the AFM membership was obvious.

How much unemployment is there in the ranks of the Federation? No definitive answer can be given because the research effort has not been made. Part of the problem is the union's definition of unemployment: "if a member is not employed full time as a musician he is unemployed."[88] There seems to be no question that the AFM represents a membership of part-time performers—only a small percentage work full time in the profession. Even superficial consideration of various sized AFM locals makes this point clear.

A local of about 1,000 members in a medium-sized city with a full-time symphony orchestra will show about one hundred Federation members fully employed in the orchestra and perhaps some fifty or sixty members fully employed in hotels and other entertainment industries. A smaller local (one hundred to one hundred fifty members) in a smaller city may have only a few members fully employed as performers. Local 802 in New York City, with a membership in the thousands, services an area in which only a minor fraction of its musicians work as full-time performers.

Another problem is the Federation's policy of open admission for all who "play for pay." With its policy aimed at discouraging amateurism and non-union activity, the AFM may include among the unemployed those members who do not wish to become employed as full-time performers or who want to be "moonlighters."

And that seems to be the crux of the issue. How many members labeled by the AFM as "unemployed" desire to be casual players, or are not capable of meeting rigorous performance standards, or are retired and keep their membership for fraternal or other reasons, or pay their dues to play the occasional MPTF gigs? And how many are fully capable, talented, and intelligent—and cannot find a full-time job as a performer?

The question never has been "is there unemployment?", but rather "how much unemployment?" within Federation membership. Automation undoubtedly added to performers' unemployment, and the MPTF was a fine idea for most AFM members—but it never was the complete response to automation, and to some it was a bad idea.

The producers of records, transcriptions, tapes, and films did not like the MPTF. They agreed only under duress to the concept of responsibility for AFM members who were not, and had never been, their employees. This objection grew over years to the point where their argument became, "Although we supported musicians across the country in the beginning of these agreements, now we have no reason to support second or third generation musicians who should have been aware of this situation before they chose music as a career."[89]

A second argument from these same producers is, "Why cut MPTF in on our business—it takes five percent off the top."[90]

A more disinterested appraisal of the funds by Thomas Kennedy[91] points out that, "Most of the payments from the fund are not received by workers who are currently unemployed. The majority of the recipients have full-time jobs in other industries ... some may be part-time musicians, but the majority do not depend on and never have depended on music as their principal source of income. No participant receives any sizable amount from the fund."[92]

Although the MPTF may have "started out as a means to force employment for exploited musicians,"[93] it was soon clear that the more valid purpose was educational, "to promote the appreciation and knowledge of good live music."[94] Kennedy accepts an educational purpose for the MPTF but makes the further point that, as an automation fund for displaced workers, the MPTF should "help the displaced workers find new jobs by financing ... retraining and relocation costs ... ."[95] The AFM has made no direct response to this suggestion other than the frequently repeated opinion that "it takes a thousand journeymen to produce one artist." A Federation official commented, "Retraining is crazy.—Most of these guys already have full-time jobs outside of music, they don't need to be re-trained."[96] The premise that there must be some realistic balance between machine-made music and live music is essential for the continuation of musical performance. After all, the machine cannot make music—only live musicians can.

In purely economic terms, the MPTF allows the Federation to share in the profits of commercial reproduction of music on records and film. It wants these profits to be of benefit to as many musicians as possible in the union. The producers would prefer to eliminate the MPTF and pay more to the performers who actually make the music—and that sentiment has been shared by the small minority of AFM members who actually do make the music.

The first evidence of this attitude appeared in 1951 and caused a "slashing attack" by Petrillo "vs. '$500-a-week elite' in Local 802"[97] in New York. Petrillo's point, of course, was that this small group of musicians were interested only in protecting and enhancing their own well-paid jobs.

Opposition to the MPTF concept continued to grow. In 1952, Local 47 in Los Angeles complained that the fund's high cost to telefilm producers was forcing them either to eliminate music or import foreign soundtracks.[98] In 1954, both the New York and Los Angeles locals objected to the new agreement signed by Petrillo with the major radio networks. The agreement did not add more live musicians but continued the practice of taping bridge, cue, and mood music for dramatic shows.[99] The income for reuse of the taped music was eligible for MPTF fees.

Open, undisguised dissent finally arose in Los Angeles in 1955 when Cecil Read was elected vice president of Local 47 (over an administration candidate). Read's campaign was based upon opposition to the contract with radio and television producers which allowed all reuse payments to go into the MPTF.[100] Read promised to "go before the International Executive Board to demand that these payments be made directly to the individual musicians involved in the material before reused."[101]

The agreement (signed in 1954 for five years) called for the continuation of scale from 1946 with payment to the MPTF of 10 percent of scale earnings for the first two years and 21 percent for the last three years. In June 1955,

al Executive Board (IEB) ruled that pro-
cease making reuse payments to the film
make them instead to the MPTF. The AFM
as justified because "there were only some
receiving re-scoring fees"[102] from films
made in the 1930s and 1940s. Those musicians in Local 47
who agreed with Read thought this diversion of monies
unfair.

The positions of both sides of this controversy very
nearly approximated the classic argument of trade union
principle (the union should do what is best for the majority
of its members) versus the principle of personal rights (an
individual should be able to enjoy the fruits of his own
labor).

Read did appeal to the IEB in New York in January
1956 to reconsider its action regarding reuse fees. He also
requested the formulation of an AFM policy which would
respect the principle of performer's rights and, "in concerted action with actors, singers, writers, directors and
other performing artists, to change the copyright law to
recognize such … rights."[103]

The IEB's response was a foregone conclusion. Read's
position would have destroyed the MPTF. The IEB's reply
three days later defines the AFM's posture at that time:

> … It is found that the various requests have for their
> ultimate purpose payments to the individual musicians
> who did the recording, instead of to the Trust Fund,
> and diverting the money now in the Fund to such
> musicians, thus resulting in the discontinuance of the
> Fund. This would mean that many musicians through-
> out the country would be deprived of the little employ-
> ment made possible by the Fund and for which the
> recording industry acknowledges it owes an obligation.
> The only ones to benefit would be the recording

musicians who are among the best paid members of the
Federation and whose mechanical product is the principal reason for the widespread unemployment among
our other members.

The Music Performance Trust Fund was established to enhance the public appreciation of live music
by furnishing free concerts to the general public and to
reduce somewhat the loss of employment which came
about as a result of the widespread use of mechanical
music. It has been of great benefit to many locals, in
which the non-recording musicians of Local 47 also
shared, and appreciated by many communities.

To grant the requests of Local 47 would wipe out
the Fund, thereby depriving musicians all over the
country of this little employment, and turn the money
over to the already well-paid musicians who do the
recording and produce the mechanical music.[104]

The request was denied.

A national official of the Federation added another
argument in support of the board's position that was not
included in the printed minutes. He said, "Read was in a
position to make these demands for the recording musicians only because of a strong AFM that had protected jobs
and 'prepared the way' for many years prior to this debate.
Whatever they had, they got because of the union."[105]

Within a month of the unsuccessful appeal to the IEB,
at a meeting of Local 47's membership, Read made his
report on the appeal and suggested that further attempts
for understanding would be futile. He also introduced
resolutions supporting legal actions and a defense fund.
When these motions were ruled out of order (procedures
had not been as provided in the bylaws), Read moved that
the officers of Local 47 who supported the national union
(President John teGroen, Financial Secretary G. R. Hen-
non, and Recording Secretary Maury Paul) be suspended.
President teGroen ruled out of order all of these motions

and the resulting favorable votes and said the action "was a clear revolt against Petrillo" and "the meeting was one of the most illegal ever held..."[106]

The revolt continued—not without its comic aspects. Scola reported that a meeting of Read supporters held before the membership meeting just described was secretly tape-recorded.[107] The *Los Angeles Times*, in a front-page story, tells of Local 47's suspended president (teGroen) and vice president (Read) both attempting to conduct the union's business from separate offices in the same building.[108]

Charges, counter-charges, threats, boycotts, and petitions followed rapidly from both sides in Los Angeles—and Chicago, New York, and Washington as well. With all this bluster, teGroen and Read (both described as "mild mannered" and "of pacific tendencies") seemed to be in substantial accord. Read is quoted as saying that "neither he nor his supporters are opposed to the trust fund," and teGroen said, "I'm not against the men getting more of the money."[109] The road to compromise might have started here. It did not. The battles were to continue for many years.

Both sides brought their arguments to the news media with statements and interviews. Cecil Read presented his case—in his own words— in a letter to the editor of the *Los Angeles Times*:

> The argument has been advanced by Petrillo that the "canned music" made by the Hollywood musicians has caused unemployment for musicians in other parts of the country.
> This point has been belabored for years by the Federation in a deliberate attempt to stir up envy and hatred against Hollywood and New York musicians.
> Recorded and filmed performances of motion-

picture and TV actors and singers has caused local unemployment all over the country. But do these actors and singers have a "moral" responsibility to every performer, would-be performer or amateur led to believe he is jobless because of sound pictures and TV networks?

Are Hollywood and New York actors and singers being deprived of work opportunities and having legitimate wage increases and other earnings taken from them?

Are actors and singers being faced with "economic suicide" because they oppose arbitrary actions of a dictator who distributes the money taken from performers to thousands of non-professionals all over the country in return for their support?[110]

Read came from Chicago and made an early reputation as a fine trumpet player. He played dance dates with Gene Krupa and Benny Goodman while still in his middle teens. After working with the Isham Jones and Frankie Masters bands and doing his share of "one-nighters," he became lead trumpet with the wGN staff orchestra in Chicago. During World War II, he was associate first trumpet of the Official Army Air Corps Band in Washington.

In 1948, he moved to Los Angeles and became one of the few financially successful studio musicians in a very short time. He was a quiet, unassuming man who was deeply religious and neither smoked nor drank; a very unlikely combatant in this particular war.[111]

In response to the charges brought to the IEB by the ousted officers of Local 47, Read and twelve other accused unionists demanded a trial and hearing before an impartial committee or board. The IEB and Petrillo agreed, and the hearing was held in April 1956. The referee was Arthur J. Goldberg, then special counsel to the AFL-CIO

(Goldberg later served as Secretary of Labor, Associate Justice on the U.S. Supreme Court, and U.S. Representative to the United Nations).

The referee's findings were submitted within a month to the IEB and reported in the *International Musician, The New York Times, The Wall Street Journal, Variety, Downbeat,* and other newspapers and periodicals across the country. In a 30,000-word report, Goldberg found Read and eleven others guilty of various actions which disregarded the constitution and bylaws of both Local 47 and the International Union. He recommended that eleven defendants be suspended for one day and that Cecil Read be suspended for one year. All defendants were to be barred from holding elected office in Local 47 for two years after reinstatement. He further recommended that they all refrain from advocating dual unionism.

The IEB accepted Goldberg's report but delayed implementation so that the defendants could present their case to the convention of the International Union in June 1956. A day-long debate in the convention ensued, during which all of the defendants spoke, a secretly recorded tape was played of the meeting called by Read and his followers prior to a membership meeting of Local 47, and Petrillo charged the defendants with an "... underground plot to steal Local 47...."[112] The convention officially voted unanimously for expulsion (although the Local 47 delegation voted against the motion[113]). The basic charge was dual unionism. The Convention then voted Petrillo the power to hold locals in trusteeship to help prevent future "47 type" problems.

The next step was litigation. Although there were indications of compromise—the AFM was helpful in keeping Read's right to work during his suspension, and AFM General Counsel Henry Kaiser had "some informal discussion with members of the dissident group"[114]—no real progress was made.

Four lawsuits were filed in late 1956 and early 1957 on behalf of the film and recording musicians. These suits were against each of the four sources of monies for the MPTF. The defendants were the AFM, the trustee of the MPTF, and the producers. Each suit questioned the legality of the MPTF and sought to stop payments, asked for the appointment of a receiver to collect monies for the plaintiffs, and claimed damage against the AFM for payments already made. The totals claimed, amounting to many millions of dollars, would not be settled until April 1964— a time span of almost seven years.[115]

While legal action proceeded, the rebel faction (without Cecil Read, who was suspended from the Federation) "swept from office" the pro-Petrillo administration of Local 47. The vote margin was better than 2 to 1.[116] Petrillo thought the election "no surprise" and offered to work with the new administration "in all matters for the common good."[117]

There were efforts toward conciliation. In May 1957, representatives from the new administration of Local 47 met with President Petrillo in New York. In a joint statement issued after the four-hour meeting, Elliot Daniels, president of Local 47, and Petrillo said that certain aspects of the MPTF were discussed, and the local had requested that film studio musicians participate in bargaining contract discussions with filmmakers. They also agreed to meet again to discuss further problems.[118]

Petrillo was true to his word. In preparation for contract talks with movie producers in January 1958, Local 47 chose a "studio committee" to work with the AFM in the negotiations. Although Petrillo had said the Los Angeles musicians would have "... damn near the last word," it took the encouragement of Herman D. Kenin, then the west coast representative of the Federation, to convince the doubting members that they would be heard.

Kenin promised that "there would be no meeting between the Federation and movie producers at which members of Local 47's studio committee would not be present" and "… the Local would have the right to ratify or reject any contract. This includes the right to strike in face of unacceptable contract terms."[119] The studio committee (some sixty strong) were studio musicians and representatives from Local 47—not all Read men.

Negotiations began in Los Angeles in January 1958 between the AFM (with the Local 47 studio committee) and the motion picture producers. The demands made by both the studio committee, for much more pay and better working conditions—55 proposals in all,[120] coupled with the MPTF demands of the Federation "… were hastily rejected as being unrealistic and resulted in the employers walking out of the negotiations."[121] In retaliation, the union called a strike.

Evidently movie makers had learned some survival techniques from the two recording bans. Soundtracks continued to be made in Europe and Mexico. An AFM attempt to induce a public boycott of these films was to no avail—and the strike continued.

In March, Read became impatient with the lack of progress in resolving the strike, and after an ineffective petition by himself and others to Petrillo to reopen negotiations and "eliminate or modify the Trust Fund,"[122] he and a small group of supporters formed a rival union, The Musicians Guild of America (MGA).

Dual unionism, the bane of trade unionists, the "worst crime" in the view of organized labor, had arrived. The Read-led MGA quickly obtained the minimal support necessary to file a petition with the National Labor Relations

Board for a representative election. The mere filing of such a petition forced both the end of negotiations and the strike. It brought the wrath and hostility of all organized labor down upon the MGA. William Schnitzler, Secretary of the AFL, speaking for George Meany, the president of the AFL-CIO, said the Guild had "committed the grievous sin of strike breaking against their union brothers."[123]

In July 1958 the National Labor Relations Board election was held. Those musicians who had two or more calls to work during the preceding eighteen months at the major movie studios were eligible to vote—some 1,400 musicians. The Guild won by a narrow margin.[124] The MGA was a legally recognized union; dual unionism was a reality.

In commenting on the formation of the Guild, Read said,

> The supporters of the Guild tried for years to work within the AFM to protect their wages from confiscation and to protect their work. We exhausted every right of appeal within the union and started the Guild out of desperation only when it became evident that the AFM strike in the motion picture studios would permanently lose this employment for American musicians.[125]

Others, AFM loyalists, viewed the beginnings of the MGA in a different light. They believed that Cecil Read had been thinking of forming a rival union since his defeat in the 1956 Convention. The strike was a product of the Read faction, and the timing of the actual formation of the Guild was fortuitous and exploited a weakness in National Labor Relations Board procedures. The resulting stalemate brought further frustration to the Los Angeles musicians, and this plus the help of a full section of the *Los Angeles Times* devoted to the dispute published just before the

NLRB election and bitterly anti-Petrillo and pro-Read, pushed the Guild to its narrow victory.

PETRILLO'S RETIREMENT AND HIS CONTINUED INFLUENCE

The years 1956, 1957, and 1958 were difficult ones for Petrillo and his administration. The dissent and then revolt in Local 47, the "trials" of Cecil Read and his supporters first by Referee Arthur Goldberg and then by the AFM Convention, the lawsuits against the Federation and the MPTF, and finally the dual unionism of the Musicians Guild of America were devastating blows to Petrillo's authority and self respect. These actions opposed his most important achievement, the MPTF, and brought about what must be a terrible disaster to a trade unionist—dual unionism.

So it was not surprising to "insiders" when, in an open letter in the May 1958 *International Musician*, Petrillo said, "I must decline to accept the nomination as President of the American Federation of Musicians at the 61st Annual Convention."[126] The general Federation membership was stunned, and the announcement made front-page news throughout the country. In an interview with *The New York Times*, Petrillo "denied ... that the revolt in Local 47, Los Angeles, had had any influence on his decision to retire." He added, "That bothers us about as much as a fly bothers an elephant. They got 250 members. We got 260,000. What do you think they're going to do?"[127]

On the other hand, a long-time AFM national figure thought the "Los Angeles problem" was foremost in Petrillo's mind. "They broke Petrillo—he simply could not understand their point of view."[128] Petrillo himself said in 1984 that "it was time for a change."[129]

The 1958 AFM Convention did nominate Petrillo in spite of his letter. Led by a band, hundreds of delegates marched around the convention hall yelling, "We want Jimmy," and displayed placards pleading, "Jimmy, Don't Leave Us."[130] The demonstration lasted almost twenty minutes. Petrillo was so moved he cried openly on the platform. There could be no question that Petrillo was the convention's choice. He certainly represented the great majority of AFM membership.

When it was clear that Petrillo would not reconsider his decision, upon motion of the convention, he recommended Herman D. Kenin as his successor. By almost a 2 to 1 majority, Kenin was elected the fifth president of the Federation[131]—Petrillo's eighteen-year presidency had ended.

But as an indication of his popularity and power (even as a lame duck), "the Chief" was still able to convince the membership to agree to hold conventions every two years instead of annually. This proposed change would have saved the AFM many thousands of dollars at the expense of diluted governance, participation by the delegates, and their loss of the considerable "perk" of attending international meetings in faraway cities at practically no personal expense. Predictably, without Petrillo's direct involvement, the 1959 Convention rescinded this action and kept the annual convention.

Petrillo's presidency had ended—but not his influence and participation in Federation affairs. Kenin, as Petrillo's hand-picked successor, was not surprisingly sympathetic to Petrillo's views. The international leadership of the AFM had changed, along with some expected changes in methodology, but the basic philosophy of AFM unionism was expected to continue.

Petrillo continued as president of the Chicago local but declined a pension from his national office as long as he continued to receive the $26,000-after-taxes salary from Chicago.[132] He did resign, however, from the Executive Council of the AFL-CIO—he had been the first member of the AFM to be so recognized by the parent group.

His influence would continue because of his national prominence. A man who played a duet with President Harry Truman at the 1954 AFM Convention, who was welcomed at the White House by Presidents Roosevelt, Truman, and Eisenhower, whose name was (and still is) recognized throughout the United States and Canada as representing the AFM, and whose legal battles in the courts and with governmental agencies had set precedents could not immediately leave the stage of union decision making. Petrillo continued to exert influence as president of the Chicago local until 1962, as director of the Federation's Civil Rights Program in the 1960s and 1970s, and as president emeritus and advisor to the International President and the International Executive Board until his death in 1984 at the age of 92.

His final defeat for elective office as president of Chicago's Local 10 was probably caused by a combination of factors. In October 1962, Petrillo's administration easily defeated a move by dissidents to cut his weekly salary from $500 to $350. This same small group of "nay sayers" (calling themselves Chicago Musicians for Union Democracy, CMUD) "had been active in insisting that a committee of players sit in on the just-concluded negotiations between Local 10 and the Chicago Symphony Orchestra"[133] (Association).

On November 12, 1962, at a regular union meeting, the CMUD nominated Barney Richards, a pianist and bandleader, to oppose Petrillo for election as president of Local 10. For the first time since 1933, there was a challenge to Petrillo's authority.[134]

The same week that the nomination was made, "61

members of the Chicago Symphony Orchestra filed unfair labor practice charges with the National Labor Relations Board against Local 10 and Petrillo. The performers claimed "Mr. Petrillo declared that symphony musicians would need permission from him and his executive board to take outside jobs" and "that the Orchestra Members' Committee, elected by members of the symphony to represent them in contract bargaining, would not be allowed to participate in negotiations for next year's Ravinia Festival."[135] Petrillo had not changed his priorities. He still favored "spreading the jobs around" and continued his long time opposition to fragmentation of the union membership into special "guilds" or groups. He believed that elected officers of the local, not elected members of the orchestra, should do the bargaining. Joseph Golan, chairman of the Orchestra Members' Committee, felt "Mr. Petrillo was irked because four symphony musicians were opposing his slate in the union election scheduled for December 4."[136]

The CMUD campaigned hard—Petrillo's administration almost not at all. The result was a defeat for Petrillo by 95 votes (1,690 to 1,595).[137] After forty years, Local 10 had a different president—and Petrillo had lost his first election.

At the 1958 Convention of the AFM, when Petrillo declined the nomination for International President, he was made "an advisor for life" to the International President and International Executive Board. He was to receive no salary unless or until he no longer held the $26,000 salaried position as president of Local 10. That time had come, and President Kenin announced that Petrillo "... would receive $10,000 a year pension from the AFM and $10,000 salary as an adviser to the union." Kenin also said that "Petrillo will receive an additional $3,000 a year as a contingency fund, for which there need be no accounting."[138] Petrillo's salaries over many years from both the international union and the Chicago local were substantial. They enabled him to live in a penthouse on Chicago's "Gold Coast" in his later years, an address that contrasted strangely with twenty and thirty-year-old suits, shirts, and ties he regularly wore.

In March 1963, Barney Richards, the man who had defeated him for the presidency of Local 10, nominated Petrillo to the honorary title of President Emeritus of the Local.[139] Petrillo accepted that honor but took little part in the political life of Chicago musicians until the administration of President Hal Dessent in 1984 and the dedication to him of Local 10's headquarters.

Petrillo's death on October 23, 1984 brought recognition again for "the most controversial and best known of the nation's labor leaders."[140] The Federation had lost a world-recognized spokesman.

OTHER PETRILLO ADMINISTRATION ACTIONS

There were other accomplishments of the Petrillo administration that did not fit into the mainstream of activities which led directly to recording ban, to the MPTF, to union discord. One of these was the decision by Petrillo and the International Executive Board to abolish subsidiary black locals in 1944.

The AFM, of course, reflected both the good and bad aspects of the society of which it was a part. In some situations, the prejudice against blacks within the Federation forced the segregation of black and white locals—with some of the black locals subsidiary to the white locals in the same locality. The Petrillo administration's ruling meant that these black locals (some twelve in all) would now be issued their own charters and would govern themselves in the same way as all other locals. While this action did not eliminate segregation, it was the first step toward equality of membership.

In 1951, with the approval of the board, Petrillo began the Lester Petrillo Memorial Fund to aid disabled members of the Federation on an emergency basis. Applicants have physical disabilities which prevent them from earning their livelihood as performing musicians.[141] Lester Petrillo, James Petrillo's son, died in 1931 as a result of injuries suffered in a football game. Originally, the fund was to be built by gifts from AFM members and others, with Petrillo making the initial personal donation of $10,000.[142]

In 1956, a resolution was adopted by the annual convention to contribute a modest amount—at first five cents per member, then ten cents per member in 1963, and, in 1977, another modification allowing suspension of contributions so long as the fund balance exceeded $500,000.[143] Gifts continue to be made from AFM and outside sources—in December 1984, a contribution was announced from the MCA Foundation, Ltd. for $25,000 in honor of James C. Petrillo. The International Executive Board serves as a trustee for the fund, which currently provides over $50,000 annually[144] in financial assistance to disabled musicians.[145] In a modest way, the Lester Petrillo Fund serves the old fraternal purpose of "taking care of your own"—one of the original purposes of the first unions. Those destitute AFM members disabled by heart disease, diabetes, Parkinson's disease, and the like deserve to be cared for by all of society. The Lester Petrillo Fund is a warmhearted "extra" supplement.

Petrillo was also an early advocate for repeal of the "20% Cabaret Tax" instituted early in World War I (and continued through World War II) to be charged in all establishments that provided live entertainment. Although this was a wartime measure designed to discourage luxury spending, it persisted through the Petrillo administration and beyond.

Another long-range goal pursued by Petrillo was government subsidy for opera and symphony organizations. He thought "the alternative meant death for musical culture in America."[146] Again, it would be many years beyond his administration before the realization of these efforts.

The year 1958 was time for a change. Time for conciliation, modification, and compromise. Time for new ideas. Herman Kenin may have been "Petrillo's man," but he was also "his own man." The decade of the 1960s was to bring change to the Federation—some old problems would be solved, and new problems would arise that would test the ingenuity of Kenin's new administration.

Chapter IV
Time for a Change—Herman D. Kenin,
"Pragmatist With a Soul"[1]

Like Petrillo, Herman D. Kenin was an experienced labor leader before he became international president of the AFM. Unlike Petrillo, Kenin came from a well traveled, middle-class background and had had an extensive formal education.

Kenin was born in 1901 in Vineland, New Jersey. His father, Samuel Kenin, had been a member of Samuel Gomper's cigar makers' union in Philadelphia before he tried truck farming in Southern New Jersey. When farming lost its appeal, the Kenin family moved to Lincoln, Nebraska, and then to Portland, Oregon. It was in Portland that Kenin attended public school and Reed College. Following three years as a night student at Northwestern College of Law, he was admitted to the Oregon bar in 1930.[2]

While in college, Kenin, who was a violinist, played with the George Olsen orchestra and then headed his own band. He explained, "I was so bad, I had to become a band leader."[3] During the Depression years Kenin practiced law, and his band played usually scarce hotel, club and radio dates in the Portland area.

In 1936, he was elected president of his Local 99 in Portland; in 1943 he was chosen by Petrillo to fill an interim position on the International Executive Board.

Now, it was necessary to give up his law practice and become a full-time union official.

He remained as president of the Portland local and member of the International Executive Board until 1956, when he was appointed the first West Coast representative of the Federation, with offices in Los Angeles. After twenty years as president of Portland's Local 99, he had to resign to move to Los Angeles and devote all of his efforts to the serious problems with Local 47 and other concerns of western locals. In 1958, as Petrillo's choice for International President, Kenin was elected by a large majority.

Years later as he recalled the election, Kenin said, "I wasn't sure I could handle the job. I wasn't even sure I wanted it. But it was Petrillo himself who persuaded me to stand for office."[4] Petrillo, he remembers, said, " 'I'm too damn impulsive to carry on this kind of job any longer. I just can't do it with these labor laws. What this union needs now is a man with patience.' "[5]

After his election at the 1958 Convention, Kenin made plain "his first endeavor would be to end the differences between the international and the rebellious Los Angeles unit."[6] Although solving the problems in Los Angeles may have remained a first priority for the new administration, there were other issues that needed to be addressed. In a speech delivered to the New York State Conference of Musicians in September 1958 (just over three months after his election), Kenin enumerated the tasks confronting the Federation and added some of his own evaluations and "new directions."

He began by reiterating his belief that "canned music …is, and will continue to be, the all-pervasive challenge to our profession and to our union."[7] Kenin went on to praise the trust fund principle to combat this challenge and then added, "Trust Funds are not major objectives of the Federation. They are … a means of [obtaining] … live jobs for living musicians." and further, " ... the Federation has always stood willing ... to exchange Trust Funds payments for direct live employment."[8]

Gone was the suggestion that the MPTF was a sort of "unemployment fund" for the AFM. Replacing this concept was a new attitude which for the first time offered the possibility for compromise. Here was a willingness to trade MPTF contributions for more live employment. Kenin the pragmatist had made his first statement.

Kenin then discussed the economic restrictions of the Lea Act and Taft-Hartley legislation. He promised to fight for revision or repeal of these laws—and he did, but with little or no success during his administration. In fact, the effects of Taft-Hartley were to be felt increasingly by the AFM in the late 1960s and 1970s.

The issue of federal subsidy to preserve "our musical heritage" was a priority that Kenin had advocated (along with Petrillo) before his presidency. The National Endowment for the Arts would become a reality during his administration.

Another task for the Federation was the repeal of the 20-percent cabaret tax. This battle had begun in the Weber administration, continued under Petrillo, and now the Kenin administration would shortly gain partial and then complete success.

Kenin then introduced the broad area of public relations and suggested a campaign to build public demand for live music. Although certainly not a new idea, Kenin's approach was unique. He discussed a new project[9]—an annual Congress of Strings for young musicians of the U.S. and Canada. The Locals of the Federation would supply scholarships to string performers, and the facilities and faculty would be supplied by industry and educators. Kenin thought the project had inherent worth and would "dramatically show the acute shortage of skilled string musicians directly traceable to the diminishing economic opportunities for serious professional musicians." What Kenin did not say was that the more proficient string players produced by this program would help make secure the jobs of those well trained and talented wind and percussion players who were already members of the symphony orchestras.

Another parallel program suggested by Kenin, to grant annual awards to "the best new dance band," did not enjoy equal success. The project, which involved industry commitments to provide recording contracts, hotel engagements, and countrywide tours, did not survive Kenin's administration.

Finally, Kenin spoke of the need for worldwide cooperation of organized musicians. He praised as a "first step" the new accord reached that year between the AFM and seventeen European countries. The agreement (1) forbade the making of recordings for an employer or producer involved in a strike; (2) prevented the making of recordings for library purposes; (3) prevented the making by musicians of recordings except for the creation of a single final product; (4) prevented the making of a soundtrack for a theatrical or TV film the major part of which was filmed in another country; and (5) prevented the making of any type of recording intended to be used to accompany a direct live performance by actors, singers, or any other classification of entertainers. Kenin's high hopes for this agreement were never realized. Too many organizations, too many conflicting motives, no practical enforcement, and too many temptations for individual gain doomed the concept.

During the course of his administration, Kenin would develop other objectives and "tasks" for the AFM. As a beginning, however, this speech indicated that the Federation would continue in the mainstream of the Petrillo administration, and pragmatic innovations would appear as solutions to old, continuing problems.

THE SOLUTION TO DUAL-UNIONISM—
AND WHAT HAPPENED TO THE MPTF

Immediately following its certification in July 1958 by the National Labor Relations Board, the Musicians Guild of America began to organize its potential membership in preparation for negotiations with the major movie studios. Cecil Read announced temporary eligibility requirements for membership:

> Any musician who was eligible to vote in the recent NLRB election or will be eligible to vote by reason of employment in the independent studios; any musician who shows any work record in the past year in radio, television, phonograph records or television film; any musician who has supported the guild's principles and given financial support up to this time.[10]

He proposed initiation fees, quarterly dues, and work dues to support the Guild. The Read faction that formed the MGA clearly was continuing their original arguments for an all (current) performer-union, but the work dues element in the fee structure indicated that they also recognized the "trade union" tenet that those who could best afford a union should contribute most to its support.

In September 1958, the MGA negotiated a contract with the major movie producers. Its provisions indicated the objectives of the MGA—and their lack of bargaining skills. The contract eliminated payments to the MPTF, emphasized live employment, and increased wage scale. It also permitted a tape library for each series with unlimited free reuse. There was agreement "not [to] use the sound-

track of any television film recorded during the agreement
for any other television film or series, during the life of the
contract and for ninety days thereafter. Similar restrictions
were made applicable to theatrical motion pictures... ."[11]
Strangely, the contract did not provide for reuse payments
on television films. The principle of "performers rights"
that Cecil Read fought for consistently for more than two
years was lost. Gorman says, "... They felt that their association did not have the economic power to extract such a
concession from the film producers."[12] A Federation sup-
porter said, "They gave away the store."[13]

The Kenin administration and the AFM were not disinterested bystanders. When the MGA contract was announced, it was immediately examined and criticized.
Their major objections were these: a motion picture made
for theatrical use could be used on television without
residual payments of any kind; a soundtrack used in one
film could be used in another if a new collective agreement
was not negotiated within ninety days after the expiration
of a current contract—placing the union under pressure
to agree quickly to a new agreement; a soundtrack used in
one film could be dubbed into any other film if money was
borrowed against a film or if the producer stopped making
film—since trade practice is "to borrow," no real regulation
existed; a soundtrack for a television film could be dubbed
into a full series without reuse fees; all contract studio
orchestras were abolished, ending any attempt for full-
time employment;[14] and the MPTF was completely removed.

Shortly after this MGA-filmmaker contract was announced, an unmistakable shift in AFM policy became
evident in new agreements negotiated between the Federation and the record industry (December 1958) and with the
major radio and television networks (early 1959). Both

contracts, for the first time, established a pension plan for casually employed musicians, included "substantial scale increases,"[15] and reduced the contributions to the MPTF. Kenin, in a speech to Local 47, commented on the agreement with the major radio and television networks, emphasizing the pension fund and "the largest wage increase in the Federation's bargaining history,"[16] His speech did not mention the MPTF but did claim, "We have negotiated handsome reuse payments for all our members engaged in the making of videotapes."[17] The Federation's change in position was even more pronounced in the pact with producers of commercial advertising—"jingles." The new contract, effective in November 1959, called for "substantial reuse payments, a 5 percent employer contribution to pensions....[A] new pay scale ... some 11 percent over the previous ... and employer contributions to the Music Performance Trust Funds have been eliminated."[18] Kenin was establishing battle lines for the coming challenge to MGA in a representation election sanctioned by the NLRB for 1960. There could be no doubt now that Kenin was trying to end differences between the AFM and "the rebellious Los Angeles unit" and that he was willing to exchange trust fund payments for more live employment with higher wages.

The NLRB-sponsored and supervised election to establish the bargaining agent choice of Hollywood's studio musicians was held in the summer of 1960. The AFM defeated the MGA by a vote of 473 to 408. The mediocre contract negotiated by the MGA with the film producers, the growing realization among the players that dual unionism was just "no good," and the change in direction of AFM policy as illustrated by their most recent agreements with the record industry, the radio and television networks, and the jingle producers obviously influenced the result. In the shortest time allowable by law, the Federation returned to power, but it still would be more than another year before dual unionism could be laid to rest.

As the new representative of the studio musicians, the AFM began discussions with movie producers about theatrical and television films and with television networks about televised programs. Kenin's administration continued the pattern of "increased concern ... for the economic interests of the film musicians and a further retreat from the aggrandizement of the Music Performers Trust Funds."[19] The contracts included higher wages, contributions to the pension fund, and for the first time, residual payments for reuse of filmed television programs, replacing an obligation for the producers to pay five percent of gross revenues to the MPTF. With the passage of time, the reuse provisions of these and similar contracts became even more important.

In these negotiations, the AFM was forced to swallow a bitter pill. The producers argued convincingly that the MGA contract had voided their obligation to make reuse payments to the MPTF under prior contracts going back many years. The revenue lost to the funds amounted to millions of dollars.

The MGA, although defeated in the movie studios, still had contracts with some television producers and small record companies. These agreements called for higher scale wages than AFM contracts, but no fringe benefits. In May 1961, on the evidence of this higher scale and as "a last gasp," the Guild "wrote to some 5,000 [recording] musicians [in Chicago, New York, and Los Angeles], asking, 'wouldn't you like to be paid Guild scales whenever you work for a record company?' and enclosing signature cards for authorizing the Guild to serve as collective bargaining representative."[20] The campaign was unsuccessful and paved the way for conciliation and compromise.

Kenin's speech to the AFM convention in June 1961 contained strong hints of things to come. He said that "... musicians' first fundamental purpose is to unite all musicians". Further on, Kenin stressed, "The Trust Fund policy was never an objective, it was rather a bold and imaginative effort to help keep our organization from being torn asunder and totally fragmentized by the sudden onrush of canned music.... History has also taught us that the rank and file musicians of this generation— and especially those who produce recordings—are substantially less than enthusiastic about the Trust Fund."[21]

These sentiments were not shared by all who attended the convention. One resolution (Number 47) wanted the convention to "go on record to instruct President Kenin to refrain from entering into any agreement which may sacrifice any income to the ... Trust Fund and that he fight to preserve and strengthen this fund."[22] The resolution's defeat by voice vote sent a signal to both Kenin and Read that it was time to reconcile differences.

Kenin, Read, their advisors and legal counsels met that same summer and by September 1961 had reached agreement. A letter dated September 5, 1961, from Kenin to the Board of Directors of the MGA succinctly sums up the understanding. After stating that "the interest of professional musicians could best be promoted by the consolidation of their total economic and political power into a single union," Kenin listed the terms of the agreement: the Guild agrees to dissolve the organization as soon as possible, while the Federation agrees to seek to induce record makers to pay fifty percent of moneys currently payable to the MPTF to musicians who made the recording and to continue to seek reuse payments for recording musicians in other recording fields; to reinstate with full uninterrupted rights all those who had been expelled because of their support of the Guild and to nullify all fines; to reaffirm its policy to grant to all musicians employed in the fields within its jurisdiction the right to ratify all contracts it negotiates; and to establish not later than April 1, 1962 in Los Angeles a recording musicians' committee which would advise on bargaining proposals, negotiations, and all other matters affecting their interests.[23]

Kenin's letter had previously been approved by the IEB, and upon receipt in Los Angeles, the members of the MGA gave their consent to the agreement, voted to dissolve the Guild, and permitted their current contracts to lapse in favor of the Federation.[24]

Dual unionism was now over, but the concessions made by the AFM were far reaching. By diluting payments to the MPTF, the Federation effectively enhanced revenue for the recording musician (both in terms of higher wages and reuse payments) and reduced monies available for MPTF distribution to the huge majority of AFM members. The pendulum had swung from the trade union principle of "the most for the many" to the performers' right "to share in the fruits of his labor." No less far reaching were the AFM's promises to allow ratification of contracts by those members immediately concerned and to support the formation of a recording musicians committee to share in negotiations.

Petrillo's forecast in 1940 that guilds or committees would form and threaten the unity of the AFM was partially realized in 1961. But he was only half right. Instead of splitting its constituency, the recording musicians committee (and others like it to come later) helped bring the Federation together and certainly created a more democratic organization. There are still AFM members today who distrust the "separateness caused by these groups within the union."[25] There are, on the other hand, these

AFM members who say, "Every time I get my Special Payments check [for recording], I say thank God for Cecil Read."[26]

The lawsuits filed in 1956 and 1957 against the MPTF and the AFM by recording musicians were also all but over by 1960. An out-of-court settlement was accepted by the various parties in December 1959. Kenin also endorsed the proposal in early 1960 in letters to locals in San Francisco, Chicago, Los Angeles, Nashville, and New York: "Under the proposed settlement the plaintiff [recording] musicians ... would receive a total of roughly $3,500,000"[27]—a substantial loss to the MPTF. Further legal delays in both New York and California postponed final settlement until 1964.

With the Federation's new emphasis on providing more financial reward to the musicians who actually make the recording or tape, the sources of revenue for the MPTF became drastically diminished. Since the early 1960s, the major source of income for the fund has been from the record producers and filmmakers—and that income is curtailed by the AFM's promise to the MGA to induce record makers to pay fifty percent of the usual MPTF payment to those who made the recordings.

Even with these restrictions, the MPTF is still big business and still the largest single employer of musicians in the world. By 1963, fifteen years since its inception, the funds had spent $50,000,000 for free live musical performances in the United States and Canada.[28] The allocation was about $6,000,000 in 1963;[29] in 1970 it was $7,370,000; in 1976 it was $9,430,340;[30] in 1981 it was $21,000,000.[31] Of course the amount of allocation depends in part on the number and price of the records and tapes sold in a given year, and in 1983 revenues fell to about $13,000,000 reflecting a drop in the record market.[32] The actual amount available for performances can be greatly enhanced by securing matching funds from local co-sponsors, a practice strongly supported by the MPTF.

The three-year contract beginning in 1984 between the AFM and the record industry greatly reduced the MPTF contribution while retaining the support for the special payments to those who made the recordings. Now the number of live performances the MPTF could support depended much more upon the market for records and tapes because of the smaller contribution formula set in the contract. Local co-sponsors were encouraged to supply sixty percent of the cost for each performance[33] to "take up the slack."

An AFM official, commenting on the agreement, said, "They wanted to cut [the MPTF] out completely, so I look at it this way: the glass is half full, not half empty."[34] Another Federation official, contemplating the numbers of AFM members who depend on fund gigs, called the MPTF, "the thread that ties the union together [the fund sponsored all kinds of live performance—symphony, jazz, chamber music and rock]—and now it will be that much weaker."[35] Still another AFM officer said, "The fund really supplies so little money now, that only the small locals will hurt."[36]

When negotiations began in November 1986 for a continuing contract with the recording industry, it was apparent early that these would be difficult bargaining sessions. When elimination of the MPTF and drastic cuts in the Special Payments Fund were proposed by industry, the talks were recessed until January 1987.[37]

The AFM bargaining team, including representatives of the locals where most recording musicians work (Los Angeles, New York, Chicago, Nashville, and Toronto), the Recording Musicians Association (RMA), and an executive committee headed by International President Fuentealba,[38] disagreed among themselves as well as with the recording industry. As a result, "… on the final day of the talks, the RMA and every Local [except Nashville] … represented at the bargaining table … walked out of the negotiation in protest."[39] The agreement reached by Fuentealba, the executive committee, and the Nashville local contained two major concessions which brought about the internal discord. The concessions called for ten percent cuts in industry contributions to both the MPTF and the Special Payments Fund, and no payments to either fund were to be made until a recording had sold a minimum of 25,000 units. This last point brought the most protest since neither the recording industry nor the AFM were able to pinpoint the actual dollars involved[40]—one source estimated, "It could be a 50% cut".[41]

Fuentealba defended the results as "… the best agreement we could negotiate, … When you look at what was on the table, where we were on Tuesday, we're very pleased with the results. We don't think anyone could've done better."[42]

Those opposed to the agreement believed that they were being disregarded and that the views of the rank and file members who do the recording work were not represented.

The agreement was ratified by those union members involved: 1,153 to 844. Following usual procedures, the ballots were mailed with a covering letter from the president recommending approval. The opposition's request to voice their views was denied by Fuentealba (since this was not standard procedure), and the recording musicians missed the opportunity to learn that at least one option to cutting MPTF and the Special Payments Fund—a reduction of wages[43]—was never presented to the industry team. The ballot also offered no choice indicating a desire for more negotiation rather than the drastic "strike or no strike" choice. Fuentealba thought there was no alternative

"... There's no going back to the bargaining table. We strike as of March 1 if this is rejected."[44]

Surely, no one knows how a strike may end; it usually involves concessions on both sides. But this agreement (in effect until January 31, 1990) is particularly burdensome for both the Federation and the "cream-of-the-crop" musicians who make the recordings. After all, the MPTF and the Special Payments Fund are forty-year legacies from the days of Petrillo and Kenin. Without a strong Federation, these benefits to both rank and file and greatly talented musicians would have been impossible, and the profession would have been greatly diminished without them.

These concessions also come at a time when the recording industry is making huge profits. Alan Dodds Frank points out,

"... On April 15, [1987] CBS Recordings reported its highest ever quarterly earnings: $67.9 million, pretax, nearly 75% of CBS' otherwise off-key earnings.... At $41.6 million, MCA's first quarter earnings were above expectations thanks to a strong boost from the studio's record division.... Warner Communications ... music division ... accounts for nearly 25% of the world market ... this year's first quarter operating profits rose 50% to $47 million.[45]

In comparison to these profits, it is instructive to consider what the MPTF actually costs. "For each recorded tape sold at retail for $8.98 ... the industry, after allowances for free goods and packaging, contributes 1.65 cents, or one-sixth of 1% to the MPTF, an amount long since built into the pricing of the product."[46]

The MPTF has strong public support and draws praise from both ends of the political spectrum. Senator Orrin R. Hatch (R.-Utah) has said, "... Not only do I give a special word of thanks as a lover of music, but I'm sure all

Americans who have heard the free music of MPTF applaud its efforts." Senator Edward Kennedy (D-Mass.) urges " ... business and community leaders everywhere to respond to the efforts of MPTF in encouraging the expansion of free live musical programs throughout the country."[47] Although recording musicians, the Federation, and the profession will have to live with this agreement for three years, it does not bode well for the next decade.

With MPTF performances now more difficult to come by, local union politics are increasingly a factor in who gets the job. Large locals regularly publish "who plays where and for how much" in their periodicals (New York's *Allegro*, Los Angeles' *Overture* and Chicago's *Intermezzo*), while many smaller locals supply much less information to the public or its membership. It is not unknown for officials in smaller locals to play an unusually high percentage of the MPTF gigs themselves.

The Music Performance Trust Funds still exists. It is still the largest single purchaser of live music in the world, but its size and influence are declining. It was a concept of foresight and ingenuity that fit the times of its inception and continues to be a major, and sometimes sole, source of live music in hundreds of smaller cities, towns, and big city neighborhoods across the continent. The record industry seems certain to continue to fight the MPTF to extinction, guaranteeing that the fund may never again be the force it once was. Strangely, given the magnitude of the fund both in dollars and performances, the record companies have never attempted to exploit the considerable public relations value of this subsidized expenditure. A move in this direction might influence the future of the MPTF.

Cecil Read, after his complete reinstatement by the Federation, continued an active role in AFM politics. He was helpful in the final resolution of the lawsuits and was liked and respected by many AFM officers.[48] One Federation local official said, "I always felt that after the L.A. thing straightened out, Read would make a good AFM man—and I was right."[49] It seems no one ever doubted Read's integrity. The criticisms were always directed toward his "crimes" against the trade union principle that problems should be solved within the union, not by litigation or dual-unionism. Another complaint was his inexperience— even naivete—in negotiating with purchasers of music. On the other hand, his negotiation with the Kenin administration which brought about the merger of the MGA and the AFM was very effective. The agreement influenced the decline of the MPTF, greatly enhanced the reuse fees for recording musicians, and opened the way for special constituencies within the Federation to organize, advise on pertinent negotiations, and ratify contracts—all specific goals of the MGA.

THE AMERICAN FEDERATION OF MUSICIANS–EMPLOYER'S PENSION WELFARE FUND AND THE SPECIAL PAYMENTS FUND—A BETTER DEAL FOR THE WORKING MUSICIAN

Both the American Federation of Musicians-Employers' Pension Welfare Fund (AFM-EPW) and the reuse fund (which carried the concept of the Special Payments Fund) began as inventive supplements to AFM contracts early in the Kenin administration. It may have been the pragmatic Kenin who devised these strategies to defeat the dual unionism of the MGA, or it may have been a Kenin convinced that working musicians deserved a better deal.

In either case, the AFM-EPW Fund began as part of a new five-year agreement beginning in January 1959 between the Federation and the record industry. The concept of a pension fund for casually employed musicians (e.g., a freelance musician who works for different employers) is of the same magnitude as those ideas that initiated the original MPTF. A freelance musician will typically work for many different employers in the course of a year, a month, or even a week. As a recording musician, he or she could be hired to play with many different groups on different recording dates—sometimes as a side musician, other times as leader, contractor, or soloist. And each of these gigs could be for a different record company.

With the new contract, for the first time, this musician would be able to build his or her individual pension credit from all these different employers no matter what performing role was played. The pension contribution was exclusively from the employer and paid as a percentage of the musician's scale salary.

At first, the AFM-EPW Fund applied only to recording musicians who were instrumentalists, leaders, and contractors "other than those in organized symphonic orchestras."[50] On July 1, 1961, under the same contract, symphony orchestras, arrangers, orchestrators, and copyists were also included in the pension plan. All employer contributions are made to the AFM-EPW Fund, which is administered separately from the Federation (as required by provision of Taft-Hartley). The pension fund has an independent administrator and a board of trustees having equal representation from the AFM and industry.[51] In addition to death and disability benefits, the fund provides for retirement as early as age 55. The musician can continue in the profession after he or she begins to collect a pension.

It was clear from the very beginning that Kenin envisioned an expanding future for the AFM-EPW (now known as the AFM-EP Fund). In the spring of 1959, he said, "Our pension plan has been carefully devised so that in the reasonably near future every working musician in every branch of musical endeavor may ... enjoy this highly prized benefit."[52] And he was right— the opportunity was there. By mid-1960, pension coverage was extended to network radio and television, some traveling engagements, and the "jingles" field.[53] In 1969 (in the fund's tenth year), over 90,000 AFM members in forty locals were covered "in phonograph, radio and TV networks, jingles, motion picture industry, traveling theatrical shows and other work."[54] All AFM members were eligible for coverage if they were employed under agreements and contracts that required contributions to the fund; additionally, this could include "full-time employees of the Trust Fund itself, full-time office and clerical employees for the AFM and of any of its affiliated Locals, and duly elected or appointed officers and representatives of the AFM and of any of its affiliated Locals."[55]

Although the AFM-EP Fund has been highly praised— one musician called it "the best thing the union has ever done,"[56] and *Overtones* said, "This Fund is perhaps the greatest accomplishment of the AFM in its history"[57]— Kenin's hope that every working musician could enjoy "this highly praised benefit" was frustrated because "only a handful of Locals have come into the Pension Plan...."[58]

Today, the freelance musician who might play at a hotel or downtown club on Friday or Saturday night, might play Sunday afternoon at a country club, and on other days or in other weeks might play for a wedding, private party, or Bar Mitzvah (and each gig for a different employer) is the AFM member who needs this benefit most. However, in less than fifty locals (out of over five hundred) does the contract call for employers' contribution to the AFM-EP. The great majority of the locals resist putting this additional cost in their agreements "so we don't price ourselves out of the market completely."[59] As in other unions and businesses, most young workers are not particularly interested in pensions; they much prefer a higher wage scale.

The concept for the Special Payments Funds really began in 1959 when, for the first time, the Kenin administration negotiated reuse fees for the performing musician of videotapes. Of course, these fees were "negotiated from" payments previously scheduled to be paid to the MPTF. The pattern of providing reuse fees to performers instead of the MPTF was continued in the jingles pact later in 1959. 1960 brought the principle of reuse fees for performers of filmed television programs. Finally, in January 1964, the new contract with the record industry provided that fifty percent of revenues previously payable to MPTF be paid instead to recording musicians—The Phonograph Record Special Payments Fund had officially arrived. This was the fulfillment of the Kenin pledge in 1961 which brought about the dissolution of the MGA.

The first year's payment totaled "some $720,000 to more than 12,000 recording musicians."[60] Each record maker bases its contribution on sales. Each musician receives payment based upon the proportion between his or her annual scale wages from recording and the total scale wages paid to all performers in the year preceding distribution. There is also a sliding scale of payments in each of four succeeding years. Unlike most royalty arrangements, fund revenue is derived from overall record sales and not on sales of a specific record. Two musicians who earned the same scale wages in a given period will receive the same amount of money from the fund even if one had played on a hit record and the other had not.[61]

By 1968, the distribution from the Phonograph Record Special Payment Fund was "about $5,000,000 ... to approximately 18,000 members."[62] In 1974, the distribution was over $8,000,000[63]; in 1978, almost $15,500,000[64]; and in 1984, $9,2000,000.[65] The MPTF's potential loss was the recording musicians' personal gain.

In 1972, a Theatrical Motion Picture Special Payments Fund was begun based on the pattern of the Phonograph

Record Special Payment Fund. The Theatrical Motion Picture Fund derives revenue from reuse of theatrical movies on television, cable networks, and videocassettes. Filmmakers contribute monies based on sales, and film musicians receive payment based on earnings of specific films, unlike the overall sales concept of the Record Fund. This Theatrical Motion Picture Special Payments Fund is administered separately by the United States Trust Company,[66] but accounting procedures are handled by the staff of the AFM-EP Fund. This arrangement helps assure accuracy in recording both pension and special payments to the individual musician's accounts.

The AFM-EP Fund and the Special Payments Funds provide good examples of actions by Kenin, the pragmatist with a soul. Both funds were practical—they defused and compromised disagreement with the MGA and within the Federation—and they provided "a better deal for the working musician."[67]

THE CONGRESS OF STRINGS—THE NOBLE EXPERIMENT IN PUBLIC RELATIONS AND EDUCATION

In 1957, a small group of musicians concerned about the growing shortage of good string players brought the problem to the attention of Herman Kenin, who was then west coast representative of the AFM.[68] For many reasons, including expectations of small financial remuneration, talented young musicians were not learning to play the violin, viola, cello, and double bass in sufficient numbers and with sufficient skill to supply the needs of symphony orchestras in the United States and Canada.

It was the marching and concert bands that attracted most attention in high schools and universities. And the numerous wind and percussion players who formed these organizations were talented, well trained, and honed to high musical standards by much competition. After all, each symphony orchestra will employ only three trumpet players chosen from the hundreds of trumpet players already in the market plus the hundreds of trumpet players that each year join the professional market. On the other hand, each orchestra needs at least thirty to forty violinists. The market had only a minimal supply, and the comparatively few university and conservatory orchestras formed a much smaller pool of talented, not so well trained players who entered the market, players who were not pushed toward high musical attainment because there was little competition. There was almost a double standard of performance in professional orchestras. The wind and percussion players gained their positions in a highly competitive market; the string players, especially those in the rear of their sections, were not of the same musical caliber.

Kenin, a violinist, was sympathetic and, as a union leader, also aware of certain public relations aspects that could be helpful to the Federation. Later that same year, 1957, the International Executive Board and Petrillo were approached with the problem and approved in principle a scholarship program for young string performers, the details to be worked out later. But with Kenin's election as International President in June 1958, the proposed scholarship program moved ahead at an accelerated rate.

Roy Harris, a noted American composer who was also an AFM member, was one of the original group of musicians who had approached Kenin earlier; it was to Harris that Kenin turned to head this "noble experiment." "A nation-wide education-labor-industry project to help correct the growing shortage of fine young string players"[69] was an attractive, educational, and public relations venture for the Federation. The AFM was emphasizing youth, live music, our "cultural heritage," and cooperation with educational and industrial leadership. The project had a winning combination of attributes.

In January 1959, an International Advisory Committee was named for the first Congress of Strings to be held at Greenleaf Lake, Oklahoma, that summer. They included James P. Mitchell, Secretary of Labor, conductors Leonard Bernstein, Eugene Ormandy and Leopold Stokowski, violinists Yehudi Menuhin and Szyman Goldberg, cellist Gregor Piatigorsky (all except Mitchell were AFM members), and representatives of the National Federation of Music clubs, Music Educators National Conference, and American String Teachers Association.[70] It was an imposing listing but did not include The American Symphony Orchestra League (the organization representing the management of United States and Canadian orchestras), which would receive the direct benefits of the project.

At first, the funding of the Congress of Strings was to be shared by the AFM, educators, and industry. The Federation, through sponsoring locals, would choose and support with $300-scholarships at least fifty talented string players. Education-Industry would provide the setting and the cost of the staff and program. The AFM also paid for the students' roundtrip transportation until cost cutting became a necessity in 1982.

The Congress of Strings at Greenleaf Lake was a success. Instead of "a minimum of fifty students," AFM locals sponsored eighty-two string players. The professional staff included the concertmaster and associate concertmaster of the Chicago Symphony and the concertmaster of the San Francisco Symphony, the principal violists of the New York Philharmonic and Cleveland Orchestra, the principal cellists of the New York Philharmonic and the Pittsburgh Symphony, and the principal double bassist of the Chicago Symphony.[71] The educational program consisted of private lessons, coaching sessions, sectional and full rehearsals, and concerts of the orchestra and chamber music recitals. The eight-week summer school was the model for annual editions of the Congress of Strings.

Succeeding years brought continued support from Federation locals as they supplied student scholarships at the rate of $300 (then $400, $500, and $600). The staff continued to be outstanding performers who held principal positions in many major symphony orchestras. The educational program continued to train the young players to be more proficient instrumentalists and to learn the techniques and "folkways" of orchestral performance. The conducting staff included the stars of the orchestral world: Eugene Ormandy, Erich Leinsdorf, William Steinberg, Max Rudolph, Isler Solomon, and Morton Gould, to name but a few.[72]

The educational setting changed through the years from a rather primitive Oklahoma state park to university campuses. In 1960, the Congress of Strings was held on the campus of Inter-American University in Puerto Rico; Michigan State University was the host through 1966. From 1967 through 1980, there were two locations each year: a university on the West Coast and the Saratoga Performing Arts Center in New York, followed by the University of Cincinnati in the Midwest. Beginning in 1981, the University of Cincinnati was the sole sponsor until the 1985 session at Southern Methodist University in Dallas, 1986 at Columbia University in New York City, and 1987 at Wayne State University in Detroit.

Although there was substantial cost for the sponsoring university, it was potentially an effective recruiting device. The university orchestras as well as the professional orchestras were short of string players. The universities that offered their facilities to support the Congress of Strings used the eight-week (later six-week) sessions to attract these highly desirable string players for their undergraduate and graduate programs. After all, it would be meaningless to attempt to train orchestral wind and percussion players if a complete orchestra were not available.

In more recent years, although AFM support for the Congress of Strings remains strong, there are those who are less enthusiastic now that the string shortage (in both quantity and quality) is not so severe. This improvement is due in no small measure to the increased financial reward offered in the past decade or so by the professional orchestras. The Federation has been and is, the major source of financial support for the Congress of Strings. Even with the contribution of the sponsoring university, the $60,000 grant from the Rockefeller Foundation in 1966,[73] and smaller awards from the National Endowment for the Arts beginning in the 1970s (the Congress of Strings had by this time became a nonprofit corporation),[74] the AFM spends many thousands of dollars each year for the program.

There are many intangible rewards for this support. Kenin believed that the Congress of Strings helped the Federation to preserve "our musical heritage."[75] Others felt the program was an investment in the future of the union. The fact that Congress of Strings alumni (now numbering over 2,500) are now members of all major orchestras in North America speaks well of their abilities and the program they represent. The positive public relations aspect of the Congress of Strings is still present, but perhaps somewhat diminished over the almost thirty years of Congresses. Some Federation members question whether the AFM now can afford this altruistic program. They say, "Isn't this the job of the American Symphony Orchestra League, or the individual symphonies, and the universities and conservatories?"[76] The answer is probably "yes"—but those organizations didn't do it. The AFM deserves full credit for supporting a program of real worth at considerable expense and without the usual monetary return. This effort is probably without parallel in labor history, begun by a Kenin with more soul than pragmatism.

THE TROUBLES OF SYMPHONY PLAYERS—ICSOM AND THE ROAD TO A MORE DEMOCRATIC UNION

The decade of the 1960s: the decade of the Vietnam conflict; the decade of the peaceful hippies and the violence of the civil rights conflict and the assassinations of President John F. Kennedy, Robert Kennedy and Martin Luther King, Jr.; the decade of protest.

Attitudes and conditions of our society necessarily reflect on and cause changes within all segments of the society. The American Federation of Musicians was not exempt. One of the protests of the 1960s was by some of the musicians of the symphony orchestras, a small minority of Federation membership.

The structure of the AFM allows complete autonomy to locals to set scale wages and make contracts and agreements to provide music within their jurisdictions. As long as the national constitution and bylaws are not violated, local control is complete.

Since a huge majority of Federation members are part of the entertainment business, playing for hotels, country clubs, nightclubs, shows, cafes, restaurants, dances, Bar Mitzvahs, weddings, and the like, it is natural that local officials for the most part are drawn from their ranks and spend most of their time supervising and supporting these musicians and their economic welfare. The nonprofit activities of symphony orchestras, as opposed to the profit oriented entertainment fields, have different priorities, different working conditions, and different goals for its musicians. It was no wonder that many local officials in the early 1960s (and before) were unfamiliar with the orchestra players' concerns. It also was no wonder that they resisted efforts by orchestra musicians to supply input and advice: such efforts threatened officials' position of authority. The majority of orchestras did not even have an elected orchestra committee to represent the union and orchestra players in the period between contract negotiations.

In 1962, almost no orchestra players participated in negotiations and no orchestra players had the right to ratify their contracts or to be represented by legal counsel of their choice.[77] Ironically, the Boston Symphony players, who did not become part of the AFM until 1942, were the only orchestra musicians to be directly involved in negotiations. Because their orchestra committee had long been their representatives, the Boston AFM local simply formalized the agreement between orchestra players and management.

Times were not good for orchestra musicians in the early 1960s: "… most musicians in major symphony orchestras were employed little more than six months annually at a yearly salary that was barely a living wage, about $4,000."[78] Musicians had little job security and were subject to immediate and arbitrary dismissal.[79] The contracts agreed to by Federation local officials were often disappointing. The officials were ignorant of orchestra players' desires and/or they had difficulty bargaining successfully with managements of nonprofit organizations. Many of these local officials were suspected of arranging "sweetheart" deals because "it was a lot less trouble."[80] Federation officials at both the national and local levels believed that the orchestra musicians were "naive and impractical" or "crazy nuts" or "babes-in-the-woods" and were incapable of being meaningful negotiators.[81]

In any case, wages and working conditions were so slow to improve that orchestra musicians became increasingly impatient, frustrated, and resentful. The evidence was broadly apparent. First in the New York Philharmonic contract negotiations in 1957 and next in 1959 (when the Philadelphia Orchestra won the right to have an observer at future negotiations), the discontent was openly displayed.[82]

The Kenin administration was aware of this unrest among symphony musicians. The 1960 Convention had voted down a resolution to form a National Conference of Symphony Musicians to exchange ideas and study and recommend legislation to the IEB.[83] As an attempt to air the problems and "to explore ways and means by which the Federation might give greater assistance to the needs of some 2,500 musicians playing in symphony orchestras,"[84] a Symphony Symposium was convened in New York in July 1960, only one month after the convention. This, the first conference in the Federation's history to deal exclusively with symphonic problems, was prepared carefully. An agenda committee representing orchestras and locals met with the IEB beforehand and was instructed by Kenin.[85] Each of the twenty-five orchestras invited had two representatives, one from the city's local and the other an elected orchestra member. Kenin made it clear that this meeting was for discussion only and that AFM bylaws could be changed only by the annual convention. The agenda included orchestra players' representation in negotiations, the ratification of contracts, pensions, a central clearinghouse for vacancies, and other items not so immediately concerned with player-union relationships. The meeting may have helped as a forum to vent pent-up feelings, but following events proved that no meaningful accords were reached.

In 1961, the Cleveland Orchestra players advised against accepting a new contract by a vote of 85 to 10. When the contract was approved by the executive board of Local 4 in the face of this strong rejection, "... a committee appointed by members of the ensemble brought a court action against Local 4 officers. They were charged with failing to represent the concert group's musicians fairly."[86] All told, there were three legal suits filed in this disagreement over the right to ratify contracts. The dispute was finally settled in 1964 by a compromise. Local 4's executive board agreed to abide by a 60-percent majority vote of the Cleveland Orchestra musicians. Some years later, another vote of the Cleveland Orchestra musicians by an even more lopsided margin, advised against the choice of a new musical director. Their advice was rejected again, this time by management.

The AFM convention in 1962, seemingly unconcerned with the dissatisfaction in the ranks of the symphony players, voted down a resolution to form a Symphony Department to advise the IEB, to give symphony orchestra members the right to elect orchestra committees to advise and consult with the local union's executive board, and to give orchestra members the right to ratify contracts.[87]

Later that same year, some Chicago Symphony musicians filed a complaint with the National Labor Relations Board against Petrillo and Local 10 over restrictions on outside jobs and denial of representation at negotiations.

As a result of these frustrating and negative situations, "the International Conference of Symphony and Opera Musicians (ICSOM) was formed in 1962 [in Cleveland], the culmination of a meeting held by the delegates of 20 United States and Canadian major orchestras. Its stated purpose was to 'promote the welfare of, and make more rewarding the livelihood of the orchestral performer, and enrich the life of our society.' "[88]

Of course this gathering of musicians from twenty orchestras was not the first opportunity for musicians from different orchestras to exchange views and information. In 1961, the Philadelphia Orchestra on tour in Chicago afforded a chance for the two orchestra committees to meet. They met twice more in Chicago along with seven, then nine, other orchestra committees (or representatives from these committees). The desire for shared information and the satisfactions of learning about others who believed in the same goals made the formation of ICSOM a foregone conclusion.

In the midst of this flurry of meetings, Kenin invited "local officers and representatives of symphony orchestras with an annual budget of $350,000 or more ... to attend the Second International Symphony Symposium"[89] in October 1962. This symposium had been postponed from 1961 because of the lawsuits involving the Cleveland Orchestra and Local 4. As was the case with the first symposium, the agenda was carefully prepared and included: ratification of contracts, hiring and dismissal procedures, continuity of these symposiums, and creation of a Symphony department and orchestra committees. Not surprisingly, no conclusions were reached, but the levels of animosity reached new highs.[90]

Shortly after this meeting (January 1963), the first issue of the official publication of ICSOM, *Senza Sordino* (a musical term meaning "without mute") was distributed. Its publication was in response to "a mandate by the [orchestra] representatives who met in Chicago in May, 1962."[91] The need for open communication among all orchestras was an important priority. As the voice of the orchestra musician, its views complemented the views of management and the Federation.

ICSOM was not welcomed by the AFM hierarchy. There were accusations of dual unionism and threats to "crush you like ants."[92] Indeed, there were serious discussions in these early meetings of affiliation with other unions—these were angry young men.[93] The all-important issues in these years, the right to have input in negotiations and the right to ratify agreements, were not addressed by the IEB and Kenin. These issues were considered the concern of the locals and "untouchable" at the national level.

The third and last Symphony Symposium in this series, held in October 1963, was doomed from the start by animosity and hostility on both sides. Kenin, using restraint, discussed the progress being made in achieving higher wages and better working conditions for symphony players. But he also faced the issue of dual unionism squarely: he promised that the AFM would fight and predicted the collapse of any rival union.[94] Considering the written record and the reports of those who attended these meetings, an inescapable conclusion is that Kenin was supportive of ICSOM's goals but would not sacrifice the AFM's constitution and bylaws to achieve them. The same sympathetic attitude was not present among some members of the IEB and some long-time local officials.

There was gradual change in the attitudes of local officials. Slowly, one by one, orchestras were permitted to elect orchestra committees. These committees were allowed to participate (first as observers) in negotiations, and the orchestra members were permitted to ratify contracts. The tolerance level for ICSOM continued to rise.[95]

In response, ICSOM made conciliatory moves. In 1965, it agreed to send observers to the 1966 AFM Convention, suggested a meeting of its executive committee with the IEB and Kenin, and requested official conference status within the Federation.[96]

But perhaps the biggest assistance in achieving a long

sought ICSOM goal—full year orchestra employment—was the 1966 Ford Foundation Grant of $85,000,000 in matching funds to U.S. symphony orchestras. "Two major objectives of the program [were] to provide symphony musicians with year-round employment and to raise 'the income and prestige of orchestra members.' "[97] Although Canadian orchestras were not included in the Ford grant, the major orchestras in Toronto and Montreal kept pace with the other ISCOM orchestras so that their musicians today enjoy comparable wages and working conditions. The Ford grant was successful: in 1965 there were only four orchestras with full-year contracts, with most symphonies having a season of thirty weeks or less[98]; in 1986 it was reported, "17 orchestras have year-round seasons, and the average season length of ICSOM symphony orchestras is 46 weeks."[99]

During the Kenin administration, ICSOM achieved its objectives from the early 1960s. In 1965, a small Emergency Relief Fund was established; in 1968, legal counsel was retained to advise on both the national and local level; 1969 brought the major goals of AFM conference status and the establishment of a Symphony Department in the international headquarters of the Federation; in 1970, ICSOM began conductor evaluations and the AFM convention established a strike fund with the loan of a $250,000 reserve from the general funds of the union.[100] During 1976, ICSOM started working with the Music Assistance Fund Orchestra Fellowships to help talented minority instrumentalists gain access to the major orchestras. In 1983, during the administration of Victor W. Fuentealba, AFM bylaws were amended to give ratification rights to all orchestra members.[101] This was an important milestone, acknowledging that most orchestra members had been exercising this right for many years.

Along the way, ICSOM itself became fragmented. In

1975, the Organization of Canadian Symphony Musicians (OCSM) was formed to attend "to orchestral matters Canadian in nature."[102] Supplementing ICSOM's agenda for the major orchestras is ROPA (Regional Orchestra Players Association), formed in 1984. ROPA collects and distributes essential information about the regional orchestras, those with smaller budgets than the major orchestras.[103]

ICSOM's grievance agenda from the early 1960s had been satisfied largely during the Kenin administration. In more recent years, ICSOM's attention has been directed toward the rights of women and minorities in the major orchestras, support for the Congress of Strings, "musical medicine" (the physical afflictions and possible remedies for orchestra players—the organization has sponsored a special medical questionnaire and has been instrumental in encouraging medical seminars and conferences covering subjects such as surgical intervention, stress, risk factors, performance anxiety, practice and performance habits, jaw and hearing problems, etc.[104]), participation in recording and video negotiations, the establishment of fair and equitable audition procedures, and the issue of Federation and local work dues.

The 1980 AFM Convention passed a resolution adding a new one-percent work dues to be split equally between the Federation and the local. ICSOM's objection was more against adding to the locals' already existing work dues pattern than to the one-half percent to support the national and international structure: in many situations, the orchestra player contributes two and one half to three percent of his or her scale salary plus regular dues to the Federation. One orchestra member said, "That's 1% of AFM membership contributing 75% of the work dues."[105] Actually, this probably exaggerates the imbalance, but even AFM national officers admit that "perhaps 1% of the membership [orchestra musicians] pays 20–25% of the work dues."[106]

Local and national AFM officers thought the work dues paid by orchestra members were justified because of the current services rendered by the Federation as well as the union's long continued pressures exerted over many years to place the orchestra players in their well-paid positions. This is, of course, the same argument presented by AFM leaders in the battles with Cecil Read and the Local 47 revolters—the argument of trade unionism. The many unemployed or partially employed AFM members also thought the work dues were justified. One such Federation member voiced the opinion (heard many times in many locals), "If I was working, I'd be glad to give 3% to the union."[107]

ICSOM believed differently. They argued that the large proportion of dues paid by a very small proportion of members was unfair. Their 1980 convention resolved to seek a repeal of the work tax or a limit on the dollar amount of the increase.[108] They were unsuccessful, and the dispute continued.

Five years later, work dues were still an issue. President Fuentealba, speaking at ICSOM's 1985 Convention, acknowledged that symphony musicians were paying an inordinately large and disproportionate amount of work dues. He promised to vigorously pursue the establishment of some sort of cap on work dues. He also promised to convene union local presidents and local orchestra representatives to discuss the services that unions offer to orchestras.[109] In a real sense, this meeting is a prolonged continuation of the "Symphony Seminars" conducted by Kenin beginning in the early 1960s and continued by President Hal Davis in the 1970s—an opportunity for conciliation and exchange of views.

Although voices of moderation on both sides hoped for a compromise on local work dues, in certain locals outraged partisans battled openly. Local officers accused orchestra players of being "pie-in-the-sky" dreamers and "spoiled brats" while orchestra players responded with threats of dual unionism and disaffiliation.

The meeting between local officers and orchestra representatives promised by Fuentealba in 1985 was held in Chicago in May 1986. The big issue was the large percentage of work dues paid by orchestra musicians compared to services the AFM provided in return. Name calling and threats continued, with calmer persons on both sides calling for reasoned debate.

In January 1987, a work dues committee (including representatives of ICSOM, local unions, and the AFM Symphony Department) appointed by Fuentealba met, making no recommendation for reduction of work dues for any segment of AFM population. The committee specifically rejected sliding scales, "caps" on dues, or credits toward per-capita tax. Instead, the recommendations concerned additional efforts by locals to collect work dues from all members and outlined the local's responsibility to provide at its own expense "competent, professional representation for contract negotiations and the processing of grievances and arbitration for symphony players."[110] The 1987 Convention followed through by mandating this professional representation with the proviso that it would be supplied by the Federation if locals were unable or unwilling to do so.[111] Because this is not the solution ICSOM desires, further conflict and compromise is certain to continue.

Not everyone thought ICSOM a good idea, or that it should be a conference of the Federation. One AFM national official thought in some respects ICSOM was justified but that, as with the highly-paid recording musicians in Los Angeles, its members enjoyed their good jobs because the strength of the Federation got them there. He also believed the Ford Foundation grant was a big mistake: because it gave the orchestra players too much too soon, they began to feel they were in a different class from other musicians. He added that the AFM should not be a group of conferences—ICSOM, Recording Musicians, ROPA, OCSM, and others—because this diluted the strength of the Federation.[112] These opinions have a familiar ring. They are the arguments of bona fide trade unionists and are shared by many in the AFM.

Disapproval of ICSOM came from still another direction. Gunther Schuller, prominent American conductor, composer, educator, and performer, views professional symphony musicians as "... embittered, disgruntled, bored [individuals] who ... hate music ... and for whom a rehearsal is an excruciating agony, at best a necessary evil." He adds, "For young, innocent musicians, it is often hard to resist the peer group pressures that exist in our orchestras nowadays, and there is unfortunately much in our modern union mentality—what I call the ICSOMization of our orchestras—that turns our profession more and more into a business (not even a creative business, for business, too, can be creative) in which attempts to preserve music as an art are constantly undermined."[113]

Orchestra managers have mixed feelings about ICSOM. One long-time manager said, "I much prefer dealing with the local offices—they're realistic and you don't have to fight off harebrained ideas."[114] Another manager appreciated the more intimate knowledge of his orchestra brought to the bargaining table by the orchestra committee. He felt dealing with ICSOM "an advantage for all over the old ways."[115]

Perhaps the kindest comments for both the AFM leadership and the musicians who formed ICSOM are those of H.W. Benson in his book, *Democratic Rights for Union Members*. He wrote, "... This kind of potential opposition, this challenge to the officialdom [could] have led, in all likelihood, to bitter, destructive crises. But it is possible for a responsible union leadership to adjust peaceably to democracy. The AFM leadership, yielding to the need for special representation, began to cultivate its own dissatisfied members, supported them in collective bargaining, and finally wooed them back into the field."[116] The pragmatist with a soul—Herman Kenin—would have approved that analysis.

THE BLACK EXPERIENCE—WITHIN THE FEDERATION; WITHIN THE PROFESSION

The decade of protest, the 1960s, brought substantial change for black people in North America. The civil rights movement, stalled for over fifty years by the 1896 U.S. Supreme Court decision which made lawful the "separate but equal" philosophy, was given new life by the Court's 1954 ruling ending segregation in public schools. This was followed by the Civil Rights Act of 1964 which banned discrimination because of a person's color, race, national origin, religion, or sex—the strongest civil rights bill in the country's history. In 1960, Canada's Parliament established the Canadian Bill of Rights. Legal theory was firmly in place.

Times were changing. President Harry Truman ordered integration of all black military personnel in 1948. Jackie Robinson broke the color line in major league baseball in 1947. There were black faces in the U.S. Congress.

Labor unions were gradually changing too, but there was a long journey ahead. Reported as recently as 1946, "The constitution of nine international unions explicitly deny the right to join on racial grounds" and "five large AFL unions instead of openly excluding Negroes, provide for admitting them to auxiliary unions."[117]

The AFM was not different from the society it represented. In 1944, there were approximately fifty black locals
in cities which also had a white local. Of these black locals,
twelve were subsidiary to the neighboring white local.
These subsidiary black locals were issued their own charters (which meant self-government) by the Petrillo administration in 1944, the "separate but equal" standard finally
having been achieved by the Federation.

Black locals in the AFM have a long history. The first
"colored" local was chartered in 1902 in Chicago, and its
affiliation "set the precedent for the AFM's recognition and
chartering of separate, 'colored' Locals."[118] Of the original fifty black locals in the 1940s, " ... the majority were
below the Mason-Dixon Line but there [were] ...
colored Locals in Boston, Bridgeport and New Haven,
Connecticut, Atlantic City, Chicago, San Francisco and
Seattle just to name a few."[119]

The official position of the AFM in those days was
ambiguous. On the one hand, black locals were chartered
and rechartered,[120] and employment ads accepted by the
International Musician such as, "Very fine opportunity for
young white musician ... " or "Guitarist, colored, desiring
...,[121] were common. On the other hand, a picnic scheduled for the 1946 AFM Convention in St. Petersburg,
Florida, was cancelled when it became clear that state
segregation laws were to be enforced. The following statement in 1954 by William P. Streeper, then department
supervisor in the office of the treasurer of the AFM, makes
clear the uncertain attitude of the Federation: "The colored musician holds no secondary class membership inso-
far as the Federation is concerned. He may be denied
admission in certain Locals ... but he is granted the
privilege of joining any other neighboring Local that will
accept him."[122]

The climate of the times encouraged the end of

segregation, and the merger of these "separate but equal" locals began in Los Angeles. The merger of Local 767 and Local 47 was achieved in 1953[123] after almost three years of negotiations.[124] The situation was not the same in San Francisco. In 1956, Local 6 defeated a proposal to integrate with black Local 669,[125] which had been subsidiary to Local 6 until its own charter was issued in 1945.[126]

The AFM Convention in 1957 was presented with a resolution (number 34) by Los Angeles Local 47 (recently integrated), which demanded that "in any ... jurisdiction where two or more Locals exist, immediate steps be taken to merge on an equitable basis ... " and, if this were not done, "that the International Executive Board be empowered to ... amalgamate [these locals]." The convention voted that the resolution be referred to the office of the President.[127] An opposing petition, signed by sixty black delegates, accompanied the resolution: "The subject matter ... should not be acted upon at this time because of the financial aspect involved with some of the larger colored Locals.... The subject matter can best be resolved by its various Locals involved, who are better informed as to the advantages or disadvantages of a merger. Under no circumstances should a merger be forced upon us, but should rather be accomplished by mutual agreement between parties concerned."[128]

There were reasons for the opposition of black delegates to enforced integration on a Federation-wide basis. A few black locals had a higher per-capita treasury than the white local in the same jurisdiction; black officers would lose their jobs and trips to annual conventions in a merger with a larger white local; members of locals would lose their sense of identity and "brotherhood"; and (in some cases) it was painful to be forced to integrate with whites who had turned them down in the past.[129]

Petrillo, in an interview with *The New York Times* in

1957, "...made it clear that he was personally opposed to segregation but that he was even more strongly opposed to compelling locals to integrate....The smaller Negro locals would be swallowed up by the larger white organization if mergers were enforced."[130] He did warn white locals that "...if a colored local wants to join you, you had better take them in. Because if you don't, we're going to force you to."[131]

Not all black musicians shared the views of the sixty black delegates who signed the petition against Federation-forced integration. In March 1954, a group of fifteen black musicians from Los Angeles, including Nat (King) Cole, sent an appeal to George Meany, president of the AFL-CIO, urging action on AFM integration. "The statement concluded: 'It is inconceivable to us how a labor union can say that it supports F.E.P.C. [Fair Employment Practices Commission] legislation when it refuses membership because of race.' "[132]

Meanwhile, under pressure begun by the Attorney General of California in 1959,[133] Locals 669 and 6 in San Francisco merged in 1960, almost four years after an amalgamation offer had been rejected by white Local 6. The merger agreement guaranteed to members of Local 669 two paid administrative posts and one position on the "new Local 6" executive board.[134]

Slowly, with pressure from President Kenin, there were other mergers in Denver in 1960[135] and in Cleveland in 1962.[136] But the AFM held its annual convention in Pittsburgh in 1962 with black Local 471 and white Local 60 as co-hosts.[137] In 1963 it seemed that Locals 10 and 208 in Chicago would merge, but in the midst of charges and countercharges, white Local 10 and black Local 208 switched sides back and forth—first one in favor of integration then the other. Finally, the mandated merger by the IEB was sustained by the 1964 Convention, and a trustee, Hal Davis (who would be the next International President of the union), was appointed to oversee the process.[138]

In December 1964, fulfilling "the unanimously expressed desire of our 1964 Convention concurred in by our International Executive Board,"[139] Kenin appointed Petrillo as chairman of the new AFM Civil Rights Department to complete "the orderly merger of its remaining dual Locals serving single jurisdictions."[140] A more popular choice could not be imagined. Petrillo at his appearance at the 1964 national convention drew sustained applause and cheers. It was obvious he had the popularity to complete an unpopular task. He said he intended to do the job " ... in such a manner as to guarantee the rights of all musicians affected."[141] Kenin the pragmatist, had scored another triumph.

At the time of Petrillo's appointment to head the AFM Civil Rights Department, there were 38 jurisdictions with two locals. By the spring of 1966, there were still about 25 cities with segregated locals.[142] Petrillo told *The New York Times*, "The problem is not one of geography or even of ancient racial antagonisms. Small, segregated locals, whether Negro or white, whether Northern or Southern, don't want to give up their prerogatives. These include autonomy, ownership of real estate, independent treasuries and the privilege of an annual paid trip for delegates to the national convention."[143]

Merger agreements differed, depending upon individual circumstances. For example, the two-year agreement merging Local 11 (white) and Local 637 (black) in Louisville (effective April 1, 1967) included: combined assets to be shared; no additional fees to be charged members in good standing of either local to become members of the new merged local; Local 637 (which was much smaller) was assured that one of its members would serve as advisor to the local president, one member would serve on the executive board, one member would be an assistant business agent, and one member would be a delegate to the national convention; the work dues were lowered to the 1% charged by Local 637 from the 3% charged by Local 11.[144]

The two-year agreement merging Locals 101 (white) and 473 (black) in Dayton (effective November 1, 1970[145]) included: shared assets; equal rights, privileges and benefits for all members; full death benefits and life membership privileges for all at the higher level of Local 101; Local 473 (the smaller local) was assured the positions of vice president, assistant secretary-treasurer, one executive board member-assistant business agent, and one delegate to the national convention; the dues structure would be that of Local 101, but members in good standing of Local 473 would keep their lower dues structure until January 10, 1971.[146]

The merging process did not go smoothly in all situations. The convention in 1968 heard requests from members of desegregated locals in New Haven and Chicago for the return of their original (segregated) charters.[147] The bureaucratic allotment of positions within the new desegregated locals was not always fair, and the black members faced the "tyranny of the majority." Because the black musician was in the minority, his or her stake in the union was much different than in the all-black local. Feelings ran high. There were reports of black resignations[148] and even talk of "joining the Teamsters where we would be able to keep our identity."[149]

There were some resignations of black musicians but no appearance of Teamster-sponsored musicians' unions. At the 1971 Convention, International President Hal Davis reported that all mergers had been completed except "... two Locals refused to merge—#274 in Philadelphia and #814 in Cincinnati."[150] These black locals could not come to satisfactory terms with their neighboring white locals, and the problem was "solved" by the cancellation of their charters by the IEB with the concurrence of the convention.

In 1975, Petrillo resigned from the AFM's Civil Rights Department (he was almost eighty-three years old) thinking, no doubt, that the task of integration was completed. It was not. Blacks were not integrated into the white locals, they were submerged. Fewer and fewer black musicians were delegates at the national and regional conventions: "There was just a sea of white faces."[151]

The 1974 Convention had only ten black delegates from a total of 1,096. This exceedingly small black representation brought a response from the AFM leadership. Acting upon a resolution at the 1975 Convention, an ad hoc committee was established to advise the IEB.[152] Its report resulted in the following amendment to the Constitution of the AFM at the 1977 Convention: "A merged Local, whose merger was the result of compliance with the Civil Rights policy of the American Federation of Musicians shall be entitled to one additional delegate to be elected from the black membership of said Local."[153]

From a high of 73 black delegates from segregated locals to a low of 10 black delegates in 1974 (16 in 1977 when the above amendment was introduced[154]), the AFM Convention has gradually increased its black representation, but it still looks like "a sea of white faces."

In contrast to the relative absence of blacks in the hierarchy of the Federation, some fields of musical performance have very high populations of blacks while in other areas it is almost a surprise to see black performers. Jazz, one of the great contributions to American (and world) music, was exclusively the province of black musicians for almost three decades. The white jazz musicians didn't arrive on the scene until the late 1920s and 1930s. Begin-ning with Scott Joplin, Bessie Smith, Jelly Roll Morton, Louis Armstrong, and their many relatively unsung (and many times unnamed) black contemporaries, Americans were introduced to jazz. Not until Bix Biederbecke in the late 1920s and Benny Goodman in the 1930s did equally talented white players join in making this new kind of music. In the heydays of swing and the "big bands" (the 1930s and 1940s) the tradition of segregation kept both white and black bands making music "separate but equal." The black bands of Duke Ellington, Count Basie, and Jimmy Lunceford and the white bands of Artie Shaw, Tommy Dorsey, and Glenn Miller all played the one-nighters and the big hotels, but not as mixed black and white groups.

The first recordings we have of a black-white perfor-mance of headliners is the famous Benny Goodman Trio—Benny Goodman (clarinet), Teddy Wilson (piano), and Gene Krupa (drums)—in 1935. Whitney Balliett tells us that John Hammond "... took a *mixed* band ... to the staid Mt. Kisco Golf and Tennis Club for a 1932 Saturday night dance,"[155] probably the first black-white group to perform live before a paying audience. Today the jazz tradition continues with many black groups and soloists, white groups and soloists, and mixed groups as well. Again it was Benny Goodman who first integrated a "big band" in the late 1930s with the addition of Lionel Hampton and Teddy Wilson.

Other areas of performance took much longer to integrate. Reedman Buddy Collette was probably the first black to play in a TV studio orchestra in Hollywood on a "Groucho Marx Show" broadcast in the 1950s.[156] Not so coincidentally, Collette also led the fight to integrate Local 47 in 1953. As recently as 1956, one white performer would not take part in rehearsals and performances when the Symphony of the Air in New York engaged three black players.[157]

In 1958, the Urban League of New York accused the New York Philharmonic, the Metropolitan Opera Orchestra, the Little Orchestra, the New York City Center Orchestra, the Symphony of the Air, the Lewisohn Stadium summer orchestra, the Goldman Band, the Broadway musical show orchestras, and the three major television and radio networks of racial discrimination. Quite a listing. The prima facie evidence was clear. The New York Philharmonic and the Metropolitan Opera Orchestra had never employed a black. The Little Symphony and the New York City Center Orchestra had each employed one black musician. The Symphony of the Air had hired three blacks in 1956 for one concert only. The Lewisohn Stadium summer orchestra and the Goldman Band had no black musicians. Twenty-six Broadway musicals from 1956 to 1958 had employed only fourteen blacks of a total of 650 musicians. And of the three major television and radio networks, NBC had no black studio musicians, ABC had one, and CBS had five.[158]

In response, the Philharmonic said that, although it had always notified the union when it had vacancies, "… in the last ten years not one Negro had shown up to audition."[159] The Little Orchestra and the New York City Center Orchestra replied that they would employ anyone qualified; the Goldman Band said that a black had never sought an audition; NBC said they had hired black musicians on a freelance basis. One day after the Urban League charges were made, the New York State Commission Against Discrimination ordered an immediate investigation "to determine the facts."[160] The commission issued no constructive report, and it would be another decade before governmental action was again invited.

But New York was not alone in supplying examples of

segregated orchestras. In 1963, The New Symphony Orchestra in Oak Park and River Forest (Chicago suburbs), over the protest of the conductor, rejected a black violinist on racial grounds.[161] After pressure from community organizations, the Symphony Association offered a public apology and announced that in the future "membership would be based entirely on musicianship and auditions would be conducted with a screen between judges and prospective players."[162]

In the early 1960s, musicians themselves were attempting to remove segregation from the performance arena. Concert artists such as pianists Gary Graffman, Leon Fleisher, and Julius Katchen, violinist Jaime Laredo, conductors Leonard Bernstein, George Szell, and Erich Leinsdorf, soprano Brigid Nilsson, and trumpeter Al Hirt, as well as the Metropolitan Opera and Hootenanny U.S.A., refused to perform for segregated audiences.[163] It was a successful strategy.

Meanwhile, a new orchestra made its debut in New York in 1965. The Symphony of the New World, "that has as its basic concept racial balance,"[164] performed with 52 white, 36 black, and 7 Oriental musicians. The musical reviews were not glowing, but hope was extended for improvement with more experience and rehearsal.

In an article in *The New York Times* in 1967, Sanford Allen, hired in 1962 as the only black member of the New York Philharmonic, gave his views about "... the unfortunate conditions that have kept Negroes from the field of classical music."[165] He makes the following points: with no black musicians in our orchestras, young black children have no role models and therefore no incentive to study for the fifteen or more years required to obtain proficiency on an orchestral instrument; even if the young black player becomes proficient, he still must gain orchestra experience in smaller orchestras before he is ready for an audition for

a major orchestra position; since many of these lesser
orchestras are in smaller cities with restrictive social norms,
blacks face still more problems; many union locals are still
segregated, and the black player may not even learn about
an audition date; the young black musician may not have
studied with the "right" teacher or attended the "right"
conservatory, and the audition may well have been pre-
filled.

But there were beginnings of integrated orchestras. In
1967, there was one black musician in the New York
Philharmonic, one in the Cleveland Orchestra, and three
in the Pittsburgh Symphony. The Symphony of the New
World was beginning to give orchestra experience to black
players who in turn won auditions to play in orchestras in
Baltimore, Syracuse, Denver, Quebec, North Carolina,
Richmond, Minneapolis, and Milwaukee.[166]

Other orchestras were beginning to hunt for qualified
black musicians, but there were extra-musical problems:
the orchestra managers who complained that no black
player ever requested an audition, the conductors who
were fearful of losing their position if they hired a black,
and the orchestra personnel managers who consistently
hired substitutes within "the old-boy-network." Donald
White, the black cellist hired by conductor George Szell for
the Cleveland Orchestra in the 1950s, had problems joining the "right" segregated local in the city so he could play
in the orchestra.[167]

But there also was optimism about the end of segregation. Henry Lewis, the black conductor of the New Jersey
Symphony in 1968, thought that, all things being equal, a
black musician auditioning for an orchestra job against a
white player might have the advantage.[168] Today this
could be called "affirmative action." The New World
Symphony continued as an integrated orchestra, and The
Chicago Symphony Orchestra maintained "a first-rate
training orchestra, which has several Negroes enrolled."[169]

There was also a new (and short-lived) cooperative orchestra in New York. The New York Symphony, conducted by Joe Eger, gave five concerts in 1968–1969 and was to provide "a fully subsidized orchestra training program geared especially to disadvantaged urban areas and to the Negro community."[170] A more substantive venture, the New York City Housing Authority Symphony Orchestra, was created in 1971 and celebrated its fifteenth anniversary with a Lincoln Center Concert. The orchestra " ... reflects the ethnic and economic levels of 550,000 residents of the ... city's housing projects ..."[171] and is supported primarily by state and federal grants.

The years 1969 and 1970 brought the most publicized case of alleged racial bias in hiring musicians for the symphony orchestra. Two black musicians charged the New York Philharmonic with refusal to hire them because they were black. The case was brought before the city's Human Rights Commission and the media for more than fifteen months. The musicians claimed they had each auditioned on three separate occasions and were rejected for racial reasons only. Both had had previous orchestral experience. The orchestra held that the musicians had been auditioned in the same way as others but did not qualify.[172]

The commission's report, released in November 1970, "cleared the orchestra management of bias charges filed last July [1969]."[173] However, the commission did object to practices used to hire substitutes for the orchestra. The report stated: "The most striking statistic to emerge from the evidence presented was that during the 1960s the ... [Philharmonic] hired at least 277 different substitutes ... who played a total of 1,773 weeks ... of these one was black and he played for one week."[174] The commission also noted that the Philharmonic had no blacks in its administration or on its board of trustees.

In response to the Commission's report (and, of

course, changing times), the Philharmonic began making accommodations for blacks on the board of trustees (a black trustee was chosen in 1969) and in administration. In 1970, Leon Thompson, a black conductor, was hired as director of educational activities to contact black musicians for auditions and to establish a training and study program for young black instrumentalists and potential black audiences. Reports on the availability of black musicians were made regularly to other orchestras.

Results of this new attitude were quickly observable. Writing in 1972, Donal Henahan said, "Now there are even minority representatives on the Philharmonic board of directors (three) and on the upper rungs of administration (two). Black faces appear in the orchestra with increasing regularity, and it seems inevitable that some will be finding their way into permanent membership before too long."[175] Henahan was wrong in his predictions of more black musicians as permanent members of the Philharmonic "before too long." In 1977, Sanford Allen, still the orchestra's only regular black player, resigned, and the Philharmonic membership was completely white. It was not until the 1980s that there was more than one black permanent member of the orchestra.

A 1974 survey of the personnel of symphony orchestras by the National Urban League and the New World Symphony was not completely negative. The survey found "in 56 symphonies across the country, of the nearly 5,000 musicians playing regularly... only 70 were black."[176] Perhaps the shortage of good orchestrally trained string players that prompted the beginnings of the Congress of Strings was also having some small effect upon the segregated orchestra. Very gradually, more black string players were able to escape the economic hazards of an expensive and long training program requiring good teachers and a good instrument. The presence of an occasional role model in a major symphony (both the

Philadelphia Orchestra and the Boston Symphony hired their first black player in 1969) and the increased financial rewards now available with the help of the Ford Foundation grants served to attract more black classical musicians. The altruism apparent in the development and support of the Congress of Strings was again evident as the AFM and ICSOM began support of programs to produce more black string players for orchestras. One vehicle was the Music Assistance Fund, an independent charitable trust begun in 1965 "for the specific purpose of encouraging talented instrumental musicians in various American minority populations to pursue professional careers in ... symphony orchestras."[177]

In 1976, Dr. Leon Thompson, the director of educational activities for the New York Philharmonic and secretary of the Music Assistance Fund (MAF), spoke to the annual ICSOM convention about a new plan to provide orchestral fellowships for non-white instrumentalists. Having approved the goals and concepts of the plan, ICSOM began to work with Thompson and the MAF to implement the program.[178]

The project, as endorsed and supported by ICSOM, involves placing a qualified black string player in a participating major or regional orchestra under the direct supervision of a section leader. The fellowship recipient is treated as a regular member of the orchestra and receives a stipend equal to the union minimum scale wage from the MAF and the orchestra for the concert year. This apprenticeship approach supplies the orchestral experience needed by talented players as they apply for their own orchestra job. Initial screening, interviews, and preliminary auditions are conducted by ICSOM. The additional time and efforts expended by section leaders is also freely given.[179]

Another project, developed by Local 76 in Seattle in 1968, made private music lessons available "to talented minority and economically disadvantaged children."[180]

Financial support comes from both the Washington State Arts Commission and Local 76. The project's evaluation in 1978 reported that recipients had gone on to the Congress of Strings, university music scholarships, and, in two cases, to positions in "nationally renowned" orchestras.

In 1972, the Los Angeles Philharmonic Association began The Los Angeles Philharmonic Orchestral Training Program for Minority Students as a cooperative venture of management and musicians. Lesson fees are partially underwritten by the orchestra, and members of the orchestra teach the lessons and coordinate the program. Results have indicated a new approach for communication between the ghettos and the art world—a means of creating a musically aware audience and not necessarily more orchestra performers (although by 1979 at least four "graduates" had won auditions for positions in major orchestras).[181]

By 1979, Leon Thompson was able to report that there were 49 black musicians who were permanent members of 28 world-known orchestras.[182] No metropolitan, community, or university orchestras were included, which undoubtedly would have increased the listing four or five-fold. The AFM and ICSOM have done (and are doing) a lion's share of the task of supplying string players, and specifically black string players, for our symphony orchestras. But the end of the black player shortage is not yet in sight. The Juilliard School of Music, which has trained roughly fifty percent of the personnel of the New York Philharmonic, in 1987 counted " ... only 15 black students in a music division of 730 students. ..."[183]

In other areas of the music business in the 1970s there were additional complaints by black musicians of unfair treatment. In 1970, Los Angeles' Local 47 (which had been integrated since 1953) faced grievances from the "100-plus Black Musicians Association" which claimed "job discrimination in disking, telefilm and feature pic fields."[184] The BMA claimed that only four blacks were hired for the 50-player Academy Award Show and demanded a 25-percent quota system to insure fair treatment. The union opposed a quota system and offered "to end any discriminatory practice brought to the Executive Board's attention."[185] Obviously, any claim of discrimination would be difficult to prove since subjective criteria of musical ability must be used by contractors and leaders in choosing players. On the other hand, the "old-boy-system" was undoubtedly used by some so that friends and relatives, deserving or not, were the benefactors.

In 1972, the AFM in Las Vegas faced similar charges of discrimination in hiring for the hotel house bands. Here unintentional hiring affronts may have occurred because "very few blacks have come to live in the city."[186] Unfair housing practices can often result in unfair hiring practice, with no fault attributed to the union.

The black experience in the union and in the profession reflects the values of the total society. The evidence does not indicate worse treatment for blacks within the union or the profession compared to all of society. In some instances, the AFM has adopted affirmative action postures long before the political climate demanded them. The record is not "black and white," but the Federation's shade of gray is on the bright side.

LEGISLATIVE SUCCESSES: THE NATIONAL ENDOWMENT FOR THE ARTS AND THE CABARET TAX

The Lea Act was passed by Congress in 1946. It was not repealed until 1980, thirty-four years later. This was a very slow return on Federation efforts to make political change. The AFM had much better political success in obtaining federal legislation in support of the arts. When President Johnson signed into law the Arts and Humanities Bill in 1965 (the enabling legislation for the National Endowment for the Arts) it marked the tenth year of political support from the Federation. The campaign started in the Petrillo administration and continued forcefully under Kenin's term.

Shortly after his election as International President, Kenin said, "I look forward to the not too distant day when Government will by direct subsidy play its proper part in preserving our musical heritage.... We shall mobilize all of our political influences to expedite its advent."[187] Kenin repeatedly testified before congressional committees over the years on behalf of legislation that would include a breakthrough on federal subsidy for the arts.[188]

After all, most countries that have symphony orchestras and opera companies give them government support and have been doing so for hundreds of years. Federal subsidies were not new in the United States. Agribusiness, the Post Office, air transportation, maritime navigation, schools, and other institutions in our society had benefited from subsidies for many years. Before the Arts and Humanities Bill became law, the federal government (in addition to the example of the WPA) had been giving arts organizations indirect aid in the form of declaring them exempt from taxation and allowing them to receive tax deductible gifts from individuals and corporations. The next steps to direct subsidy seemed logical and inevitable.

The 1958 congressional authorization providing land for the establishment of a national cultural center in Washington, D.C., represented "the first break-through toward subsidy."[189] Next came the bill which created a National Arts Foundation and a Federal Council on the

Arts in 1964. Finally, in 1965, the crowning legislation provided direct government subsidy to the arts through the National Endowment for the Arts. "The Congress found that 'the encouragement and support of national progress and scholarship in the humanities and the arts, while primarily a matter of private and local initiative, is also an appropriate matter of concern to the Federal government'...."[190]

The Endowment distributes funds for individual musicians and musical organizations through a system of grants and matching grants upon application and through the advice of the National Council on the Arts. Over the years, the council and its Music Advisory Panel regularly have included many members of the Federation, ICSOM, and others "who are widely recognized for their broad knowledge of, or expertise in, or for their profound interest in the arts."[191]

Funds appropriated for the arts began with the comparatively modest amount of $2,534,300 (including matching funds) in 1966. Appropriations gradually increased so that by 1986 the amount was $165,958,000. Of course, funds earmarked for orchestras were a fraction of these amounts. For example, in 1972, 93 orchestras received $5,370,800 in Federal funds; in 1985, 162 orchestras received $9,315,500.[192]

These are still very modest amounts in relation to the total federal budget. A better perspective is obtained by considering that "... The Pentagon [in 1972] spends $140 million on public relations *alone*, nearly twice as much as the entire budget of the National Endowment for Arts and Humanities ...."[193]

Kenin, who was a guest at the White House when President Johnson signed the Arts and Humanities Bill, thought the bill "... a notable if long overdue legislative accomplishment for musicians and all others who share our concern for the development of our nation's artistic and cultural resources."[194] It was indeed important fiscal legislation for the AFM.

The Federation had long had a difficult time negotiating for professional wages and longer employment with the nonprofit orchestra associations. In the early 1960s, an average symphony orchestra derived only 52 percent of total budget from ticket sales (the range was 29 to 75 percent).[195] The gap was filled by private and public contributions. The addition of federal subsidy (and the Ford Foundation grants beginning in 1966) made an easier path towards a living wage and year-round employment for orchestra musicians. Although many interests (e.g., symphony orchestras, museums, artists) had worked with the AFM for the establishment of ongoing federal subsidy for symphony and opera orchestras, its achievement was a significant artistic and monetary victory for the Kenin administration.

For many years, the Federation had blamed the so-called "20 percent cabaret tax" for eliminating jobs for musicians. The cabaret tax, which was a levy on admission to establishments that supplied live entertainment, began during World War I and continued into the Kenin administration. The AFM argued that this artificially raised cost was "responsible for the decline in demand for live music, hence for the decline in work opportunities for musicians."[196]

Kenin, speaking before the New England Conference of the Federation in 1959, said, "the two greatest deterrents in musician employment were automation and the 20 percent Cabaret Tax."[197] The AFM was prepared to lobby and spend money to repeal this "tax deterrent." That same year, Kenin met with fifteen industry, trade union, and educator groups (including restaurant and hotel associations, A.G.V.A., and the hotel and restaurant workers) interested in relief from the tax[198] to plan joint efforts.

This congressional lobbying by many different organizations plus an extensive survey of the effects of the cabaret tax on employment, paid for by the AFM and completed in 1955 by A.W. Zelomek Associates, an independent company, had positive result. The study illustrated (among many other factors) that the elimination of the tax would create another 41,000 jobs for musicians. Congress was impressed, but not totally. In May 1960, the tax was reduced to 10 percent. This encouraged the Kenin administration to underwrite another survey by the same company to measure the results of the reduction in the tax.

The second survey was released in July 1963, and showed remarkable agreement with the 1955 study. One such agreement concerned the increase in man-hours of employment available to musicians if the tax were eliminated. The first survey predicted a 68 percent increase. The second survey, based on an actual reduction of half the tax, reported that there was a 34.2 percent increase in man-hours of employment.[199]

Again, Congress was impressed with the second study and the continuing lobbying. In December 1965, the cabaret tax was completely abolished. Although the AFM received help from other unions and employers, the credit for this success should be shared by both the Petrillo and Kenin administrations. It was a good example of continuity of purpose in the international leadership.

NOT ALL LEGISLATIVE BATTLES RESULT IN VICTORIES: PROBLEMS WITH TAFT–HARTLEY AND LANDRUM–GRIFFIN

The decade of the 1960s proved to the Federation that legislation could be as implacable an enemy as automation. The Taft-Hartley Act, passed over the veto of Pres-

ident Truman in 1947, outlawed the closed shop, secondary
boycotts, and jurisdictional strikes and set the stage for so-
called "right-to-work" state legislation.

The AFM felt the effect of the act almost immediately
because of its injunction against payment by employers to
union funds: Taft-Hartley made the Recording and Transcription Fund unlawful. The brilliant restructuring of the
fund, which produced the Music Performance Trust Fund
with its administration separate from the Federation, saved
the AFM from any prolonged negative effects for some
years.

But Petrillo recognized the potential danger for the
union early on. In 1950, he warned that other aspects of
Taft-Hartley would be applied at "… the opportune time
when, armed with all of the legal ammunition of the Taft-
Hartley Law, plus a sympathetic administration and Attorney General, they will move in and deal the knock-out
blow against labor."[200] He was right.

The "opportune time" was not the early 1950s. In
1954, AFM Counsel Henry Kaiser explained to the AFM
Convention in some detail the potentially devastating
effects of the boycott provisions of the Taft-Hartley Act.[201]
The mere fact that this explanation was necessary is proof
that "the worst was yet to come."

The leak in the dam of complacency that eventually
became a flood of problems was caused by the Bureau of
Internal Revenue. In 1948, the IRS (on the basis of a 1947
Supreme Court decision) ruled that a band leader is

> … an employer for tax purposes if he holds himself out
> as being available to furnish music to purchasers
> thereof, has the right to select, hire, discharge, and fix
> the compensation of the members of his orchestra, has
> primary control over the operations of his orchestra,
> arranges details relating to engagements, and furnishes
> the music arrangements, and other equipment as may

be necessary and negotiates the conditions including
the financial terms for the engagements. But when a
purchaser of the services of musicians hires an individual to gather together a group of musicians and retains
the privilege of accepting or rejecting the selected
personnel and instrumentation, and instructs the individual as to the price he will pay each musician, the
purchaser is the employer of the musicians for tax
purposes. And when an orchestra is operated on a
cooperative or partnership basis, and all members have
a voice in the management, the members are the
employees of neither the purchaser nor the leader.[202]

This was a devastating ruling for the AFM because
from its beginnings in the nineteenth century the Federation has always faced the dilemma of who was the employer of musicians: the "father of the bride" or the
musician who led the band. If the leader was an employer
on Friday, what was his status on Saturday when he was a
sidemusician? If he was an employer on Friday, what was
his standing with the union compared to Saturday?

The Federation's position has always been that the
musicians were the employees of the purchaser of music,
whether or not the bandleader was "an employer for tax
purposes." Some band leaders who disagreed formed the
National Association of Orchestra Leaders (NAOL), first in
New York and then in other major metropolitan areas, to
voice their opposition to the AFM.

As was the case with dual unionism in Los Angeles,
the NAOL sought recourse through the courts and brought
antitrust actions (beginning in 1960), claiming that they
were the employers of musicians and objecting to the
union's surcharge on traveling bands and alleged arbitrary
fixing of scale wages and number of players to be hired.[203]
Essentially, "... the orchestra leaders want freedom from
the AFM, to which they now belong. They want to be

recognized as employers (hence, could not be members of the AFM) and, being so recognized, to be freed of what they call arbitrary rulings by the union."[204]

The complaints against the 10 percent traveling tax and the payment of local work dues by traveling bands drew the most attention. The NAOL claimed the traveling tax was for the support of "dead" locals. They argued that the working professionals "were supporting a union dominated by those who outnumber them but don't work in the field [of music]."[205] Furthermore, as employers, the Taft-Hartley Act makes it unlawful for them to collect the surcharge and work dues and remit to the union as required by AFM bylaws.

The Federation's position was that the traveling tax and work dues were forms of dues voted legally by the members of the union and that band leaders were employees who only collect the amount of tax from the purchaser of the music. The U.S. Supreme Court settled the argument by ruling in 1963 to uphold opinions of lower courts "that a bandleader ... violates the Taft-Hartley Act when collecting and turning over dues to headquarters from band members."[206]

The AFM lost that battle, but 1964 and 1965 were better years for the Federation. The 1963 Convention was faced with the loss of major funding for support of the union by the ruling of the courts regarding collection of the 10 percent traveling tax. To replace this income they enacted an increase in per capita dues. Because it was a very close voice vote, a roll-call procedure was used. Each local's delegates voted as a unit and this single vote was commensurate with its official membership. The dues increase was approved by over 44,000 votes.[207]

Some AFM members thought this weighted vote system violated the Landrum-Griffin Act of 1959 and began litigation. This law, passed by the Congress after corruption was exposed in several unions, contains a "bill of rights" for union members assuring freedom of speech and assembly. It also contains safeguards to assure fair voting proceedings and requires unions to file financial statements.

The U.S. Supreme Court, in a ruling in December 1964, unanimously upheld the AFM voting system. The decision was of crucial importance to the Federation and many other unions which also used the weighted vote. The AFL-CIO and the U.S. Solicitor General both filed friend-of-the-court briefs in behalf of the AFM position[208] thus helping establish this important victory for the Federation.

In 1965, the Federation won another court case involving the Landrum-Griffin Act. The traveling band leaders objected to paying local work dues in other jurisdictions because they did not vote to impose them. The court ruled these work dues were a legal obligation upon all AFM members out of consideration for services rendered while in those jurisdictions.[209]

Litigation continued, with the National Association of Orchestra Leaders continually challenging the Federation under antitrust laws and the Taft-Hartley Act. In 1967, in Chicago, the complaint concerned attempts to enforce the (now banned) closed shop and restraint of trade by fixing the prices orchestras could charge. The objections also included the AFM welfare and pension plans, which the NAOL claimed was unlawfully including "participation in their benefits by employers [i.e., members of the NAOL]."[210]

The ongoing disagreement regarding the status of musicians—are they employees, employers, or independent contractors?—is reflected in the class action lawsuit filed in U.S. District Court in Chicago against the AFM-EP Fund as recently as December 1985. The plaintiffs claim they are "independent contractors and/or supervisors not employees...."[211] There continues to be no resolution to the basic question of employment status for musicians. The Chicago suit may take many years before a final court determination is reached.

Meanwhile, the National Labor Relations Board was kept busy during the latter part of the 1960s and the early 1970s with the varied complaints of the NAOL. Some cases were decided in favor of the AFM, others were victories for the NAOL. Still other cases continued through the sometimes long and seemingly endless legal processes. All cases pertained in one way or another to the employment status of musicians: the AFM contending that the players were employees of the purchaser of music and the NAOL countering with the argument that the bandleader was the employer of the sidemusicians and the leader in turn was an independent contractor in his relationship to the purchaser or that the leader and the other musicians were all independent contractors.

By 1973, there were some sixty cases pending against the AFM and its locals. It was time to reach agreement with the General Counsel of the NLRB.[212] In 1978 that agreement was made. The settlement specified exactly what the Federation could and could not do to be in compliance with the law. A side letter gave assurances that the vital functions of the Federation could continue within the parameters of the Taft-Hartley and Landrum-Griffin Acts. Although the agreement settled the many pending cases, it was not a happy occasion for the AFM. It certainly did not halt the inroads on established Federation activities.

In 1982, the U.S. Court of Appeals ruled that orchestra leaders, not hotels, are the legal employers of orchestra musicians. The Court said,

> ... It is a "common sense conclusion" that hotel orchestra musicians are not hotel employees, and that the musicians' union is not their proper bargaining repre-

sentative. The Court said that there was no evidence "to demonstrate any significant hotel regulation over the means by which bands produce the music." Instead, the Court said, "the band leaders exercise all the significant control over the manner of their own and their musicians' performances." Hotels involved in the legal action can only dismiss an entire band, the Court said, stating that the leaders have all day-to-day control over individual musicians' terms of employment.[213]

Again, Taft-Hartley rules and regulations immobilized the AFM. Now the union can no longer negotiate with a hotel or offer individual musicians the protection of concerted actions.

In 1983, Local 47 (Los Angeles) lost a long-running dispute with the NAOL over union bylaws prohibiting working for non-members. The NLRB ruled that Local 47 could not discipline its members for working with non-member leader-employers.[214] A founding principle of the AFM was lost. The ruling offered the Federation no recourse to protect the trade union standard of working only with other union members.

The 1980s have brought the AFM and the Associated Actors and Artistes of America (the parent union of Actors Equity and the American Guild of Variety Artists) to the realization that legislative change is the only practical answer to these problems that all entertainment unions face.

First in the U.S. Congress and then in the New York State legislature, the AFM is pressing its case. The legislation in Congress attempts to amend the Taft-Hartley Act to recognize the purchaser of music as the employer and "any individual having the status of an independent contractor who is engaged to perform musical services shall be included in the term 'employee.' "[215] This did not please the NAOL nor the over one hundred booking agencies which belong to the ITAA (International Theatrical Agencies Association) who claimed it would force 100,000 "lounge" performers to join unions against their will.[216]

Both then International President Victor W. Fuentealba and Local 802 (New York) President John Glasel maintained that the bandleaders' concern is unwarranted. Fuentealba said, "We are not trying to interfere with legitimate bandleaders who are employers ... We are [only] seeking added protection for our members."[217] And, of course, the AFM under no circumstances would represent the great majority of nightclub performers.

Another amendment sought by the Federation would allow new employees to join the union within seven days rather than the 30-day limit now specified by Taft-Hartley. Because of the temporary nature of work in the entertainment industry, the 30-day period is meaningless.[218] Essentially, what the AFM seeks is the same special consideration given to the unions in the apparel and construction industries where intermittent employment patterns resemble those for casual musicians.[219]

The initial bills detailing these amendments to Taft-Hartley were introduced in 1980 (although the AFM began lobbying for Taft-Hartley reform as early as 1977[220]), and in every year through 1987 the legislation has been reintroduced. If the past history of positive legislative changes sponsored by the AFM is any criterion, it will be many years before these proposed amendments become law.

One of Kenin's minor achievements, early in his administration, was the establishment of a nonpartisan political action fund to help the Federation follow Samuel Gompers' concept of "rewarding our friends" in these legislative battles. The fund called "TEMPO" (Task Force for Employment of Musicians Promotional Organization), after a program for voluntary contribution begun by Local 771 in Tucson in 1961.[221] Announcing the expansion of TEMPO to the national arena, Kenin reminded the 1962 AFM Convention that under the law no union funds may be expended in behalf of federal candidates and the voluntary contributions acceptable to TEMPO must be great enough to provide "... meaningful support at election time."[222]

Since 1962, contributions to TEMPO have been minimal although successive Federation administrations have been forceful in their advocacy. Typically, donations to TEMPO reported for 1985 indicate dismal results. For example, Local 802 (New York) with over 14,000 members contributed just over $300 and many locals made no contribution at all.[223]

The absence of "meaningful support at election time" from TEMPO for its political friends in both parties may help explain in part the mediocre legislative results the Federation has achieved.

The twelve years of the Kenin administration were eventful and productive. Valuable achievements included the settlement of the Los Angeles dispute; the change in direction of the MPTF and the addition of the Special Payments Funds; the AFM-EP fund, the first pension plan for the casual performer; the Congress of Strings; the compromises with ICSOM; the careful compliance with the mandate of civil rights; the successful endeavor in sponsoring the National Endowment for the Arts; and the final elimination of the Cabaret Tax. Even the ability to live with the restrictions of Landrum-Griffin and (especially) Taft-Hartley Acts during the tumultuous 1960s was a pragmatic success.

Kenin's death in 1970 was a great loss to the Federation. He was a brilliant, responsible leader during a period that demanded thoughtful, careful change and growth—a time for a pragmatist with a soul.

Chapter V
Modern Times

THE DAVIS PRESIDENCY

In 1970, FOR THE FIRST TIME IN its long history, the Federation faced a change in leadership that did not conform to the orderly procedures of the annual conventions. Herman Kenin died of a heart attack on July 21, 1970, only one month after being reelected International President of the AFM for the twelfth year. His death was marked by messages of condolence from President Richard Nixon, national and international labor leaders, many important personages in the fields of entertainment and, of course, musicians from all over the Western world.

Hal C. Davis, who had been vice president of the AFM for six years, was elected to succeed Kenin by the International Executive Board.[1] In turn, Victor W. Fuentealba, a member of the board, was elected to replace Davis as International Vice President. That special meeting of the IEB in July 1970 brought to prominence the two men who would lead the Federation until the 1987 Convention.

The new president brought to his office the same kinds of practical experiences as a performing musician and labor leader as had all of his predecessors. As a percussionist, starting in 1930, he played theaters and nightclubs and for eleven years was a staff musician with radio stations KDKA and WCAE in Pittsburgh. As a long-time member of Pittsburgh Local 60-471, he served on the executive board and became its president in 1956. In 1963 he was elected to the International Executive Board, becoming vice president of the Federation in 1964.[2] He was also vice president of the Pennsylvania AFL-CIO and a member of that state's Council On The Arts.[3] It seems that no one joins the AFM primarily to become a union political leader—the first priority is to want to be a professional musician.

Early in the Davis administration it was readily apparent that there would be close continuity with previous objectives and procedures of the Federation. Speaking at the AFM Convention in June 1971 (his first convention as President), Davis said, "... The basic purpose of the American Federation of Musicians is the same today as it was seventy-five years ago—namely to protect and advance the interests of musicians, create job opportunities and enforce good faith and fair dealings among all our members. This was our goal in the beginning. This is our goal now. And this will be our goal for years to come...."[4] Later, at the same convention he said, "... The most critical problem facing all musicians today is the continued threat of displacement by canned music...."[5] Both comments could have been made by either Petrillo or Kenin.

The strongest indication of the commonality of purpose of these AFM leaders is the program called "Young Sounds." In 1968, President Kenin appointed a special committee chaired by IEB member Victor Fuentealba to consider how the Federation could be more appealing to young musicians. The Fuentealba Committee's recommendations were approved by the 1969 convention, with final guidelines established shortly afterwards by the IEB.

The Young Sounds program was designed to enable the young performer (ages fourteen to twenty-one) to join the Federation with reduced annual dues and initiation fee payable in installments and refundable in full up to ninety days from the date of application. The musician then had the opportunity to play for youth-oriented engagements only, with special instruction and orientation supplied by the union. The program was to be implemented by locals on a voluntary basis.[6] Kenin believed Young Sounds would "... reach and teach the young musicians...familiarize him with the AFM and protect him from the growing problem of exploitation...."[7]

Obviously, both Davis and Fuentealba agreed with Kenin because all three administrations attempted to emphasize the importance of Young Sounds. What was left unsaid was the AFM's continuing problems with attracting the young musician who loves to play, wants exposure at the expense of higher pay, and who, in the rush for fame and glory, gladly works for less than the established older musician.

Young Sounds was not successful—the Federation is still trying to appeal to the young performer. Although other approaches to the same problem are being explored now by the AFM, it is clear that the successive administrations have been equally aware of the need to do something to attract more young musicians.

In retrospect, the relatively short Davis presidency was in large part characterized by this continuity with the past. Davis implemented Petrillo-Kenin programs such as the Music Performance Trust Funds, the American Federation of Musicians-Employer's Pension Funds, and the Special Payments Funds; the Congress of Strings; participation in and ratification of contracts by involved segments of the Federation (members of the International Conference of Symphony and Opera Musicians, the Organization of Canadian Symphony Musicians, the Recording Musicians Association, and so forth); the Symphony Symposiums; the merging of segregated locals and the integration of black musicians in the mainstream of AFM governance;

support for the National Endowment for the Arts, state and provincial arts councils, and for performing royalties; the resolve to seek changes in the Lea Act, Taft-Hartley, and Landrum-Griffin; the advocacy of TEMPO; and cooperation in the escalating battle against "canned" music and tape and record piracy.

Davis was also well aware of the continuing problems within the Federation. One of these problems was money: how should the mechanisms of the union be financed. Since 1963, when the 10-percent traveling surcharge was eliminated, per-capita dues were the primary source of income—and the $6.00 annual fee per member was inadequate. The 1971 Convention, under Davis' encouragement, gave him the power to appoint a Federation Finance Review Committee to "... review all existing sources of income, examine new possibilities, invite suggestions, and evaluate the long range needs of the Federation. ..."[8] The committee, chaired by Eugene Frey, President of Local 1 (Cincinnati), reported their findings to the 1972 Convention.

After informing the delegates that the AFM had a deficit operation of approximately $200,000 in 1972 and estimating a five-year shortfall of close to $2,000,000, the committee's major recommendations were to change to biennial conventions and increase the per-capita dues from $6 to $8 annually.[9] The committee also noted that the AFM was the only AFL-CIO union which met annually and paid full per diem compensation to its delegates.

Eventually, annual dues were increased, effective in January 1974, but the request for biennial conventions met with disapproval. For delegates representing small and medium-sized locals who work all year as union officials for little or no money, the annual trip to the convention, with AFM per diem and paid hotel bills, was considered just payment for their labors.

ly, the financial problem did not disappear
way solution. The 1977 Convention, facing
it financing situation, was told by Davis that
running a twentieth century operation with
a horse and buggy income." The delegates responded by
voting to increase annual dues from $8 to $10 but insisted
on keeping annual conventions.[10]

While surviving these partial victories on the internal
financial front, the Davis administration suffered a major
defeat at the hands of the United States Congress. The
long-awaited revision of copyright legislation was passed in
1976 with performance royalty pointedly excluded. This
lack of success on an issue which since the Petrillo administration had received high priority was especially painful
because it indicated the ineffectiveness of a potentially
powerful coalition. Before committees of both the Senate
and House of Representatives, the AFM argued for performance royalty along with AFTRA (American Federation of
Television and Radio Artists), Actors' Equity, the AFL-CIO
Unions for Professional Employees, and others.[11] All to no
avail because the broadcasting industry was in vigorous
opposition.

As a sop to some interests in the musical world, the
final version of the 1976 Copyright Act did provide protection for composers, arrangers, and publishers (but not
performers) by providing minimal compensation for the
use of copyrighted music in jukeboxes. From 1978 through
1981, this charge per jukebox was $8; in 1982 and 1983 it
was $25; from 1984 through 1986 it was $50; and in 1987
it was $63.[12]

There was a hiatus in the initiation of new programs
for the Federation during the Davis administration. This
may have been caused by the great amount of effort
required of an impoverished AFM to implement those ideas
inherited from Petrillo and Kenin. Or it may have been

due to the increasing pressure of litigation pending before the National Labor Relation Board and further inroads by canned music. Or it may have been caused by an administration better versed in caretaking than creative leadership. In any case, the dilemma of increasing AFM membership and decreasing musical employment during the Davis presidency produced no "new directions."

In 1978, a sad historical event repeated itself. On January 11, 1978, Hal C. Davis died of a heart attack. Like Kenin, rather than return to his suburban home after late union business, Davis died in a New York City hotel.[13] Although the Davis administration of barely seven and one-half years produced no major developments for the AFM, during his time in office the Federation assumed a more militant stance. There were more symphony orchestra strikes for improved contracts,[14] and through his insistence the AFL-CIO effectively sponsored a three-month boycott of the Ringling Brothers and Barnum and Bailey Circus.[15]

Again, an emergency meeting of the International Executive Board was called (on January 14, 1978),[16] and Vice President Victor W. Fuentealba was elected International President. His successor as vice president was David Winstein, a member of the IEB and president of Local 174-496 in New Orleans.[17]

VICTOR FUENTEALBA'S ADMINISTRATION

Fuentealba, in the long tradition of AFM presidents, was first a performing musician and then a labor leader. Like Herman Kenin before him, he supported his law school education by working as a professional musician. Fuentealba played clarinet and saxophone, joining Local 40-543 in Baltimore in 1941. Upon graduation from Maryland Law School in 1950, he combined musical engagements with a legal career as a member of the Baltimore, Maryland, and American Bar Associations. In 1956 he was elected president of the Baltimore local, a position he held until becoming International President. Along the way through the AFM hierarchy, he also became a member of the executive board in 1967 and AFM vice president in 1970.

Although Fuentealba approved of many aspects of the "continuity and implementation" efforts of the Davis administration, he did not attempt to hide his impatience and frustration with "the old school of labor relations"—he had planned to be a candidate for International President in 1978 in opposition to Davis. In a interview shortly after his election as International President, Fuentealba said, "... We're going to have to sell ourselves to the younger musician now and change our methods of operation in some cases...."[18]

The new president lost no time in making his views known. Within six months of his election by the executive board, Fuentealba renewed previous efforts to lobby Congress for legislation to establish performance royalty for recordings. It was a strong effort involving a letter-writing campaign to Congressional leaders by AFM members. But again the effort was too weak and the opposing broadcasting interests were too strong so that the lobbying failed.

The 1978 Convention, which marked Fuentealba's first election by the primary governing body of the AFM, was the springboard from which the new president's "changes in methods of operation" were to begin. At the convention, Fuentealba told the delegates, "... High priority must be given to recruiting new members and improving the [Federation's] image in the eyes of the public...." And he noted (in retrospect, far too optimistically), "... There is no reason in the world why the American Federation of Musicians cannot double its membership within the next five years." He also suggested biennial conventions because the AFM was still in financial trouble.[19]

Only cursory attention was given to the suggestion for biennial conventions by the delegates. And, not surprisingly, Fuentealba proposed Young Sounds as the continuing program needed to attract young musicians. After all, he was the chair of the committee that originally suggested it to Kenin and was AFM Vice President when the plan was continued under the Davis administration. The convention agreed, but despite the support of Kenin, Davis, and Fuentealba, Young Sounds has yet to be successful.

His election by the convention gave Fuentealba the courage to go ahead with more far-reaching efforts to change the direction of the Federation. The first of these was the appointment of a new general counsel for the AFM in September 1978. Henry Kaiser, friend and confidant of Petrillo, Kenin, and Davis, a man who had served the Federation since 1941, was instrumental in the establishment of legal principles in AFM contractual obligations and was well known to thousands of AFM members through his statements in the *International Musician* and his appearances at many conventions, was replaced by Cosimo Abato from Baltimore.

Abato was well qualified. His law firm represented some sixty diversified labor unions. He served his labor law apprenticeship as an attorney in the Office of the Solicitor of Labor, United States Department of Labor, and as a trial lawyer with the National Labor Relations Board Fifth Regional Office. In addition, he had been a professional musician in both Baltimore and New York.

Fuentealba realized the impact this new appointment could have. In his introduction of Abato to the 1979 Convention he said,

> … I made what was one of the most difficult decisions that I have ever had to make in my lifetime. I knew

that it was going to be a most controversial one. . . . It was
my opinion that the interests of our Federation would
be better served if a capable attorney could be found
who had also been an experienced musician [to be our
general counsel]. . . . [20]

Henry Kaiser had done much work preparing an
agreement with the National Labor Relations Board, and
Abato lost no time in joining the fray to help the new
administration find "new directions." By November 1978,
only two months after his appointment as general counsel,
he had concluded negotiations with the general counsel of
the NLRB on a revised side letter accompanying the settlement agreement of 1978 between the AFM and the NLRB
which had been prepared by Kaiser.[21] Of course, the point
was to resolve these issues as soon as possible.

An AFM official explained the "new directions" by
pointing out that the Davis administration wanted to delay
resolution of NLRB cases as long as possible—to give
ground as slowly as possible—to hope (and work) for
legislative change in Taft-Hartley. Besides, the Federation
could not afford the cost of all these suits. This new
administration wanted to "clean up everything" and attempt to negotiate future disputes.[22]

But Fuentealba did not have the luxury of developing
new directions to the exclusion of old problems. One
continuing problem was financial since the AFM was again
in a deficit budget operation. Since the president saw no
practical way to reduce internal expenses, the administration attempted to reduce per-capita dues to the AFL-CIO.

The AFL-CIO declined to reduce these dues but suggested three budget-balancing ideas that might help the
AFM financial condition: (1) increase AFM per capita dues
from $10 annually to $10 monthly; (2) hold biennial
conventions; and (3) merge city and town locals into
regional groups.[23] Neither the IEB nor the 1979 AFM
Convention took the first or third suggestion seriously.

Although withdrawal from the AFL-CIO would have saved the AFM approximately $400,000 a year, this alternative was also immediately dismissed.[24]

The 1979 Convention faced a budget deficit that was estimated to be as great as $400,000. Several motions were directed at a remedy. Fuentealba proposed a one percent work dues levied on all AFM members who work under national contracts (e.g., the recording, film, and broadcast industries) to finance and maintain a network of national contract offices. When this proposal was defeated with a proviso to review it again (after further study) at the 1980 Convention, another $2 increase in per-capita dues was approved. More important was the vote to switch to a biennial convention in 1981.[25] Fuentealba had achieved what only Petrillo (in 1958) at the height of his popularity had done. With great reluctance, the delegates had agreed to deprive themselves of a substantial "perk" in the interests of fiscal stability.

Slowly, Fuentealba's strategy for building a stronger Federation by offering more services became evident. Although his work-dues proposal was defeated, the August 1979 *International Musician* announced that for the first time there would be a full-time Vice President for Canada (in Toronto) financed by a one percent work dues on all Canadian engagements. Vice President for Canada J. Alan Wood resigned as president of the Toronto local and assumed his full-time duties in the same city.[26]

The leaders of the Federation were concerned not only about reaching out to young performers, but also about the decline in membership of the traveling lounge musician. In many situations, the young player was the traveling lounge musician, and almost from the beginning of the century through 1963 these traveling lounge players had done more than their fair share in supporting the AFM. In more recent years, the traveling lounge player frequently had to pay local work dues as he or she moved from gig to gig while receiving a minimum of service and (many times) a maximum of inconvenience. Finally, the Fuentealba administration, for the first time, arranged to meet with representatives of this group to discuss problems peculiar to their kind of musical activity.

Following the format of the Symphony Symposiums begun by Kenin and continued by Davis and Fuentealba, representatives of the IEB met in February 1980 in Kansas City with representatives of traveling lounge musicians. Like the meetings with symphony players, this meeting attempted to bring the complaints of the traveling musicians directly to the ears of the administration. Is it fair to demand four percent work dues in one city just a few miles from a city which has work dues of two and one-half percent, or even zero percent? Since the work dues were based on varying scale wages, even two percent work dues on a high scale wage meant more money than four percent of a lower scale wage. What service is offered for that amount of dues? Is the service better in the first city? Worse still, when claims were made, the defective procedures in the international offices frequently precluded positive results—procedures took too long, and the actions were ineffective. How can the traveling musician reach anyone in the national office in an emergency? (Many AFM members did not know about the toll-free "hot line" established for them in 1978.)

Like the symphony meetings, this meeting was inconclusive but it did bring the plight of these musicians to the attention of the administration. One board member thought the meeting was a good idea, but with the decline in the number of traveling musicians within the AFM it was "... too little, too late—like locking the barn after the horse is gone...."[27]

As the 1980 AFM Convention approached, there were some signs of dissent to the Fuentealba administration. The spokesman for this opposition (the Committee of 100) was Phil Lampkin, a retired union official from Las Vegas. The complaints centered around the perceived abrupt method in which Henry Kaiser was dismissed as general counsel, the report Fuentealba made in the *International Musician* (April 1979) concerning his meeting with a subcommittee of the AFL-CIO executive council regarding approval for permanent monetary relief from per-capita taxes, and a letter written to AFL-CIO President George Meany in September 1978 by Fuentealba, implying that the AFM might be forced to disaffiliate from the AFL-CIO.[28] Because the AFL-CIO disputed Fuentealba's interpretation, the disagreement had made national headlines.

By May 1980, the Committee of 100 had chosen Jerry Spain, the president of Local 6 in San Francisco, to be their opposition candidate at the annual convention.[29] Either the national press exaggerated the conflict or the Committee of 100 did not make a serious effort, because Fuentealba "triumphed over Jerry J. Spain ... by a two-to-one margin...."[30]

On the financial front, the 1980 convention finally passed an increase of one percent work dues based on scale wages, with one half of the dues going to the International treasury, the other half to be kept by the local. Although the original motion presented by the IEB called for a 2 percent levy, this was still an important victory for Fuentealba.[31] The burden of financial support for the Federation which so long had rested upon the traveling musician had now shifted to the working musicians in all areas of the profession. This may be a good trade union principle, but given the high population of unemployed or minimally employed musicians in the AFM, there have been continuous complaints from those few "full-time" players in the union who believed that they are paying a disproportionate share of Federation expenses.

The work dues controversy did not stop with the end of the 1980 Convention: in fact, it continues to be a

contentious issue. The 1981 Convention voted over-
whelmingly to keep the one percent work dues in response
to the motion by the San Francisco and Reno locals to
abolish the levy. The convention also reaffirmed the biennial convention system, setting the next convention date in
1983 and marking the first time since the World War II
years of 1943 and 1945 that the AFM had missed a
convention.[32]

That was the good news. The bad news was that the
AFM continued to lose members, a decline from an estimated membership of 320,000 in 1976 to approximately
280,000 in 1981. And there were also fewer locals in 1981.[33]
Many delegates felt the new work dues helped to acceler-
ate the defection rate in the membership ranks.[34]

With the help of this new income source (the one-half
of one percent work dues that was meant for the Federation), the Fuentealba administration continued its agenda
for adding and improving AFM services. Four new administrative assistants were approved by the IEB in October
1982 and began their assignments in early 1983. This
additional layer of more highly trained staff was designed
to help locals avoid labor-law pitfalls, negotiate agreements, meet with prospective employers and, especially,
"organize the unorganized."[35] Fuentealba was trying an
approach to attract more AFM members by giving assistance to the many smaller locals that were understaffed (or
had no staff at all) in their music business battles.

Then, in early 1983, came the Musicians' Referral
Service, a new way to assist Federation members in fur-
thering their employment opportunities. Questionnaires
appeared regularly in the *International Musician,* and interested musicians returned the completed forms to the
president's office where pertinent information was entered
into a computer and made available to bands seeking new
members.[36] Although originally welcomed by young players, its success so far has been minimal.

By mid-1983, in time for the biennial convention, the AFM was solvent, thanks to the work dues levy passed in 1980. Now the main issues before the delegates were all aspects of the same problem: how to attract and keep Federation members.[37] The emphasis was upon bringing the traveling lounge musician back to the AFM.

After "... lengthy and often cynical debate...,"[38] the convention approved a motion giving the IEB exclusive power to regulate wages and working conditions for traveling members. Also approved were proposals to eliminate the 10 percent-over-scale charge traveling musicians had previously been required to demand, a recommendation that locals assign someone to service these musicians, and measures "... to ease the financial penalties imposed on former union members within the traveling musician ranks who wish to return to the fold...."[39]

These measures designed to make the AFM more attractive to the traveling musician were just the first shots in what became a continuing campaign. Later in 1983, the Federation hired a new public relations firm (Budd Arthur Associates, Inc. of Chicago) to help in "recruiting new and old members."[40] In 1984, the IEB made further attempts to give better service to traveling musicians by developing a new contract which could be subject of a civil court suit; the IEB also made arrangements to hire local attorneys at Federation expense to enforce these contracts.[41] This new procedure replaced the longstanding preference of the AFM for arbitration, an option which was too lengthy to please the traveling musicians.

But 1984 was not a good year for the Federation in this battle. In January 1985, J. Martin Emerson, then International secretary-treasurer, reported that the number of employees in his department was reduced from thirty-five to seventeen, "... principally due to an extreme drop in the number of claim cases which used to emulate from traveling members who in large part have left the Federation."[42] In March 1985, Mr. Emerson reported, "... An effort to recruit new members is not only timely but vitally needed in order to stem a continuing slide in the international membership which during 1984, decreased approximately 15,000 to a total of 231,000 members in the United States and Canada."[43]

The decreases in AFM membership was one of many increasing problems for the administration. In a report to Federation members in January 1985, Fuentealba said, "... With the increased use of synthesizers throughout the music industry and the concessionary bargaining that has been taking place throughout the labor movement during the past several years, it is apparent that our negotiating team faces difficult negotiations...."[44] In an earlier statement, Fuentealba had gone even further. He indicated that the greatest single danger for the Federation was the electronic synthesizer, one of which "can replace an entire orchestra."[45] and he was right. The synthesizer, through various techniques employed by one person, can "sample" and then reproduce the timbre of each orchestral instrument, combine them, and "manufacture" the sound of the full orchestra.

The synthesizer plus the increasing use of canned and taped music (with and without live performers) and the deterioration of AFM membership was a full cup of troubles for the Fuentealba administration. As Petrillo said, "... Vic [Fuentealba] is okay but he has a very tough job. If we can only hold our own."[46]

Still another problem became apparent in 1985: "the graying of the union." At a meeting in Denver in March 1985 of the Western Conference of the AFM, Fuentealba discussed the problems associated with the fact that a large percentage of the Federation's membership were "Life Members." In effect, although a Life Member was defined differently by individual locals, great numbers of AFM members paid reduced or no dues.[47] For those locals that carried life insurance policies for their members, without outside help, this aging process meant default or bankruptcy. And it was a near political impossibility for such locals to expect their own membership to levy (or increase) dues for Life Members.

The stage was set for the major controversy of the 1985 Convention. Although it has always been the locals (rather than the Federation) that had introduced and established "Life Memberships," it became a Federation problem when locals lost working members while older, retired players remained in the AFM. It soon became impossible for many locals to support the benefits (including life insurance) for members who contributed little or nothing to the union. To attempt to meet their financial needs, the local typically increased its work dues; the younger working musicians objected, some resigned, and the problem intensified.

The convention's solution was a compromised version of a resolution presented by the IEB which prescribed a Federation-wide definition of "Life Member" and established standard reduced dues for these Life Members. The bitter debate over this issue revealed some disappointing statistics. There were over 50,000 Life Members in a total membership of approximately 231,000—a proportion certainly out of balance. In the roll-call vote that concluded the debate, the majority of locals rejected the resolution although it was supported by those large locals which were in financial difficulties because of a disproportionate number of older members.

The convention assumed it had reached a solution to the problem, but the arguments continued at the local level. Many older members felt they should have been "grandfathered," that is, their dues and paying status should have remained and the new dues should apply only to those who were not yet Life Members. Some locals paid the increased dues from special resources of their own. Other locals noticed the almost immediate resignations of many older players who had "hung on" in expectation of the life insurance pay off. One union official said, "... The Federation took the locals off the hook and put the onus on the convention."[48] Another local official argued, "... The fraternity of the union was violated— there must have been another way."[49]

The 1987 Convention attempted to find that other way. In response to no less than seventeen resolutions on this subject submitted for its consideration, the delegates chose a substitute resolution recommended by both the Law and Finance Committees. The resolution lowered the eligibility age to sixty-five, permitted those who resigned or were expelled because of the earlier dues requirement to be reinstated upon payment of back dues, and allowed individual locals to reduce Life Members' dues to as low as twenty-five percent of their regular per-capita dues. Although still a compromise, this "other way" may be more acceptable to more Federation members.[50]

The Fuentealba administration's thrust towards more service for the working musician continued with the addition of staff administrative assistants. More regional meetings were called "... to assist... local officers in their constant efforts to provide better services for their membership."[51] With the adoption of biennial conventions, this intensified contact was of heightened importance.

The Symphony Department of the AFM's International Office had been established in 1969 by Kenin, and Fuentealba recognized the importance of the work-dues-paying symphony player. Just as he had expanded the Office of the Vice President for Canada to a full-time position, he now began to enlarge the scope of the Symphony Department. With the appointment of Lewis Wal-

deck in January 1983 as head of this department, he
increased Waldeck's staff to meet the increased work load.
In September 1986, he appointed Lynn Johnson as the
head of the first West Coast branch of the Symphony
Department in Hollywood.

The efforts for more members and better service
continue. One recent meeting of the IEB approved no less
than sixteen requests from locals for either reduced dues
or initiation fees. The same meeting approved seven
voluntary merger requests.[52] Both categories of requests
indicate the realities of AFM life: lower dues may make
happier members and perhaps more of them, and a
merged local might give better service than two understaffed locals.

Not until the January 1987 negotiations with the
record industry was there any overt indication of dissatisfaction with the Fuentealba administration. These sessions
produced a split in the AFM negotiating team, with only
Fuentealba's executive committee and Local 257 (Nashville) agreeing to a contract which would allow the industry
to pay into MPTF and the Special Payments Fund only after
a recording sold more than 25,000 units. The RMA and the
large locals where most recording musicians live (New
York, Los Angeles, Chicago, and Toronto) walked out
before this agreement was made, believing that they were
ignored by the president. Although the pact was approved
by the recording musicians (1,153 to 844), the RMA and the
large locals claimed that at least one substitute proposal
was withheld (a trade-off of lower wages for restoration of
fund cuts) and that the voting musicians should have been
given the opportunity to request further negotiations—
especially since auditors for the MPTF could never accu-
rately estimate contributions with a "sales trigger" of
25,000 units.[53] Although Fuentealba insisted that there
could be no further negotiations (only a strike/no strike

vote) and that he had not ignored the other participants,[54] relationships between the AFM president and the large local presidents and the RMA worsened rapidly.

In April 1987, *Daily Variety* reported that a series of resolutions sponsored by both the New York and Los Angeles locals would be presented to the 1987 AFM Convention in June. The thrust of the resolutions was to work towards "increased democratization"[55] and specifically called for: a guarantee for union members to ratify national contracts (players have done so since the 1960s, but this privilege does not appear in the bylaws); the power for locals and individual members to request membership lists to lobby members about contracts; and the appointment of the American Arbitration Association to conduct AFM International elections.[56]

Then followed charges and countercharges in the *International Musician,* the various periodicals of the large locals, and in *Variety* until on June 1, 1987 a letter was sent to all convention delegates castigating the present administration and calling for a "draft" of J. Martin Emerson (the International secretary-treasurer emeritus) as a candidate for AFM President. The letter was signed by the presidents of the New York, Los Angeles, Chicago, and Santa Ana locals, as well as the president of the AFM New York State Conference and the secretary-treasurer of the Joliet local.

This June 1 letter was the basis for an article by Henry Schipper in the June 10, 1987 issue of *Variety.* Mr. Schipper believed that the biggest issues from the opposition's view were the alleged autocratic behavior of Fuentealba (stemming from the controversial negotiations with the recording industry) and a perceived insensitivity towards the locals.[57]

"Marty" Emerson came to the 1987 Convention in Las Vegas (June 15–19, 1987) as an "alternative" candidate obviously favorably inclined to accept a draft.[58] On June

17 he formally announced his candidacy along with a slate of Bobby Herriot (president of the Toronto local) as Vice President from Canada and Serena Kay Williams (secretary of the Los Angeles local) as International Secretary-Treasurer. Their platform called for "... conciliation, unity and statesmanship"[59] with democracy, fairness in mergers, return to local autonomy, an AFM headquarters in a less costly permanent home, and more service to locals of all sizes.[60]

Another letter sent on June 16 to convention delegates extolled the virtues of President Fuentealba and suggested that the real bosses, if Emerson were to be elected, would be the larger locals and the RMA. The letter was sponsored by no less than fifty delegates calling themselves the Committee to Re-Elect President Vic Fuentealba.[61]

When J. Martin Emerson won the election (708 to 650), for the first time in the history of the Federation a sitting president had been denied reelection. *Variety* quoted Emerson as saying, "... No one is as surprised as I am.... In the end, I think Vic's dictatorial attitude, his seeming disregard for humanistic issues, did him in." Emerson added, "... My hope is to restore togetherness, brotherhood and sisterhood, what a union is all about.[62]

Fuentealba similarly expressed surprise at the voting, "...which he attributed to the Emerson campaign's ability to 'brainwash' AFMers into 'blaming me' for the erosion of the Music Performance Trust Fund ....."[63] He also indicated in an interview with the *Las Vegas Sun* that he might run again in two years,[64] and in the *International Musician* he referred to his coming "... two year sabbatical."[65]

The president-elect (who would not assume office until September 1, 1987) was born and raised in Washington, D.C. He had attended the New England Conservatory and played trombone with the big bands of Tommy Dorsey, Gene Krupa, Sonny Dunham, Ted Fiorito, and

Meyer Davis. Then came union business. He served twenty-two years as a board member and secretary of the Washington local before becoming International secretary-treasurer in 1975. Emerson was a trustee of the AFM-EP Fund and the Lester Petrillo Fund, project director of the Congress of Strings, a member of the board of directors of Wolf Trap Farm Park (in Washington), and a founding member of the National Association of Jazz Educators.[66] He was given the title International Secretary-Treasurer Emeritus when he chose not to seek reelection in 1985.[67]

The new International president clearly fits the mold of his predecessors—first a working musician, then long experience in the union business and a journey through the AFM hierarchy before assuming this top position.

One of the last photographs of Joseph N. Weber, who served the federation as its international president from 1900 to 1940. Although illness forced his temporary retirement for one year (1914–1915), his was the longest tenure of any AFM president. (Courtesy of the *International Musician*)

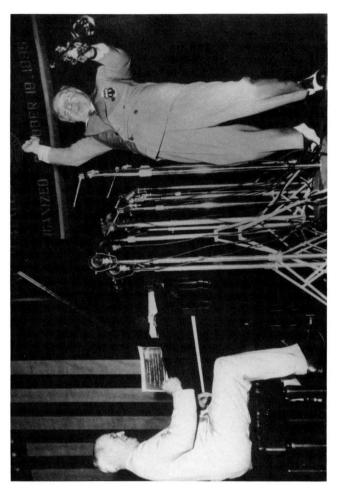

James C. Petrillo and President Harry Truman show their elation at the conclusion of a chorus of "Hail, Hail, the Gang's All Here" at the 1954 AFM convention. (Courtesy of the *International Musician*)

AFM President Herman Kenin testifies at Senate Subcommittee hearings on revisions in the copyright laws. With Mr. Kenin are National Counsel Henry Kaiser (*left*) and New York Counsel Jerome Adler (*right*). (Courtesy of the *International Musician*)

Attending his first AFL-CIO executive council meeting as a newly elected member of the council and a vice president of the Labor Federation, AFM President Hal C. Davis *(left)* poses with AFL-CIO President George Meany in February 1976. (Courtesy of the *International Musician*)

In April 1978, AFM President Victor W. Fuentealba *(left)* is pictured with California Congressman George Danielson at hearings on Danielson's bill to create a performing royalty for sound recordings. (Courtesy of the *International Musician*)

TOP: The 1986 Congress of Strings Orchestra. (Courtesy of the *International Musician*)   BOTTOM: Delegates to the 1987 AFM convention in Las Vegas. (Courtesy of the *International Musician*)

International President Emeritus Victor W. Fuentealba conducts the swearing-in ceremony for new international officers at the 1987 AFM convention. *From the left:* Richard Totusek, John Glasel, Vince Di Bari, Robert D'Arcy, Eugene Frey (all IEB members), J. Martin Emerson (International President), Mark Tully Massagli (International Vice President), J. Alan Wood (Vice President from Canada), and Kelly L. Castleberry II (International Secretary-Treasurer). (Courtesy of the *International Musician)*

An AFM panel of witnesses testified in favor of S. 1346 (the performing arts labor relations amendment) during a December 1987 Senate hearing. The delegation included (*left to right*) AFM General Counsel Henry Kaiser, AFM President J. Martin Emerson, Nashville Local 257 President Jay Collins, and AFM National Legislative Director Ned H. Guthrie. (Courtesy of the *International Musician*)

Concert soloist Miriam Fried. (Photo: Christian Steiner. Courtesy of ICM Artists)

The Juilliard String Quartet: Robert Mann, Joel Smirnoff, violin; Samuel Rhodes, viola; Joel Krosnick, violoncello. (Photo: Don Hunstein. Courtesy of Alix B. Williamson)

The Chicago Symphony Orchestra with its conductor and musical director, Sir Georg Solti. (Courtesy of the Chicago Symphony Orchestra)

Recording session at Paramount Studios in Hollywood. (Courtesy of the Recording Musicians Association)

Music Performance Trust Fund concerts at (TOP) City University of New York (Hoffmeister Winds Quintet and (BOTTOM) Terry Clark and His Orchestra at New York City's Bryant Park. (Courtesy of Music Performance Trust Funds)

A Saturday night dance. (Courtesy of Local 1, AFM)

Kid Thomas and the Preservation Hall Band in the French Quarter, New Orleans. (Courtesy of the *International Musician*)

TOP: Teddy Wilson, piano; Benny Goodman, clarinet; Lionel Hampton, vibraphone; Phil Flanigan, bass; Panama Francis, drums. A 1982 performance. (Courtesy of the *International Musician*)　BOTTOM: Willie Nelson performing at the 1985 AFM convention. (Courtesy of the *International Musician*)

Chapter VI
The Union Business

DESPITE RECENT DOWNWARD TRENDS in membership, the American Federation of Musicians is the largest entertainment union in the world. The business of the Federation is big business. From a Depression-induced low membership of about 100,000 in 1934,[1] there was a steady, gradual growth until the mid-1970s: in 1951, over 240,000 members;[2] in 1960, over 266,000;[3] in 1970, over 300,000;[4] in 1976 331,000.[5] From this high point there has been a gradual decline in membership each year: in 1983 just over 246,000;[6] in 1984 about 231,000;[7] and in 1985 approximately 225,000.[8] In 1987, the AFM Convention's official roll-call vote was based upon a membership of 210,000 in all fifty states, Puerto Rico, and Canada (about 10 percent). In general, AFM membership peaked shortly after most other unions in the United States, but in the past decade, membership loss has approximated that experienced in other labor organizations.

The Federation's constitution and bylaws attempt "… to strike a compromise between adequate national authority and effective local representation."[9] Although these governance documents are subject to change by each convention (which is the international union's primary source of control and power), the membership, like those of other large unions or stockholders of big corporations, tends to perpetuate policies and elect the same leaders in office for long periods of time.[10]

The (now biennial) convention, held in June of odd numbered years, exercises legislative functions and elects International officers. Each local elects its own delegates to the convention based upon the number of its members: 200 members or less receive one delegate; if between 201 and 400 members, two delegates; more than 400 members, three delegates.[11] For the election of International officers, each local is entitled to one vote for each 100 members (or major fraction thereof) but no local can cast more than ten votes except on questions affecting a change in the bylaws. In that case, by voice vote, standing vote, or (upon proper request) roll call, each local will cast as many votes as it has members. This arrangement is evidence of the dichotomy between small and large locals that has existed since the days of the National League of Musicians in the nineteenth century.

Resolutions to amend the bylaws or to further the business of the convention may be submitted by members, locals, or the IEB and must be published in the *International Musician* one month before the convention.[12] Before they reach the floor of the convention, all resolutions are first referred to various committees of delegates appointed by the president. Each resolution carries the committee's recommendation with it. This power of the president to appoint committees is probably one of the reasons for the longevity of AFM administrations. Not surprisingly, the president's views, for the most part, are reflected by the committees.

All new candidates for International office usually submit pertinent information to the *International Musician* for publication before the convention. These candidates for President, Vice President, Vice President from Canada, Secretary-Treasurer, International Executive Board (five positions), and Delegate to the Convention of the AFL-CIO (usually six positions) occupy themselves with "politicking" before, after, and during convention sessions until the actual elections.

The convention also sets the salary for all members of the IEB: President, both Vice Presidents, Secretary-Treasurer, and the five elected board members (the delegates to the AFL-CIO Convention are not paid). The highest salary is the President's—$70,000 annually as of July 1, 1985 (plus 4 percent annual increases through 1989), an increase of $6,000 from the salary set by the 1981 Convention[13] and $20,000 more than the President's salary in 1970.[14] Judged by the annual remuneration given to other leaders of entertainment unions, this is not too much, and may be too little. In 1985, Ken Orsatti, national executive secretary of the 58,000-member Screen Actors Guild earned $80,000; Ed Lynch, president of the 11,500-member National Association of Broadcast Employees and Technicians, earned $73,200 in 1984; Sanford Wolff, national executive secretary of the 65,000-member American Federation of Television and Radio Artists, earned $95,000 in 1984; Alan Eisenberg, executive secretary of the 36,000-member Actors Equity Association earned $56,973 in 1984.[15]

Other annual salaries voted by the 1985 Convention were $15,500 for the Vice President (a part-time position); $57,000 for the Vice President for Canada; $57,000 for the Secretary-Treasurer (these three officers are also entitled to a 4 percent annual increase through 1989); and $14,000 for each of the other five members of the IEB (also part-time positions).

As the AFM's legislative body, the convention decides "where the money comes from." For many years,the primary source of funds was the tax on traveling musicians. In 1963, with the threat of a Taft-Hartley ruling against this tax, the convention tried to rely upon increased per-capita taxes. When this proved to be inadequate, it adopted the work dues levy in 1980 as the main source of revenue. Of course, monies are also derived (to a lesser degree) from initiation fees, annual per-capita dues, income from investments, fines, and other sources.

Over many years, the detailed body of bylaws which was created by earlier conventions (and continually altered and increased by each succeeding convention) forms the legal structure of the AFM's continuing activities. Some union officials feel there are too many bylaws, stating this reliance on bylaws has inhibited the Federation's external operations and has been partially to blame for its difficulties with Taft-Hartley and other national legislation.[16] This belief may be spreading. The 1983 Convention made decisions upon 87 resolutions and recommendations, while the 1985 Convention dealt with only 40. But the 1987 Convention drastically reversed this trend. A total of 99 resolutions and recommendations were considered, at least partially, because of dissatisfaction over the plight of Life Members, "democratic" procedures, and the status of Canadian members and locals. In the future, the Federation may well continue to make internal changes via resolutions and recommendations while pursuing external change through negotiations with purchasers of music.

The International Executive Board, and especially the President, has general supervision of the affairs of the Federation between conventions. The International administration has great power and authority despite the considerable amount of responsibility reserved for the locals.

Among the many duties of the IEB, perhaps the most important are the negotiations for national contracts in network radio and TV, TV videotape, educational TV, commercial announcements (jingles), recordings, electrical transcriptions, theatrical motion pictures, some traveling shows, TV films, and non-theatrical non-TV documentary and industrial films. Since "the troubles in Los Angeles" and Kenin's promise to allow participation in and ratification of contracts by those affected by them, these negotiations are not as simple as they once were. The much more democratic process now demands input before the negotiations start, player representation during negotiations, and (usually) a ratification by mailed ballot to be returned by qualified individual musicians indicating their approval or disapproval. The 1987 Convention further stipulated the inclusion of dissenting opinions along with the ratification ballots.

Another important IEB responsibility is the supervision of authorized booking agents who provide service for the membership. These authorized agents sign contractual agreements with the Federation which promise at least scale wages and favorable working conditions for the musician and set ceilings on the fees to be charged. Listings of these booking agents are provided regularly in the *International Musician* and in a separately published booklet. Given the restrictions of Taft-Hartley, these agreements are only moderately helpful to Federation members. Because the AFM can no longer insist on booking agent service exclusively for its members, the agents can use contracts (even for AFM members, unless they object) which allow higher commissions and lower wages.

The IEB meets at least two times annually. The diversity of the agendas (all published in the *International Musician*) is amazing. In addition to ongoing negotiations, a given meeting might adjudicate disputes between members, between locals and members, between locals and/or members with purchasers of music; rule upon requests of locals to raise or lower per-capita dues, initiation fees, or work dues; decide upon mergers of locals or authorize the appointment of a trustee for a troubled local; and deal with appeals from members or locals from previous decisions. The IEB has "... general supervision of all matters pertaining to the Federation and shall have complete jurisdiction and power relating to the Federation or any of its members or any Local thereof, as well as of all matters and questions in which the ... Federation or any of its locals or members may be interested, or by which any of them may be in anywise affected."[17]

Another great responsibility of the IEB is the complete control of wages and working conditions for the traveling musician. With the union's new emphasis on better service and "a better deal" for the traveling player, this task becomes greater. Recently, the IEB adopted a ruling that for purposes of calculating work dues, there would be a national minimum of $40 per day for traveling engagements—a figure considered much too low by some big-city locals.[18] It may be too low, but by setting this price the influence of national control is put to work to accomplish national policy. The 1987 Convention confirmed the rank and file's approval of this policy. The delegates voted a "cap" of 3 percent work dues for traveling members who work in nightclubs, hotels, lounges, and taverns.

The international officers fulfill other duties as well as participating as members of the IEB. The Secretary-Treasurer's office is responsible for all matters regarding claims, charges, conventions, fines, collections, and so forth as well as the publication of the *International Musician*. The Vice President for Canada has a fully staffed office in Toronto and is responsible for all Federation affairs in Canada. The President's office, however, includes the bulk of staff and assistants that provide for the ongoing functions of the AFM.

The International headquarters of the union in New York contain departments under the President's control that supervise unfair and defaulter lists, strikes, lockouts, boycotts, bylaw interpretation and rulings, booking agents, foreign and domestic tours, field services, membership services, organizing and recruiting, symphony and opera affairs, and supervision of national and international contracts. For many years there has also been a representative of the President to lobby Congress in support of specific legislation. There are no archival or statistical departments but the President's office has, especially in recent years, created a strong force to interact with and serve the locals.

Starting in 1936, a staff of International representatives was established to assist locals in conforming to Federation bylaws, developing local contracts, and working with music purchasers, all tasks originally performed by the state or province representative. Each International representative is assigned a particular geographic area and reports directly to the President's office.[19] The administrative assistants were added in 1983 to bolster this effort and, particularly, to conduct hearings, encourage mergers, and investigate potential labor law violations. The President's office also maintains a full-time West Coast representative in Hollywood (the first West Coast representative was Herman Kenin, appointed by Petrillo) to oversee Federation affairs in that part of the country. The office is now enhanced by a representative of the Symphony Department (added by Fuentealba).

Who are these International officers elected by the 1987 Convention to work with President Emerson? They were, first of all, working musicians—then came union experience, with progressive steps up through the hierarchy. Their positions call for knowledge of how music is made and the music business. To be effective, they need to be good negotiators, have an understanding of financial matters, and be both flexible and pragmatic. In fact, the successful IEB member would have been a good business leader and politician given other circumstances.

International Vice President Mark Tully Massagli also

serves as president of Local 369 in Las Vegas, a position he has held since 1979. He is also president of the Nevada State AFL-CIO and president of the South Nevada Central Labor Council. He holds degrees from San Fernando Valley Junior College and the University of Nevada. His musical experience has been "on the road" and in Las Vegas with a jazz trio. International Vice President from Canada J. Alan Wood played tuba professionally with numerous radio and television orchestras and with the Toronto Symphony. Until his position became full-time in 1979, he also served as president of Local 167 in Toronto. International Secretary-Treasurer Kelly L. Castleberry II also served as a local president (Number 136 in Charleston, West Virginia) until election to his present position in 1985. Castleberry's formal education was at Marshall University and West Virginia State College. He played clarinet and saxophone in show bands in the East and Midwest.

The International Executive Board's five members present a varied cross section of music/business education and experience. Robert D'Arcy has been a member of the Federation since 1937. An officer of Local 161-710 (Washington) since 1950, he is now the local's president. A working musician all his adult life, he has played theaters, hotels, restaurants, night clubs, radio, and TV and is a highly respected society orchestra leader. D'Arcy is also a lawyer who is a member of the Bar in Maryland and the District of Columbia. Another long-time AFM member, Vince DiBari, has been vice president of Local 47 (Los Angeles) since 1973. He played trumpet in the pit of the Paramount Theater while attending Loyola University and later was a music major at UCLA. DiBari's professional career includes ten years "on the road" with the big bands and work in virtually every major motion picture studio along with many nationally broadcast radio and TV shows.

IEB member Eugene Frey, a clarinetist, was a member of the Cincinnati Symphony for seventeen years before becoming president of Local 1 in Cincinnati in 1958 and IEB member in 1975. Frey holds two degrees from the University of Cincinnati and has been a member of the Planning Section of the Music Panel of the National Endowment for the Arts. IEB board members John Glasel and Richard Q. Totusek are also local presidents in New York City and Spokane, Washington, respectively. Both are also businessmen: Glasel has a music publishing company and is co-owner of a music paper and reproduction service; Totusek owns several tax accounting offices in the Northwest. Totusek holds two degrees from Gonzaga University and has taught at Georgetown University, Fort Wright College, and Spokane Conservatory. He describes himself as an all-idiom pianist working as a show, jazz, and commercial performer. He also played French horn with the Spokane Symphony. Glasel, a trumpet player, holds degrees from Yale and has played in jazz groups, big bands (Sidney Bechet, Eddie Condon, Benny Goodman, Woody Herman, and others), the New Haven Symphony, and the Little Orchestra Society. Additionally, Frey and Glasel serve on the board of trustees of the AFM-EP Fund. All in all, a well-educated, long experienced, diversified group.[20]

Although the executive power of the President and the IEB is substantial, much authority is reserved for the locals. Since all of the United States and Canada is (since 1943) within the jurisdiction of some local, each member of the AFM is simultaneously a member of a local and of the International organization. Normally, there should be no local with fewer than fifty members, but the IEB may grant a charter if there are less than this number if it is "... in the best interests of the Federation."[21] In these days of declining membership, there are probably several of these very small locals. One international official estimates there are now approximately 500 locals—down from over 700 in the mid-1970s.[22] The largest local is in New York City, whose peak membership has been well over 30,000,[23] and is now (as of 1987) just over 14,000.[24]

The locals' members elect officers, business agents (who are sometimes appointed) and executive boards. Local members also set initiation fees, regular periodic dues, and work dues. A portion of the initiation fee is shared with the International treasury along with a $12 annual per-capita dues and a one-half percent work dues. Usually, the local executive board also sets scale wages for local engagements and negotiates local contracts and agreements. Other tasks include recommending booking agent agreements to the IEB, ajudicating disputes, setting fines, "policing" working places for musicians within their jurisdiction, and offering a variety of services to both local and traveling members.

Initiation fees (including the International's share) range from $15 to $275, with an average of $62. Annual regular dues (including the International's share) range from $15 to $85, with an average of $37.[25] Work dues range from one percent to 5 percent of scale wages for local members, with a ceiling of three percent for traveling musicians. Typically, there is no "average" local, but the larger locals tend to have higher initiation fees and regular dues. The variance in work dues depends on the local's financial situation, not the size of the local.

Remuneration of local officials also varies widely based upon the local's size and the regional employment situation. Since the AFM keeps no records of these salaries, an educated guess is that a very small local may pay its officers nothing except waiver of dues; locals with between 100 and 300 members may add $500 to $1,000 annually to the dues waiver; larger locals may pay officials in the $10,000 to $20,000 range,[26] but even the largest local,

Number 802 in New York City, paid its full-time president only \$37,700 in 1983.[27] Is it any wonder that local presidents like Mark Massagli, Robert D'Arcy, Eugene Frey, John Glasel, and Richard Totusek are also IEB members? It's the only way they can afford to be in the union business.

Not surprisingly, a great range of business talents and ethics are represented in the elected local officials. At one extreme is the secretary-treasurer of one of the larger unions who regularly played "dark dates" (i.e., cash, unreported engagements) in his own city[28] and the executive board member of another local who somehow played a huge percentage of MPTF jobs year after year without any attempt to help others in his local.[29] There are young rock musicians who travel constantly and report they never see local officials except when, "... they come around to collect work dues."[30] And there are local officials who establish unrealistically high scale wages and then refuse to be flexible in making adjustments.[31]

The International staff knows about many of these "bad apples" through reports and gossip. One staff person commented, "Lots of dumb things are done out there. What can you expect when they're not paid to do the job?"[32]

But there are local officials who are better "business" people and are dedicated to the job. The official of a larger local who tolerates the use of tapes in a "downtown" performance because he knows the promoters are short of cash now but will use live performers next time; the official of a small local who "carries" a musician down on his luck until he plays a few gigs and pays up his dues; the official who knows there is much non-union work done in his city by performers who also hold good union jobs in the local symphony and who is still able to "wave the carrot, not the stick"; and the official who recruits among the purchasers

of music rather than the players themselves are all examples of the sort of businessman/politician needed to "do the
job."[33] "Knowledgeable," "practical," and "pragmatic"
seem to be the key words that describe a successful local
official.

Part of the problem the Federation faces in improving
the business and political skills of its local officials is that
there is no real training and development program for
them. Another part of the problem, given the very low
salary schedules, is finding the dedicated people who are
willing to serve in these positions, hold another job to
support themselves, and still carry on the (sometimes
thankless) responsibilities of trade unionist. This last is
undoubtedly a factor in the recent rash of mergers of two
or more locals.

Who are these elected local officials? The presidents
are rarely women or blacks, although women and blacks
do serve with some frequency as secretaries, treasurers
and executive board members. They are usually part-time
musicians and attorneys, retail store clerks, state, county or
city employees, insurance agents, housewives, recep-
tionists, schoolteachers (of music and other subjects), private music teachers, and retired men and women. They
are musicians in all phases of the business. Increasingly,
symphony players will probably take a larger part as their
field retains its stability while membership falls in other
areas.

The locals are (or should be) in business to serve their
own members and those traveling musicians within their
jurisdiction. All locals are involved in negotiating and
enforcing union contracts; indeed, some locals do little
else. But even the smallest local, with good leadership,
does more. Keeping in constant contact with purchasers of
music and promoting ventures that might be helpful in

advancing the cause of live music can be (or should be) part of the job for all locals.

The larger locals can offer more to benefit their members; the larger the local, the more services it can offer. Some examples: referral services on the local level to match the AFM service at the national level; credit unions (many lenders think musicians are a poor risk); emergency relief funds; payroll processing; hospitalization and health insurance plans; optical and dental programs; life insurance programs; in-house booking services; engagement payment guarantee; legal services; programs to assist in drug or alcohol problems and other professional counseling and referral services for troubled musicians. Some large locals even sponsor "senior citizen" orchestras for their members.

Another layer of governance between the locals and the International is the series of conferences (groupings of locals in the same geographical area) whose meetings (usually annually) serve as a forum to discuss common problems. The meetings also enable International officials and/or staff to conduct informal training programs for the local officials who are the delegates. These conferences— Western, Canadian, New England, Tri-State, International Upper Peninsula, Southern, etc.—more than a dozen all told, are more important now in these days of biennial conventions to supply a necessary communication link between locals and the International.

The AFM, a member union of the AFL-CIO, is also affiliated with the Canadian Labour Congress, the Music Educators National Conference, the National Association of Jazz Educators, and the North American Band Directors' Coordinating Council.[34] Its foreign affiliations have included the British Musicians Union, the Philippine Musicians Union, the two Mexican musicians unions

(Sindicato Unico de Trabajadores de la Musica del Distrito Federal and Sindicato Nacional de Trabajadores de la Musica de la R.M.),[35] and the International Federation of Musicians.[36] This last organization offers the greatest hope for cooperation among musicians on an international scale. It "... is composed of thirty-eight affiliated unions representing 330,000 musicians worldwide [and] was founded in 1948 to protect and further the economic, social and artistic interests of musicians organized in member unions."[37]

Chapter VII
Ways of Musical Life:
Professions Within the Profession

THE WAY THINGS WERE

A HISTORY OF THE AMERICAN FEDERATION OF MUSI-
CIANS and its predecessor, The National League of
Musicians, is really a history of the performance of instrumental music[1] in North America for the past century. Just
as it is impossible to separate the history of the Federation
from the history of performance, it is equally impractica-
ble to view the union without regard for the individual
musicians who make up the AFM—the professional performers. Certainly, some of the types of performance that
once were an important part of the musical profession are
gone. But many others have evolved into segments of
today's musical job market.

Long before the Civil War, touring minstrel shows and
river boat bands employed the first of the North American
traveling musicians. Then came burlesque from about the
1880s, followed by the beginnings of vaudeville before the
turn of the century. And "show biz" meant meaningful
employment for musicians. In its heyday during the 1920s
there were "... 2000 vaudeville theatres in the United
States and Canada."[2]

In 1913 the famous Palace Theater in New York
started two shows a day which was the hallmark of big time
vaudeville ("small time" vaudeville meant anywhere from

171

three to eight or nine shows a day). But by 1932, the Palace had replaced vaudeville with double feature movies along with a news reel and a comic short feature. By 1933, vaudeville was dead, the victim of the Depression, "the talkies," and radio. Burlesque and vaudeville may have died, but the entertainment they provided has lived on (in much diminished form) in Broadway musicals, a few resort hotels, the nightclub shows of Las Vegas, Reno, and Atlantic City, the show bars in a few large cities and some late-night TV shows.

During the days of silent film, the best job in the music business was in the theater orchestra. In the larger cities, this meant employment for several orchestras with the opportunity for players to meet in some centralized area (usually a bar) during intermissions to play poker, exchange news, and compare wages and working conditions. In terms of trade union principles, the Federation probably was never stronger. But with the advent of the sound motion picture in the late 1920s, as we have seen, thousands of musicians lost their jobs.

It seems there have always been fairs, carnivals—and circuses too. There still are fairs, carnivals, circuses, and now ice shows, but for the most part, when music is desired, it is canned. Only the largest shows employ live musicians today, but in a much smaller band supplemented by recorded music. An international official complained, "... They come in and say, 'It is a complete tape show, but let's see if we can hire a few players to take the heat off you from the locals—if it doesn't cost too much.'"[3] Such tapes were made by a full orchestra or band either on a "dark date" or under the mistaken impression that the tape was to be used for rehearsal only, or from a recording made during performance without knowledge of the players. As Petrillo said, "They were playing for their own funeral."

Then there was the first big band era— not the bands of Benny Goodman, Duke Ellington, or Glenn Miller but the bands of Patrick S. Gilmore, John Philip Sousa, and C.A. Cappa. The spectacular band extravaganzas probably began with "the series of concerts put on in New York and Boston by Monsieur Antoine Jullien in 1853–54."[4] Jullien, a great showman and promoter (who learned a great deal from P.T. Barnum) fashioned his 100-piece orchestra show with bombast and circus-style advertising. Although the nucleus of his orchestra was forty imported musicians, he was soon followed by Patrick S. Gilmore, who adapted Jullien's methods to spectacular band shows with American musicians. The Gilmore sensational concert in New Orleans (in 1864) eclipsed Jullian's efforts. He used a band of 500, a chorus of 5,000, plus cannons and church bells.[5] By 1872, Gilmore outdid his own previous efforts. For the World Peace Jubilee, he used a chorus of 20,000 and an orchestra of 2,000 along with cannon, anvils, and chimes.[6] In 1878, Gilmore reversed the trend of bringing performers to America by taking his 66-piece band on a successful tour of Europe.

But it was left to native-born John Philip Sousa to thoroughly establish the military band tradition in North America. After serving as leader of the U.S. Marine Band from 1880 to 1892, he formed his own band (made up of many members of the famous Gilmore band[7]) and toured the United States, Canada, and Europe to wide acclaim.

In 1892, there were at least two leading bands in competition with Gilmore's: Cappa's Band ("C.A. Cappa, Bandmaster; Music furnished for all occasions") and Bayne's Band ("William Bayne, Bandmaster; Music furnished for Balls, Lodges, Clubs and Private Parties").[8] After the Sousa band's many successful years, there were many more bands on the national scene. Frederick N. Innes, Arthur Pryor, Giuseppe Creatore, Edwin Franko

Goldman, Bohumir Kryl, Henry Fillmore, and others all directed bands in the Sousa tradition. Some organizations toured, providing continuous work for musicians. Other bands played only in their home cities and provided, at best, occasional weekend or summer employment.

While the band extravaganza may have begun in 1853, the history of municipal bands predates Monsieur Jullien by a quarter century. The Allentown (Pennsylvania) Band was formed on July 3, 1828, and still plays annually from Memorial Day to Thanksgiving.[9] Our Shamokin Band (Pennsylvania) counts its history from 1865, and since that date (the ending of the Civil War) there have been many other municipal bands formed that still provide employment for wind and percussion players. The Ashby (Massachusetts) Band beginning in 1887,[10] the Long Beach Municipal Band (California) in 1909,[11] the Hagerstown (Maryland) Municipal Bank in 1915,[12] the Racine (Wisconsin) Band in 1923,[13] and the Daytona Beach (Florida) Municipal Band in 1930[14] are all examples of bands that regularly perform today. Although most band seasons are short and do not approach full-time employment for their members, they do offer the casual musical engagement so lacking in the smaller cities for performers. And for their audiences, they offer the rare opportunity to hear live music.

The municipal band tradition has not died out completely. Thanks in part to MPTF monies and co-sponsors (city, chambers of commerce or business interests), "music in the parks" exists in United States and Canadian cities from New York, Chicago, and Toronto to Rochester (New York), Sioux Falls (South Dakota), and Hamilton (Ohio).

Another band tradition, the industrial band, has now all but disappeared. Organizations such as the Lukens Steel Company Band (Coatsville, Pennsylvania), The

Armco Band (Middletown, Ohio), the Anglo-Canadian Leather Company Band (Huntsville, Ontario), and the Packard Band (Warren, Ohio) were conducted by Sousa Band alumni and provided live music for their hometowns. The band personnel (except for an occasional "ringer") were employees of the company and only rarely members of the AFM.

Perhaps the most famous of these organizations, the Armco Band, evolved into a professional band. Under its conductor, Frank Simon, the band broadcasted nationwide on a regular basis over NBC from Cincinnati. Simon included many members of the Cincinnati Symphony Orchestra as part of his regular personnel.

The military band tradition has not declined. From the first public performance of the U.S. Marine Band on August 21, 1800,[15] the military bands of both Canada and the United States have prospered. The major service bands in Washington advertise regularly in the *International Musician* when they have vacancies and attract Federation members for their auditions. One recent opening in the Marine Band for a clarinetist drew a crowd of 34 highly trained and talented potential members.[16]

The conventional military bands on ships, air bases, and Marine, Navy, and Army installations (50 in the Army, 20 in the Air Force, 17 in the Navy, and 10 in the Marine Corps[17]) are generally small and uniform in instrumentation. But the "official" service bands in Washington and the military academies are multi-musical-force units containing choruses; jazz, rock 'n' roll, and country combos; military marching bands; concert bands; orchestras; and chamber music ensembles. The 1982 Defense Department budget proposal listed three military bands in Washington with budgets larger than that of the National Symphony Orchestra.[18] In that year the proposed budget for all military bands called for a greater expenditure than the entire appropriation for the National Endowment for the Arts.[19]

The AFM has changed its attitude toward military musical organizations. From Petrillo's advice in the 1950s to cut band units, the Federation has reversed itself and now objects to budget reductions for military bands.[20] Since there are now many musicians in the armed services of both the United States and Canada who are Federation members, the International office frequently expresses views to enhance their careers.

The second big band era,—the one we associate with "swing"—began with Benny Goodman, who became the "King of Swing" on August 21, 1935 at the Polomar Ballroom in Hollywood; it lasted through the years of World War II. But there were dance bands that played the big hotels and ballrooms and traveled the country before 1935, and there are dance bands still traveling today.

In the early 1930s there were the "sweet bands" of Guy Lombardo, Wayne King, and Hal Kemp. Before that were the swinging black bands from the 1920s through World War II—Fletcher Henderson, Duke Ellington, Earl Hines, Count Basie, and Jimmie Lunceford. And at the height of their popularity in the decade between 1935 and 1945, Goodman's contemporaries were Glenn Miller, Tommy Dorsey, Harry James, Russ Morgan, Stan Kenton, Artie Shaw, and perhaps a thousand more.[21]

The big bands played clubs, ballrooms, hotels, and theaters in the large cities and were regularly broadcasted "live" from the engagement. They also played "one-nighters" on the road, sometimes for months on end. When the band was booked at the Little Club of the Park Central Hotel in New York or the Joseph Urban Room of the Congress Hotel in Chicago for twelve or eighteen weeks, it was a great job. The music was exciting (that is, there was opportunity for improvisation), the audience was enthusiastic, and the pay and working conditions were satisfying.

But the one-nighters were grueling. The band might finish playing at 1:00 A.M. and drive one or two hundred miles to the next booking. This gave the players a "twofer"—a chance to sleep in the early morning and again that night for the price of only one day at the hotel or motel. Other schedules would call for an early morning departure from one city followed by an all-day bus or car ride which ended at the next city with barely time to change clothes and eat a sandwich before taking a seat on the bandstand. It was, and is, a business only for the young.

There were always many musicians ready and willing to join the big bands, but for most, it meant part-time work and on-the-job training in the smaller, less prestigious bands first. This meant risking work without pay (if the club owner was less than honest) or being stranded "in the sticks" with only candy bars for supper. Then gradually, by word of mouth, through an audition, or with a little help from friends, a good player could join the top echelon. Most wind and percussion players who rose to the professional ranks generally came directly from the many high school bands without additional formal music education.

Today, there are "ghost" swing bands traveling the country without their famous leaders. The Tommy Dorsey Orchestra, the Russ Morgan Orchestra, the Glenn Miller Orchestra, the Duke Ellington Orchestra, and the Guy Lombardo Orchestra (along with many others) keep the sound of the swing era alive. They still play conventions, private clubs, charity balls, dance halls, and concerts. They still play the music that made their namesakes famous— the dance music of the 1930s and 1940s. The job is for both the young player and the old-timer who are available for casual work.

The big band era will not come back; there are very few new big bands—McCoy Tyner and Juggernaut are exceptions and the Tonight Show Band with Doc Severinsen is a one-of-a-kind. Economic realities dictate the advantages of a trio or quartet over the eighteen to twenty-six player dance band. And of course, the disc jockey is less expensive still.

THE CLASSICAL ESTABLISHMENT

Since early in the Petrillo administration (1941), conductors and instrumental soloists have been members of the Federation along with their colleagues in the symphony and opera orchestras with which they play. Originally, the AFM wanted them as members to present a unified front in order to bring the Boston Symphony into the Federation and to strike the record companies. Their presence within the union today emphasizes the strength of the AFM in the world of classical music. Although players in major orchestras (along with soloists and conductors) probably make up less than two percent of the Federation membership, they represent by far the most highly organized segment of the profession.

These world-famous, highly talented soloists lead a not so glamorous, stressful, well-traveled life. Today's stars—pianists Emanual Ax, Jorge Bolet, Vladimir Horowitz, Alicia de Larrocha, Garrick Ohlsson, Rudolf Serkin, Andre Watts, Alexis Weissenberg; violinists Boris Belkin, Yehudi Menuhin, Nathan Milstein, Itzhak Perlman, Isaac Stern, Pinchas Zuckerman; cellists Lynn Harrell, Yo Yo Ma, Nathaniel Rosen, Mstislav Rostropovich, Peter Wiley; and many others—are members of the international "jet set" and perform in recitals and concerts dozens of times each year.

From childhood, they are committed to studying with famous teachers and to hours of daily practice. The practicing continues throughout their professional life-time. Fritz Kreisler (a famous violinist from earlier in the century) is reported to have said, "If I don't practice for one day, I know it. If I don't practice for two days, my wife knows it. And if I don't practice for three days, everyone knows it."

The constant travel from one city to another, or from one continent to another, the hours of practice in strange hotel rooms, eating in good and bad restaurants, the musical interchange with good and not-so-good orchestras and conductors on almost a daily schedule—all seem worthwhile to these geniuses when balanced by the personal satisfaction of performing well and hearing the applause of appreciative audiences.

Their fees are high, over $40,000 per concert for some soloists,[22] and they are worth it. The presence on an orchestral program of a great soloist will sell out the concert (and the series of concerts) in many cities. The star system works—audiences will come to see and hear the soloist despite the program or the quality of the orchestra or conductor.

The same phenomenon applies to star conductors but perhaps to a lesser degree. Audiences come to hear Leonard Berstein's Mahler, James Levine's Brahms, or Georg Solti's Beethoven. Only rarely are there "child-prodigy conductors"—Loren Maazel was an exception. Most great conductors begin their careers as orchestral players or rehearsal pianists in the opera studios and through diligence, talent, and luck move from smaller orchestras to great orchestras in major cities of the world. Those conductors who choose to stay as musical directors of a single orchestra for the greater part of each season must be politicians and administrators as well as musicians and are rewarded with authority, administrative detail, and six-figure annual salaries. Those conductors who choose to be guest conductors jet from orchestra to orchestra across nations and continents are rewarded with prestige, travel fatigue, and much larger six-figure salaries. Lesser conducting talents fill positions with smaller, less prestigious orchestras, but always there are far more potential conductors than orchestras. It seems everyone wants to be a conductor.

Chamber music performers are another segment of the classical establishment, but there is room for only a very few on North American stages. String quartets dominate the field, although a few pianists and an occasional woodwind player make the grade. Most chamber music players have studied (and practiced) their instruments from childhood, have had good private instruction, have attended conservatories or prestigious schools of music, and have either "graduated" from an orchestra position or moved directly into an ensemble early in their professional careers. A great many chamber music ensembles are associated with universities or conservatories: the Juilliard String Quartet, the LaSalle String Quartet (The University of Cincinnati), the Cleveland Quartet (The Eastman School of Music), and the faculty who make up the Yale Chamber Music Series are some examples. These performers supplement their performing careers (on campus, in nearby cities, and on national and international tours) with teaching duties at their institutions. In effect, their institutions subsidize their performances—chamber music recitals are not good "box office." Chamber music performance is a highly desired, very overcrowded field that gives its practitioners prestige, job satisfaction, hard work, and annual salaries comparable to principal positions in major orchestras. Additionally, these performers participate in the (usually) very good retirement systems of our major universities.

Unlike the decline of the big professional bands, the symphony orchestra is alive and well in most large cities in the United States and Canada. According to the American Symphony Orchestra League, there are more than 1,500 North American orchestras,[23] and John Chancellor says, "… Symphony orchestras had audiences of about 23 million people [in the 1982–1983 season]."[24]

The picture is not quite so rosy for the professional musician. Only the major orchestras (numbering probably less than 35) and some of the regional orchestras (less than a half dozen) offer the possibility of an annual wage above the poverty level. The ASOL classifies orchestras by the size of their annual budgets: in 1986 a major orchestra's budget is over $3.6 million, a regional orchestra's budget is from $1.0 million to $3.6 million, metropolitan and urban orchestras have budgets reaching down to $135,000.[25] In contrast to these figures, in 1968, the ASOL listed only 26 orchestras with budgets of $500,000 to $4 million and 56 orchestras with budgets from $100,000 to $499,999.[26] Clearly there has been a noticeable improvement in the financial health of our orchestras and the corresponding rise in wages—thanks in great part to ICSOM since the early 1960s, the Ford Foundation grants in 1966, and the militancy of the Federation during the 1970s. This growth is especially gratifying since the Association for Classical Music has estimated the classical music audience as only between 3 and 6 percent of the population.[27]

The first major North American orchestra was founded in New York in 1842. It was followed by orchestras in St. Louis (1880), Boston (1881), Chicago (1891), and Cincinnati (1895). By the beginning years of the twentieth century there were orchestras in Dallas, Honolulu, Minneapolis, Philadelphia, San Francisco, Toronto, and many other cities. With the exception of Boston (which formed its "Pops" Orchestra in 1885, thereby providing almost year-round employment for its symphony musicians[28]), these symphony positions provided only part-time jobs that needed to be supplemented with other work. The lucky players obtained other employment in music, freelance playing, or teaching. Others took any sort of work to subsidize their symphony jobs.

This part-time symphony employment was not confined to the first half of the century. Advertisements in the *International Musician* throughout the 1950s emphasized its prevalence: "The Springfield (Ohio) Symphony Orchestra desires to contact musicians interested in combining symphony work with full-time industrial or business employment; openings in all sections ... "[29] and, "Mobile Symphony desires first oboe, first clarinet ... on part-time basis, willing to work in other employments ... "[30] are some examples.

The mixed amateur-professional status of smaller orchestras is acknowledged by notices in AFM publications. In 1953, Detroit's Local 5 granted permission for its members to play with amateur orchestras with "... rehearsals gratis, but [they] must be paid the symphony concert price for any concerts... ."[31] As recently as 1985, Local 10-208 in Chicago agreed to allow its members to play with the Evanston Symphony, provided "... there is a proper contract to cover union members."[32]

But the growth of the symphony orchestras did not always progress smoothly. In the 1950s there was a movement to merge the Rochester Philharmonic with the orchestras in Syracuse and Buffalo[33]—and again in 1969 to merge the orchestras of Rochester and Buffalo.[34] Other orchestra boards in other cities became interested, but the movement failed because of the protests of civic leaders and interested locals of the AFM.

The improvement in financial respectability for the orchestral musician began with the first 52-week contract in the 1965–66 concert year of the New York Philharmonic. This was followed the next year by the full-year contract with the Philadelphia Orchestra. The Boston Symphony had a 50-week contract, and the Cleveland Orchestra reached a 48-week year in the 1966–1967 contract. That same year, the Chicago Symphony had a 47-week concert year.[35] Now that the so-called "big five" had gained this long sought goal, other major orchestras followed suit. For the first time orchestral musicians, performers who had reached the top of their profession, began to achieve economic parity with university faculty who taught orchestral instruments, many of whom had not reached the same professional excellence.

Finally, at least in the major orchestras, today's players receive an honorable living wage, and what were seasonal part-time jobs now provide year-round employment. This is not true in the regional orchestras. These organizations are the best of the part-time orchestras. They play an eight or nine-month season (or less) with salaries that fall far below a living wage. Regional orchestra players must have other employment to survive. Typically, great numbers of these musicians hold full-time positions on the faculty of local universities or as music teachers in the public schools. Some are highly trained and talented housewives who are satisfied with part-time work, while others are music students from the local colleges or universities. Occasionally, additional string players or a rare solo wind player will be imported from a nearby city or university for concerts.

In many respects, these regional orchestras are comparable to triple A or double A teams in professional baseball. They provide live entertainment for their local audience, a modest wage for local players, and an important feeder system to the "major leagues" of the major orchestras.

Auditions for "major league" orchestras are not what they once were. No longer can a dictatorial conductor hire (and fire) at will. No longer can cronyism nor sexual and racial partisanship have as great an influence in choosing new orchestra players, nor can secret or closed tryouts be held. Today's major orchestras are committed by contract to a standard of fairness unheard of only a decade ago.

In this tremendously overcrowded field, it is usual to have 100, 200, even 300 musicians apply for a single vacancy. These numbers apply in part because since 1964 it has been standard practice for major (and regional and urban) orchestras to advertise their available positions in the *International Musician* so that all Federation members can be notified and the orchestras can prove they are equal opportunity employers. Some orchestras screen applications for obviously unqualified musicians; other orchestras make a point of giving fair hearings to all who apply.

Although each orchestra follows slightly different procedures, standards today are based upon a Code of Ethical Audition Practices approved by the AFM, ICSOM, and MOMC (Major Orchestra Managers Conference) in 1984.[36] The code permits the use of taped performance by the applicant in lieu of or in addition to written resumés. Because tapes have proved to be an inadequate substitute for a live audition, there is still no alternative for the huge expenditure of time and money that can be incurred by players traveling to the audition city. In some cases, a returnable deposit is also required to inhibit "no-shows." The musical material to be performed at these first round auditions is made known to all applicants so there can be no surprises, except for the music for sight-reading. Some orchestras go still further in attempting to eliminate as many inequities as possible: they hold these auditions with the applicant behind a screen. The auditioning committee for the first round audition is composed of orchestral musicians; the final audition committee includes some players and the conductor, whose verdict is almost always final. In some orchestras, if all players on the final audition committee disagree with the conductor, he or she cannot prevail. Even if the conductor has the last word, a fair minded person cannot but be influenced by the opinions of his or her musical colleagues.

You can beat the system. There are some auditions that end with a "no decision": despite the hundreds of applicants, the audition committee insists it cannot find a suitable performer. That may be because the players are all below the level of that orchestra, or because the artistic standards of the committee are unrealistically high, or because the committee intends to begin a new round of auditions in which (not surprisingly) a player well known to the orchestra will be the new winner. Nothing is perfect, but the new code seems to be a step in the right direction.

There are objections to this audition procedure. Jean Martinon, when he was conductor of the Chicago Symphony, believed that the principal player in the section, not the conductor, should have the final say in choosing a second player. He explained that sometimes there were extra-musical factors that enabled (or hindered) good ensemble performance.

Philip Hart, a former orchestra administrator, views the old system of encouraging an orchestra to hire the students of its players (without open auditions) as advantageous. This system, he argues, enabled each orchestra to keep its own individual sound.[37] A Chicago Symphony musician disagrees. He believes that with all the international clinics and teaching seminars these days, each orchestra would still produce a "homogenized" sound.[38]

Who are the players who win the auditions and survive the two or three year probationary period before they become tenured members of a major orchestra? They are, first of all, talented, well-trained musicians who have studied (and practiced) their instruments for many years. Except in rare instances, they will have served an orchestra apprenticeship in a lesser organization. They own or are buying a professional-grade instrument (or instruments) which can cost anywhere from a few thousand to two hundred thousand dollars. They have attended a conservatory or university school of music and received a professional musical education. They must prove during their probationary years that they can get along with others and promise to become a congenial colleague.

At this point, their preparation parallels that of the aspiring chamber music performer. In many cases, the potential orchestral player is the potential chamber music performer. If job prospects are too dim in chamber music (and for the wind player, they are almost nonexistent) the young performer begins to audition for whatever orchestra job is available. If this fails, he or she may try for a college or public school teaching position (if qualified to teach) where a regional or urban or community orchestra offers playing experience.

Competition continues to hone the skills of these performers as they continue their route towards a major orchestra position. The repeated auditions will eventually offer a winning opportunity for the ones who are persistent, thickskinned, talented, experienced, at the right place at the right time—and lucky. The winners are increasingly women and young.[39] Given the known propensity of conductors to be teachers, some cynics have suggested that the movement toward women and youth is a mechanism to create a more malleable and dependent musical association. Others are convinced the youth movement is greatly beneficial. The tragedy is that there are so many fully qualified applicants for any orchestral vacancy. For each outstanding talent that is permitted to be heard in our orchestras, there are probably 99 equally outstanding talents that will fall silent. A terrible waste.

The full-time, year-round schedules of today's major

orchestras are a blessing for the orchestra members, but not a total blessing. From too little music performance and disagreeable summer jobs (away from music), the orchestra player now plays and plays and plays. Finding relief from the boredom and physical and mental stress of demanding performance schedules has called for innovative strategies.

The first step in this direction was to introduce revolving seatings in the string sections. It began in the Chicago Symphony in 1971[40] as an effort to relieve boredom and enhance musical interest for the players buried deep in sections of as many as twenty or more like instrumentalists. On a regular schedule, players move to different chairs within the section; it seems the closer to the conductor the player sits, the less boredom and the greater musical interest he or she experiences. The experiment worked. Today most major (and a few regional) orchestras use revolving string section seating.

Rotating personnel in various ways when the entire orchestra is not required for a composition or complete concert is also helpful. It allows various musicians either a night off or a challenging first chair experience.

Another innovation within the past decade is the opportunity for major orchestra members to perform as soloists or in chamber music ensembles. For the string player who felt the anonymity of section performance, or a second or third chair wind player, or even the principals of sections, this new opportunity presented a different way of life. Other efforts in this direction are needed.

What's the work like? For members of major orchestras, their commitment to the orchestra means seven or eight services (either rehearsals or concerts) per week with special provisions for unusual situations and out-of-town engagements. Since each service is usually two and one half hours in length, a work week of twenty-some hours might sound quite easy to the uninitiated. It isn't.

Because major orchestra players are at the top of their profession, they are expected to produce music at that level every rehearsal and concert, every week. Just as with professional baseball players in the major leagues, errors and mistakes are not gladly tolerated. To play well consistently despite some inadequate conductors and with occasional physical or mental stress is difficult. At this level, orchestra performers are expected to know the symphonic (or operatic) literature well enough that programs can be presented with a minimum of rehearsal even with guest conductors and unknown soloists. The challenge is always there.

The regional orchestras have much shorter seasons and their work weeks can be greatly varied. Rehearsals can be in the evenings and on weekends to avoid conflicts with the many players who hold other full-time jobs. Generally, the rehearsals are grouped around concert dates, which means some very busy weeks surrounded by many days of inactivity.

Major and regional orchestras play concerts of all kinds as frequently as possible. There are subscription concerts, pop concerts, run-out concerts, tour concerts, and children's (or young peoples') concerts. Since orchestras today are much more of a business than they ever were, public performances are very important. After all, rehearsals don't bring in any money.

All orchestras are interested in creating a larger audience in their locale. That is one of the major reasons for the prevalence of children's concerts given by almost every orchestra in the United States and Canada. The first concert "... for young people (of which there is record) was presented in Cincinnati, Ohio on the Fourth of July in 1858 by the Philharmonic Society...."[41] Some fifty years later, the San Francisco Symphony played its first youth concert. This was followed by youth concerts in Seattle

(1912), Detroit, (1914), and Cleveland (1921).[42] Today it is difficult to find an orchestra of any kind that does not present a series of youth concerts on a regular basis.

Given the long history of youth concerts, their frequency today, and their presumed importance in audience building, it is difficult to believe that there never has been any scientific research to test the worth of this activity. According to the American Symphony Orchestra League,[43] orchestras still have no reliable method of determining which music to play for which age groups, how long the program should be, the value and kind of audience preparation, the use of narrators, the time of day or week that is most appropriate, and a host of other needed information. This is too important an activity to leave its programming to young ambitious conductors who need to learn the score to a Beethoven symphony at the expense of alienated young listeners. Orchestra members (and orchestra managements) are concerned about "the graying of the audience." Perhaps it is time to test ways and means of "greening" the audience.

What does the job pay? Much more than it used to. In the major orchestras, there has been a dramatic improvement in the past two decades: from annual contracts in the $4,000 to $5,000 range for a partial year's work, the "big five" now have minimum wages of $1,000 per week on an annual basis. Other major orchestras are not far behind.

Many members of an orchestra make more than the minimum wage. Although personal contracts for orchestra personnel are closely guarded secrets, we know that in 1974 only 52 of 99 members of the Cleveland orchestra worked for scale wages.[44] One AFM local official estimates that today one half to two thirds of major orchestra players are paid above scale,[45] in some cases double the scale for concertmasters and other important principals.

Major orchestra benefits also include paid six-week

vacations, sickness/accident pay, health and welfare plans, accident and life insurance, instrument insurance, and generous pension plans. There are also provisions to protect the musicians from indiscriminate dismissal (once probationary years are passed) and demotion. Major orchestra tenure is much like that practiced in most United States and Canadian colleges and universities. Dismissal and/or demotion can occur only through procedures agreed to by both union and management.

From the three- or four-page master contracts of twenty years ago, contracts for major orchestras today are at least ten times longer. Great attention is paid to number and type of services allowed per week, details of the various health and welfare plans, seniority pay, definition of principals, travel arrangements (including travel insurance, per diem, meal allocation, type of hotel/motel room, length of tour), and hiring and dismissal procedures.

These contracts seem very good to the thousands of musicians who each year audition for major orchestra positions, although they probably seem outrageously expensive to many non-musicians. But when viewed as the peak of the profession, and compared with average or median salaries of other professionals such as doctors or dentists, the major orchestra player is not overpaid.

Regional orchestra contracts are different, and sometimes there is no contract. Some players will receive a personal contract for a set number of services. Others will be hired as freelance players and paid by the service. When there is a guaranteed annual wage, it is likely in only a few cases to be in the $10,000 to $20,000 range and can be as little as $2,000 or $3,000 (or less) for per-service orchestras. In many regional orchestras, higher wages are paid to a small core of players (a string quartet and/or a woodwind quintet, etc.) who perform as ensembles in the community in addition to fulfilling orchestral duties. Fringe benefits for regional orchestra players are minimal, and in many orchestras there are none. Is there any wonder that regional orchestra players envy the major orchestra contracts?

There is a world of difference between major and regional orchestras, but there should be no doubt that the public, the profession, the players, and the union need both for better musical health. Together, these two types of orchestras supply live music for large and small communities, prepare professionals with the experience they need to make music at the highest levels, and enable the musician who (for whatever reasons) does not enter a major orchestra, to gain a modest wage and enjoy making music.

The musician's role in the classical establishment is different from his or her job in any other music market. As conductor, soloist, chamber music player, or member of the symphony orchestra, the classical musician is part of the effort to preserve and advance our cultural heritage. This added burden of responsibility complicates the already complex relationship that exists among performer, management, and audience.

The symphony player, in whatever sized or ranked orchestra, performs art music and is employed by a nonprofit organization which is supported in part by individual donations and corporate and public funds. The public's financial interest in our orchestras is substantial. Most orchestras earn less than half of their annual budget, with the balance supplied by fund raising and governmental agencies (e.g., the National Endowment for the Arts or state, provincial, county, or city grants or appropriation).[46]

The community's involvement is essential for the continued health of the orchestra. This explains in part the huge expansion of orchestra marketing departments, the growth of "mini" series, "pop" series, and miscellaneous concert promotions.[47] Entertainment and commercialism are no longer the dirty words they once were,

because without sufficient public desire to support an
orchestra, the orchestra dies.

FREELANCING

Classically trained musicians do not always belong to
the "classical establishment." Some join other highly
trained and talented musicians freelancing in our major
cities in the United States and Canada.

A freelancer, the original and most prevalent job
classification for performers, has no guarantee of job
security; he or she is simply available for any type of
musical engagement. Freelancers spend a great deal of
time making contacts with contractors who are the gate
keepers to the freelance job market. They also need to
spend much time practicing their instruments and honing
their sight reading skills. In their business, the one thing
that can't be faked is musical ability.

Successful freelancers might hold a minimal employment base: in New York it could be the City Center Opera
or City Ballet; in Nashville it might be the Nashville
Symphony Orchestra; in other cities it could be a part-time
teaching job. Other successful freelancers want no base job
or other low paying obligations. In either case, they rely on
friends and contractors for per service chamber orchestra
jobs, recording sessions for a jingle or soundtrack, gigs
with a pick-up group to play background music for a pop
singer, or even sessions as street musicians. A classical
musician might respond to the traditional one-liner, "How
do you get to Carnegie Hall?" by saying, "Practice." The
freelancer would answer the same question by saying,
"Make friends with contractors!"

Recording sessions at midnight or practicing in a

backstage dressing room or spending an enormous amount of time on the telephone are all part of the job for freelancers. So is working constantly for days on end without rest and then hitting a dry period when there is no work at all.

There are rewards for extremely talented and lucky players. With the right recording sessions along with reuse payments (which can be higher than the original sessions because they continue for several years) and well-paying concert jobs, they can far outearn colleagues who have the security of a major orchestra contract.[48] For some freelancers, money is better than prestige. They resign from major symphony orchestras because they cannot stand the regimentation or the strain of playing for what they consider musically inadequate conductors.

Today, the trend is moving in the other direction. One reason why young players are seeking and accepting major orchestra positions is "... the narrowing of ... [the] rich freelance market...."[49] Among other factors, the synthesizer is replacing many musicians in the recording studio and orchestra pit.

In 1961, when Herman Kenin promised to establish a recording musicians' committee "... to advise on bargaining proposals and negotiations and all other matters affecting their interests,"[50] he laid the foundation for the Recording Musicians Association. The RMA, a conference within the Federation[51] of musicians who make recordings of all types, was first established in New York City in the early 1970s. The second chapter was formed in Chicago, and by January 1983 a third chapter was begun in Los Angeles.[52] In March of that same year, the RMA had chapters in Nashville and Toronto that joined with the New York, Chicago, and Los Angeles groups in submitting ideas to the AFM leadership for new contract negotiations.[53] In a very short time, recording freelancers have

joined members of ICSOM as legitimate sources of expertise who welcome the opportunity to interact with AFM
administration.

For the freelancer, the jingles business is a difficult
market. Not many years ago there were five major centers
for the recording of advertising jingles: New York, Chicago, Los Angeles, Nashville, and Toronto. Today, although many national jingles are recorded in those cities,
in every other city of substantial size in both the United
States and Canada there are many recording studios where
local and regional jingles are made daily.

According to an AFM survey, 73 percent of the companies that advertise the production of jingles were not
signators to the Federation's contract.[54] This does not
necessarily mean that there are large numbers of non-
union musicians; it means that great numbers of union
musicians (freelancers and classical establishment players
also) are accepting unreported and "cash" dates and that
jingle producers are also using synthesizers and pre-
recorded material originally intended for other use. Conditions are not improving. *Allegro* reports, "... The actual
amount of available recording work continues to dwindle.
At the same time, the proportion of non-union work ... is
growing dramatically...."[55]

A series of articles in *Allegro* during 1985 spelled out
some specific problems faced by the recording musician.
Not necessarily in order of importance, the major difficulties seem to be these:

> (1) The prevalence of non-union work by both non-
> union musicians and union musicians. The "dark"
> date defeats the AFM contract concepts of reuse,
> residual royalty, and pension payments. Eliminating
> these payments is an obvious goal of jingle pro-
> ducers.

(2) The replacement of acoustical instruments (even full orchestras) by the synthesizer. Jack Gale, the author of these informative articles, traces the development of this problem from the end of the 1960s when the multi-track and punch-in capability of advanced taping equipment became available to small "home" studios using young non-union players and singers. With the added techniques of echo, equalization, and sophisticated processing, varying degrees of acoustical sound distortion gradually became acceptable as "new" sounds. The 1970s brought lower priced, higher quality multi-track recording equipment and a corresponding increase in electronically processed wind and string instrument sounds which were more or less altered from their original state. The use of completely synthesized sounds in the 1980s was the logical next step. And it was inexpensive. No more worries about orchestration, copying parts, and balancing instruments and voices in an expensive studio. In fact, no studio was needed at all: the synthesizer was simply plugged into the tape recorder and one player could replace a full orchestra, including percussion and bass. No musician objects to the synthesizer as long as it is used for its own special sounds—after all, the synthesizer performer is probably a member of the Federation. The conflict arises when the synthesizer replaces other instrumentalists.

(3) The advanced ability of electronic equipment to record acoustical instruments enables less talented performers (presumably non-union) to make jingles and background tapes in home studios anywhere on the continent. The engineer can "bleep

out" wrong notes, and multi-track capacity allows the player any number of takes until he or she gets it right. It is this technology that enables producers (when time schedules allow) to record in Europe and elsewhere to take advantage of still lower wage scales.

(4) Many players are unfamiliar with the union contracts. Reuse agreements are complicated, and policing compliance begins with a knowledgeable performer.[56]

Still another concern is that caused by "over-dubbing." This technique enables three violinists to replace fifteen violinists, or one trumpet player to fulfill requirements for a complete section.

A purely musical problem faced by recording musicians is caused by the multi-track capability of the new equipment. The "laying on" of individual instruments on top of existing music doesn't allow the give and take of musically aware performers for intonation, balance, and rhythmic dependency. It can never be "a conversation among equals" as good ensemble playing always has been.

One of the ultimate goals of the freelancer is to become one of the very few musicians who get frequent work in the Hollywood studios. These players come from the symphony orchestras, recording studios in other cities, Broadway shows, traveling bands and combos, and even directly from colleges and conservatories to this Mecca of high pay for musicians.

As always in the freelance field, superior technical control of the instrument and musicianship are prerequisites. Then come the contacts with contractors and with other musicians who might make recommendations to contractors. Not only is it necessary to play the right notes at the right time, but versatility and knowledge of styles is of utmost importance. A ballad from the 1930s is not played the same as a tune from the "top 40" or a passage from a Beethoven symphony.

The musicians who "make it" understand that there is little or no rehearsal time (it's too expensive) and that they are expected to get it right the first time. If they can't, or if they are unreliable in any way, the contractor will call someone else next time; there are many more capable and qualified musicians then there are jobs in the studios. And even fewer freelancers "make it" now that some full length movies and television shows are scored for synthesizer only. Some early examples in the 1980s are the movies *Chariots of Fire* and *Out of Bounds*, and the television series, "Miami Vice."

Some very talented and fortunate musicians move within the system from the role of player to that of arranger or composer/conductor. David Rose in the 1940s moved from Chicago's NBC staff orchestra to network musical director (of Mutual Broadcasting) in Hollywood, to arranging and eventually composing. John Williams and Henry Mancini are other musicians who changed from performer to performer/composer/conductor and function in various combinations of these roles.

The studio player may not find the music he or she is required to play aesthetically satisfying, but there is great gratification in performing well and gaining the respect of one's peers. Besides, the freelancer can always play chamber music or join a jam session with friends for musical rewards not offered in the studio.

Another goal of freelancers in the New York area is the pit orchestra for the Broadway musical. The field is limited. Even with Local 802's pact with the League of New York Theatres and Producers which specifies the minimum number of players who must be hired in each theater, the number of jobs is less than 400, including off-Broadway and off-off-Broadway. Today there are only 30 long-established Broadway theatres (from the 70 in the 1920s) and, obviously, not all of them produce musicals.[57] In 1970, there were twenty new musicals; in the 1985–1986 season there were only ten[58]—not a very promising trend.

Again, the contractor is the keeper of the gate and all hiring is through that powerful position. Of course, it is not unknown for conductors, composers, and even directors and producers to mention names of favored players for the orchestra (with positive results), but for most musicians the way to break in is through the player who already has a job with a Broadway show.[59]

Under the current contract with the League of New York Theatres (which expires in September 1990)[60] each full-time member of the orchestra hires his or her own substitute, subject to the conductor's approval after the first subbing appearance. For newcomers to the Broadway scene, making themselves known to the performers who play their instrument in the various shows may be the only practical way to eventually become a full-timer too. This approach makes sense. The contractor knows a huge pool of well qualified, experienced players. He will certainly hire from this group because he knows the orchestra will be of high quality. The way to know the contractor is by appearing in the orchestra first as substitute.

The long running Broadway musical pays well—$720 weekly in the 1987–1988 season (rising to $760 and $798 in the remaining years of the contract) along with possible cost of living adjustments,[61] health insurance, pension contributions, and instrument loss and maintenance allowances. But the job can be boring. A bass player remarked that after two weeks he would know any show well enough to read the daily newspaper during performances.[62] Perhaps that's why substitution is a viable ploy—

full-time players need a break to play other gigs for variety, fun, or to maintain contacts.

If a Broadway company goes on tour, the entire orchestra may make the trip if there are short stops at many cities because it's less expensive than the cost of rehearsals in each city for new players and in some areas the specialized performers may not be available. If the show tour includes long engagements in a few cities, the conductor takes only a skeleton musical crew. It may be only the concertmaster, lead trumpet, and a percussionist (or possibly a woodwind doubler) who make the trip. At each tour stop, local musicians are hired through local contractors. After a brief (never long enough) rehearsal, the show goes on. In some cities there are complaints about the quality of local musicians; in other cities the players are as good or better then the New York originals.

When a musical tours without its New York orchestra, the producer may ask for new orchestrations so that today it is not unusual to see a Broadway show on tour with two synthesizers and perhaps six other musicians in the pit instead of the 26 musicians who played for New York audiences.

What causes still more anguish for the Federation and its live musicians are the shows on the "dinner theater circuit" that are presented using a complete tape recording of the New York performance instead of live musicians. No wonder Local 802 contracts in New York so zealously guard the minimum number of players in each Broadway theater. The contract in force now even includes a schedule of premiums to be paid for the use of synthesizers and a freeze on current minimum employment guarantees until 1993.[63]

The "club date" field is almost a misnomer. The AFM lists these jobs under "single engagements." In various areas the field is known as casuals, one-nighters, or just jobbing. Furthermore, these gigs are rarely played in clubs: they are worked in private homes, fraternal buildings, catering halls, hotels, country clubs, synagogues, churches, ballrooms, restaurants, and stores.[64] The music is for weddings, debutante balls, bar mitzvahs, country club dances, fashion shows, office parties, organizational affairs, birthday and anniversary parties, and so forth. Truly, music for all occasions.

The purchaser of such music will typically call a booking agency, bandleader, or musician to arrange for the type of music, the number and kind of instrumentalists, time, place, date, and cost of the entertainment. The agent or leader calls together others and, if the players are all competent club date musicians, they need never have met to produce a successful performance. The leader calls out the name of the tune, the key, and sets the tempo. From then on musicianship takes over.

"Versatility, the ability to read music and a good repertoire all rate high on every leader's list of requirements"[65] for a good club date musician, especially since the job could call for up to twenty players. The musician in demand knows as many as two hundred standard, current, and show songs (and can play them in various keys), knows the few songs (about thirty) that set the Dixieland repertory and the equally limited tunes for ethnic affairs, can "double" various woodwind or brass instruments, and can play in various styles—jazz, top 40s, R and B (rhythm and blues), rock, and more.

Besides the booking agencies, the entrée to the club date field includes the society band offices that specialize in this area of performance. The bands of Meyer Davis, Lester Lanin, and Peter Duchin provide the music "for weddings and debuts of … the Astors, du Ponts, Rockefellers, Fords, Dukes, Drexels and Firestones."[66] These incorporated society band offices are big business, with dozens of bands and thousands of musicians trained to play in "their" style. These bands play thousands of tunes in "all sorts of styles"[67] and have been part of the business since the 1920s.[68] The auditions for the important "name" band offices are demanding. A woodwind player is expected to play saxophone (tenor and/or alto), clarinet, and flute (or possibly oboe or bassoon). The audition consists of playing tunes in various styles, transposing alto saxophone parts on clarinet, and a short course in "proper deportment."[69]

Of course there are many band offices of lesser quality; booking agents (and purchasers of music) cannot expect all musicians to be all things to all people. Specialization is surely a factor when the huge range of various types of engagements and the equally large range of musical styles are considered; there are limits to versatility.

In contrast to the "classical establishment," there is a great deal of non-union performance in the club date field, and not only involving non-union players. A union musician in a large east coast city regularly plays "cash dates" whenever possible and joins many others moonlighting on second jobs in the underground economy of unreported income.[70] Other musicians are hired by band offices and booking agencies as individual contractors, sometimes over the protests of the player. This is steadily becoming a more prevalent practice because it saves the hiring agent or office from paying health and pension fringes and social security tax, and the player avoids paying work dues. The contracts frequently do not meet AFM minimum scale. Non-union players abound and are particularly attracted to cash dates that allow unreported income. After all, most single engagement players must have a regular job that provides a living wage. This is also the employment field for the DJs (disc jockeys), who find no difficulty in providing complete versatility. Their musical talent is limited to providing the best recordings.

Still another type of single engagement is the appearance of big name performers who play casino hotels, perform on the college circuit, and appear with symphonies and in the few clubs which feature music for listening. A relatively recent phenomenon is the "top-of-the-market" tours by current rock stars who perform in giant coliseums and open air theaters for audiences of many thousands and receive the highest fees in the business.

Steady engagements can be for several days to a week, two weeks, four weeks, or more. If the job is for weekends, for example, it is probably on an ongoing basis. Indeed the term "steady" for this kind of employment emphasizes the intermittent job life so typical for most musicians. Motels, lounges, restaurants, nightclubs, taverns, and bars are usually the locale for steady engagements; these businesses book soloists, duos, trios, and quartets, up to big bands. The purposes of the musical entertainment range from unobtrusive background music for dancing to showcases for stars of the musical profession to dazzle an audience that has come primarily to listen.

The musical menu available in the hotels, clubs, bars, and restaurants of our largest cities on any given weekend is indicative of both the catholic taste of the public and the amazing versatility of musicians. There is music from classic harp, piano, and strings to dixieland, jazz, bluegrass, country-western, blues, new wave, rock/jazz fusion, soul, punk, heavy metal, techno-pop, and reggae.[71] All this in addition to the local symphony and/or opera performance. With minor exceptions, there is music for everyone.

Non-union as well as union players are employed in the steady engagement field, but almost without exception the "big names" are Federation members. And DJs also compete in the field, working at discos of various economic levels in competition with live music.

Ways of Musical Life

One category of traveling musi[...] engagement field is rapidly disappear[...] scene. Hotel and motel chains incr[...] expensive to hire a DJ locally for the[...] trio for weekend dancing than to pay[...] housing and perhaps discounted foo[...] who tour the chain.

Of all the varied types within the musical profession, it is the young rock bands that are least likely to be AFM members. Only when the band succeeds or seems on the verge of creating potentially big selling recordings is there a tendency to join the union.

The lure of music and the examples of rock, heavy metal, punk, new wave, and techno-pop bands that have made popular records or have appeared in huge concert halls are strong incentives for new bands. Typically, the young players have obtained only basic instruction on their instruments and have spent hundreds of hours listening to and imitating their various musical models until their own style emerges.

The next step after joining together to form the band is on-the-job training in almost any room that will have them. Because money seems to be only a minor consideration at first, it is not uncommon for unscrupulous club managers to actually make bands pay for lighting and publicity efforts while they play for a percentage of the admission charge—and that without any audit by the band. Then come the one-nighters and split weeks on the road. Not with the four or five customized buses and crews of "roadies" used by established stars, but in a small rental truck for equipment and a crowded car or two.

Without the protection of standardized contracts (provided by the AFM and some legitimate booking agents), the band is at the mercy of people who can and do exploit them. Without specific obligations regarding housing,

, length of performance, equipment to be supplied, onies to be paid (and when), the band members are more frequently victimized than not.

From the band's view, there is one advantage to this way of life. Payment is usually made in cash and quickly becomes part of the underground economy as unreported income. On the road, especially in smaller towns and cities, the band's contact with the Federation is minimal. One player said, "We always played over scale—the union meant nothing to us."[72] Another rock musician was unaware of the AFM's coverage of all musical engagements. He said, "I thought the union was [only] for the orchestras and the big cities."[73] The rock band members are almost always young: understandably, it's a young person's game.

Even James Deering, who complains in his book, *Making Money Making Music*, "... The union is catering to older musicians, not today's trend-setting performers," also says, "... A body that will guarantee musicians a minimum wage is desperately needed ... If the older wiser union musicians in locals across the country can become more responsive to the needs of today's young musicians, the union could reverse the current trends of 'not joining until I absolutely have to.'"[74] Indications are that the Federation is trying desperately to become more responsive.

At home or on the road, one of the immediate goals of these bands is to make a hit record. In these days of highly developed and relatively inexpensive recording equipment, it is possible to make a recording in almost any city or town on the continent. But here too, without a protective manager, booking agent, or AFM contract, the band would likely make a "demo" or full recording with the proviso that payment will be made when the recording "took off," a promise more frequently broken than kept. Besides, it takes more than recording techniques to make a hit record. Videos, tours, radio and TV exposure, and a knowledgeable sales campaign are all part of the package for success.

It is only the entertainment professional—including actors, dancers, football, basketball, and baseball players, and musicians—who clearly demonstrates the tremendous distance (financial and otherwise) between the stars and the ordinary practitioners of their business. In the music profession it is difficult to comprehend the great gulf that exists between Leonard Bernstein, Isaac Stern, the members of the Juilliard Quartet, a principal player in the Chicago Symphony, a successful Hollywood studio musician, Willie Nelson, Randy Travis, Chick Corea, Sarah Vaughn, The Talking Heads, B.B. King, Wynton Marsalis, and Bruce Springsteen and a section violinist in a metropolitan orchestra, a clarinetist in a park band, and a drummer who plays the v.f.w. dance every other Saturday night. And yet, for over ninety years the AFM has represented a huge percentage of these highly diversified talents and personages, an achievement equalled by no other labor organization.

THE ULTIMATE WEAPON—STRIKE

Unlike other workers, Federation musicians cannot resort to half-way measures such as the slow down, the "job action," and the strict observation of and adherence to rules.[75] Faced with an impasse in negotiations, unless the AFM can mount a campaign to pressure or embarrass management's position, a strike is not only the weapon of last resort—it is the only weapon.

In these days of declining union membership in a great many industries, "... it is down to about 19 percent of the total work force, from nearly 25 percent in 1979,"[76] concessionary bargaining has become commonplace and the AFM negotiating teams are hard pressed.

Perhaps the most widely publicized strikes by musicians in the twentieth century involved the recording industry. Under the Petrillo administration in 1942 and again in 1948 (for a total of 38 months) the AFM refused to make recordings. The strikes were successful, resulting in the establishment of the Music Performance Trust Fund.

Much earlier, the AFM had been involved in another important strike. In 1919, the Federation (along with the International Alliance of Theatrical and Stage Employees, IATSE) supported Actors' Equity in their dispute with the Producing Managers' Association. The main issue was the establishment of Actors' Equity as the actors' bargaining agent. After a strike that lasted thirty days and affected over fifty shows in eight cities, the managers signed a five-year contract which firmly established Actors' Equity as the "actors' voice."[77]

More recently, in the 1970s, "there have been strikes by musicians of 16 major American orchestras, many of them the first in the long histories of the organization."[78] The more militant attitude of the orchestra players began in the early 1960s and was responsible for the formation of ICSOM. With the Ford Foundation grants in mid-decade that made possible year-long contracts, the players intensified the struggle for honorable salaries and working conditions they believed were essential to continue high artistic standards.

In retrospect, it must have been somewhat surprising to orchestra players (and AFM local officials too) that successful strikes could be launched against nonprofit organizations that were operating with a deficit budget. The strikers were successful, for the most part, in achieving their goals, because all the orchestras were completely unionized and management was able to enhance their own efforts in gaining more financial support through better-run fund drives and more successful grant applications.

Not all strikes are won by the Federation. In August 1980, "the 5,000 musicians who score movies and filmed television programs joined the more than 60,000 actors who have effectively shut down production...."[79] The musicians wanted reuse payments for reruns of television films and programs, payments that already had been won by actors, directors, and writers in the 1960s. The actors in the 1980 action were striking for higher residuals.

After nearly six months, musicians returned to work without having won their "repay for replay" proposal.[80] Although the Federation gained somewhat higher wages and a concession to make a separate agreement on home video, the key demand was lost. In reporting the settlement, *The New York Times* said, "... [The] musicians suffered a strategic blow when members of the Screen Actors Guild and the American Federation of Television and Radio Artists ... crossed musician picket lines..."[81] after their own dispute was settled. The article also stated that during the strike, producers used music previously recorded and had new music recorded abroad. For the AFM, it was clear that closer cooperation with other unions, both here and abroad, was essential to insure the success of such a strike.

In the same year, 1980, a lockout by the Metropolitan Opera Company concerned the 17 unions that make possible the performances in this hemisphere's most famous opera house. Since the contract with the orchestra traditionally forms the pattern upon which all other agreements are signed,[82] the orchestral issues attracted national and international attention.

The major issue for the orchestra was a request for a four-performance week rather than the five performances required in their current contract. This "... would make the opera orchestra [schedule] comparable with major symphony orchestras...."[83] The Metropolitan Opera management claimed they could not meet the additional expense of hiring the extra musicians required for a full schedule of seven weekly performances.

On September 29, 1980, the Met formally announced the cancellation of the 1980–1981 season although all musical activities had been halted four weeks earlier. Negotiations continued periodically between the orchestra and management with federal mediators until an accord was reached on October 25, 1980, and made the front page of *The New York Times*. A four-performance week was agreed upon, with the "fifth performance" becoming a rehearsal.[84] In essence, the orchestra "... won on principle and the Met won on money."[85] But in retrospect, the orchestra won a good deal more. All agreements since 1980 between the orchestra and the Met have been settled early, with the four-performance week firmly established, reasonably good continuing wage increases, and a pension plan which serves as a model for the major symphony orchestras.[86]

The Met management completed agreements with all other unions and opened its season on December 10, 1980. In a disagreement such as this, the public lost the pleasure of more than eighty performances, and the orchestra musicians surely lost financially for their weeks of unem ployment. "... But the company lost something too," wrote Donal Henahan at the time, "a measure of public confidence in its administrative acumen. The 1980 labor crisis must go down as a mark against the management led by Mr. Bliss who reversed himself again and again during the four months of negotiations and ended up giving the orchestra the four-performance week that it had asked at the start."[87]

Another work stoppage in Las Vegas aroused public attention in 1984. On April 2, 1984, some 30,000 bartenders, waiters, stagehands, and musicians struck forty hotels and casinos. The unions were seeking a wage and benefit increase of about 8 percent. Management wanted to freeze wages for two years and eliminate the guaranteed 40-hour work week.[88]

Unlike previous strikes, hotels and casinos forced the unions to bargain with them individually (rather than through an association) and chose to remain open, hiring non-union employees to serve in restaurants, mix drinks, and change linen. Generally, the strike closed many showrooms and restaurants, but gambling continued and showgirls crossed picket lines to work as cocktail waitresses and hotel clerks.[89] By April 6, 1984 there had been 142 arrests for violence on the picket lines, followed by calls for an AFL-CIO boycott of the national hotel chains involved in the dispute.[90]

What seemed to be the first major breakthrough occurred on April 27, 1984, when the two Hilton hotels reached tentative agreement with two of the unions on wages and fringe benefits, but by this time the dispute had caused almost 500 arrests and the strike had lasted 26 days.[91] By April 30, 1984, *The New York Times* reported that a Las Vegas official said the strike was hurting the hotels and that the Hilton hotels were now only negotiating with musicians and stagehands since other unions had been satisfied.[92] The Hilton hotels' agreement with all unions on May 4, 1984, appeared to be a major break in the conflict. It wasn't. But on May 21, 1984, eleven other hotels (including one casino) reached agreement with all unions. This was the turning point.[93] Strikers voted to return to thirteen more hotels on May 25, 1984, [94] and on June 6, 1984, all unions except the stagehands had reached agreements. The members of the culinary and bartenders unions had reached accord two weeks earlier but remained off the job pending settlements with musicians and stagehands.[95]

For practical purposes the strike ended on June 15, 1984, when the stagehands agreed to contracts with the remaining major hotels and casinos. The strike lasted 75 days, cost Las Vegas over $100 million, caused the arrest of over 850 people, and ended with a compromise of AFM goals.[96] *The New York Times* reported that both the stagehands and the musicians were being pressured by the other two unions to settle quickly.[97] That pressure was evident in the musicians' agreement, which "freeze wages for five years, increases health and welfare benefits, maintains house orchestras and relief bands and maintains a 14-week displacement clause. The clause allows traveling bands [i.e. lounge groups]… to replace regular hotel orchestras for a maximum of 14 weeks every year."[98]

To say that the Las Vegas local won or lost this strike depends upon how one views the half empty (or half full) glass. It was certainly a stressful period. In September 1984, the IEB was still disposing of cases brought to it which accused AFM members of crossing picket lines during the strike.[99]

An opinion of negotiations in a climate of concessionary bargaining is provided by Barry Kornfeld in describing talks with record company management in 1983. Mr. Kornfeld, supervisor of the national contracts department of Local 802 (New York), writing in *Allegro*, tells of the agony of indecision when faced with final demands by managements that may well have the upper hand in terms of overseas recording and/or non-union musicians at home. He concludes that a strike is a big gamble and a severe hardship with no guarantee that the Federation would win. The negotiating team finally concurred that a settlement (that is, a compromise) now was worth more than the attendant risks of a strike.[100]

Labor relations in the symphony orchestra scene for

the 1986–1987 concert year reflect a mixed bag of results. There have been strikes and lockouts in Columbus, Honolulu, Tulsa, and San Diego, along with (for the first time) a bankruptcy in Oakland. On the other hand, there have been contract improvements in Boston, Chicago, Cincinnati, Minnesota, Cleveland, Toronto, and elsewhere.[101] These are not altogether discouraging results, but certainly they are not the nearly unanimous improvements major orchestras enjoyed a decade ago. Perhaps, in certain localities, orchestra management is reaching the upper limits of fundraising in their communities.

The Fuentealba administration has been accused of being "… afraid to strike."[102] But given the national anti-union climate, the patterns of concessionary settlements in other industries, and the problems faced by the Federation, to strike or not is a difficult decision.

HOW DO WOMEN AND
THE OLDER MUSICIAN FARE?

From its very beginnings as a part of the AFL, the Federation has been open to women members. But women were not always welcome in some of the locals before they became part of the AFM. Many of the unions that began around the nucleus of an all-male town marching band were slow to accept women musicians; and in 1892, the Toronto Orchestral Association passed a motion "… denying membership to 'members of the female sex.'"[103] The same Association "… within relatively recent memory [permitted women to pay] lower yearly dues because they were not covered by … Welfare and Death Benefit."[104]

In a twenty-five-page article on "Civil Rights in the American Federation of Musicians" published in 1954 in the *International Musician*, only one paragraph is devoted to women members. It indicates that women are welcome in all locals and that "... several Locals have elected women year after year to serve as Secretary-Treasurer-Business Agent."[105]

There seems no doubt that women can join the AFM freely, but their advancement within the hierarchy of union governance does not seem to be as unhindered as for men. Obviously, this is a statement that also could be made about the general electorate.

In 1951, there were only 29 women delegates (out of a total of over one thousand delegates) to the AFM Convention.[106] By 1985, the official listing of the AFM locals indicated that over 15 percent of the 549 locals had either a woman president (less than 2 percent) or a woman secretary or treasurer. No woman has ever been elected to an International office. But Gloria J. McCullough (then president of Local 364-409, Portland-Lewiston, Maine) was a candidate for the IEB at the 1983 Convention, and Serena Kay Williams (then secretary of Local 47, Los Angeles) was a candidate for International Secretary-Treasurer at the 1987 Convention. Slow progress—but still improvement.

The music professions have yielded reluctantly to equality of the sexes. Although there have been occasional female conductors since at least the eighteenth century in Vienna,[107] it was not until the 1850s that Josephine Weinlich brought her Vienna Ladies Symphony to perform in the United States.[108] Later, in 1888, an orchestra of American women (The Women's Fadette Orchestra of Boston) toured the continent under the baton of Caroline B. Nichols.[109] By 1904, *Billboard* was carrying advertisements for the Nellie B. Chandler Ladies "White" Orchestra (July 2, 1904) and the James Ladies Band (February 6, 1904).

The first woman to conduct the New York Philharmonic was Antonia Brica at a summer concert in 1938. She was followed by Nadia Boulanger who conducted a Boston

Symphony Concert in 1938 and a New York Philharmonic concert in 1939.[110] Then there were the conductors of the all-women orchestras: Ethel Leginsky, who organized the Women's Symphony Orchestra of Boston; Antonia Brico, who founded the New York Women's Symphony Orchestra in 1935; Ruth Haroldson, who began conducting the California Women's Symphony Orchestra in 1945; Billy O'Day, who began the Miami Symphony Society Strings in 1947; and Ethel Stark, who began conducting the Montreal Women's Symphony in 1939.[111]

In more recent years there are accomplished, talented women conductors who have "paid their dues" in years of training and experience: Joyce Brown, the first black woman to conduct a Broadway show (Purlie) in 1970,[112] Judith Somogi, the first woman to conduct a New York City Opera debut (on March 17, 1974)[113], Frances Steiner (Glendale Symphony)[114], Beatrice Brown (Scranton, Pennsylvania Symphony),[115] Lisa Redfield,[116] Margaret Hillis, Catherine Comet, Eileen LaGrange, Eve Queler, and others. But we still have no major orchestra whose music director is a woman.

There have been obstacles faced only by female soloists. It is not uncommon for concert series committees to object to a woman pianist on the basis that "we already have a woman on the series." The same committee would probably not object to an all-male series.[117] Other examples of sexual prejudice are the oft heard comments, "If you were a man, I'd hire you immediately" or "You played great—sounded just like a man."

More than a decade ago, Susan Starr, an important piano soloist, listed the popular myths that abound about the so-called limitations of women performers, myths that apply both to soloists and orchestral players:

> Woman don't have as much strength or power as men.
> Women have smaller techniques than men.

Women pianists "bang" when they try to play power-
fully, rather than produce a huge but round tone.
Women are not as ambitious for a performing career.
Women are more temperamental and more likely to
demand special attention or treatment.
Women are more likely to get married and quit, to get
sick and cancel, or get pregnant and cancel.
Women may not play their best during their menstrual
periods, making their performances erratic or un-
predictable.
Women lack the physical stamina to travel, live out of a
suitcase, and perform everyday; women need more
time between concerts.[118]

Unfortunately, the myths Starr enumerated in 1974
are still heard today, but perhaps somewhat more muted.
The proof of their fallacy is the many more women in the
upper ranks of the musical professions. The equality of the
sexes is closer to reality today both in our society and in the
music business.

It has not been easy for women to gain equality of
opportunity in our major symphonies, either. Thanks to
Norman Schweikert of the Chicago Symphony, who has
been researching the personnel of major orchestras for
some years, we know that there have been women principal
players in our major orchestras since the 1920s. Unfortunately, these principals have been for the most part
harpists, a "female instrument." Helen Enser (horn, New
Orleans, late 1930s) and Helen Kotas (horn, Chicago,
1941–4)[119] are the earliest principals on a so called "mas-
culine" instrument. Enser and Kotas were shortly followed
by Dorothy Ziegler, principal trombone in the St. Louis
Symphony beginning in 1945, who had previously played
in the National Symphony. In 1952, Doriot Anthony
Dwyer became principal flute of the Boston Symphony.

To gain positions in the highly competitive world of

major orchestras, women faced both the competition from their male peers and the additional prejudice of some conductors who believed that too many women in the orchestra made it "like a kitchen." Or the evaluative comment that "the more women [in an orchestra], the poorer the sound."

Sir Thomas Beecham has been quoted as saying, "If the ladies are ill-favored, the men do not want to play next to them, and if they are well favored, they can't,"[120] a comment refuted by Hans Kindler (then conductor of the National Symphony)[121] and others. On the other hand, Efrem Kurtz, "with a view to increasing the self-confidence of women members of orchestras," commissioned the French designer Gisele de Biezville to create a new costume for the women in the Houston Symphony.[122] Perhaps the most outspoken conductor on this topic has been Zubin Mehta, who has said of women in orchestras, "They become men. Men treat them as equals: they even change their pants in front of them. I think it's terrible."[123] And, "I just don't think women should be in an orchestra."[124] It appears that Mehta has changed his mind because, as conductor of the New York Philharmonic, he now has approximately twenty women players, including principal flute, piccolo, and bassoon.

The number of women in our major symphony orchestras has grown gradually over the years. Of course, there was a boom in female players during World War II, but many stayed on when normal employment patterns resumed. "In 1948, there were 109 women in the major orchestras of Baltimore, Boston, Chicago, Cincinnati, Cleveland, Detroit, Indianapolis, Los Angeles, Minneapolis, New York, Philadelphia, Pittsburgh, Rochester, St. Louis and San Francisco. In the same orchestras there were 100 women in 1953."[125] Regional and metropolitan orchestras usually have more female players, reflecting in part the necessity for orchestral training before joining the major orchestras.

Phyliss Lehmann, writing in *Symphony Magazine* (December 1982), reported that in the 1980–1981 concert year, 40 percent of the regular personnel of ASOL orchestras were women, including the concertmaster in Honolulu and the principal trumpet in St. Louis. Although the major orchestras in this survey were only about 26 percent female, the less prestigious orchestras had nearly 50 percent women players.

Women are regularly winning their share of auditions. A study of "Women in Major Symphonies: Why a Minority?" by Dr. Gilda M. Greenburg, reports that in the 1980–81 season, "Although there were over 1,100 musicians applying for jobs, only 47 were successful in obtaining full-time positions. Twenty of the 47 instrumental positions were filled by women."[126]

More recent research has shown that this favorable trend is continuing. The American Symphony Orchestra League reports that major symphony orchestras contained 28 percent female players in the 1982–1983 concert year. The figure for the 1972–1973 concert year was 22 percent. In metropolitan orchestras the corresponding figures were 50 percent and 40 percent.[127]

In 1984, Gideon Toeplitz, executive director of the Houston Symphony Orchestra, reported, "...The number of women musicians in the top 15 U.S. orchestras has doubled in the past three decades.... In the 1962–63 season, today's top 15 orchestras averaged 11 women musicians. The total climbed to an average of 22 in the 1982–83 season."[128]

Not only are women musicians entering our orchestras on a more equal basis these days (there has even been an increase from one to three female head librarians for our 34 major orchestras over the past decade[129]), but union-management contracts now routinely make allowances for pregnancy leave.[130] In Carnegie Hall on March 27, 1981, the Detroit Symphony played a concert with seven pregnant women on stage. "Just ten years ago the same management required several musicians to take leave without pay in their seventh month of pregnancy."[131] Progress is being made.

There have been women instrumentalists in jazz almost from the beginnings of that art form. Most of the players we know about were pianists (Lil Hardin Armstrong, Edna Mitchell, Jeanette Salvant Kimball, and others), and all of them were black. Dolly Jones Armenra and Valaida Snow were black women who somehow escaped the sexist ban on wind performance and were both fine trumpet players of the 1920s and 1930s.[132]

If Benny Goodman paved the way for black and white players to make music in the same big band, then Woody Herman is the leader who brought about integration of the sexes in the big band. Margie Hyams played vibes for Herman in the 1940s along with trumpeter Billie Rogers.[133] A few other isolated examples followed with other bands.

But the growth of all-women bands in the 1930s and 1940s was really an affirmation of sexual prejudice because there were no musical opportunities. Advertisements in the *International Musician* such as, "Wanted: Girl musicians for mid-West territory band, steady work, good salary"[134] or "Wanted: Girl musician for nationally known dance and show band"[135] were common. There were even notices from the Department of Defense for women musicians for WAF bands.[136]

Phil Spitalny's Orchestra, perhaps the most famous of the all-girl orchestras, made its debut at the Capitol Theater in New York in May 1934. Two years later the orchestra began its long-running radio show, the Hour of

Charm, and made many tours during about twenty years of popularity.[137]

Many other all-girl bands followed this pattern: Freddie Shaffer's All-Girl Band, the Hormel Girls' Caravan, and Eleanor Krannick's The Co-Eds Orchestra are some examples. The Sweethearts of Rhythm was an all-female, racially integrated big band of the swing era that held its own musically with the far more popular male segregated bands of the day.

It was not until the 1970s that sexual integration became more than tokenism in the freelance field. The Broadway hit Purlie in 1970 had a pit orchestra of twenty-six including two women. This was considered a normal male-female ratio for the time by conductor Joyce Brown.[138] The armed services bands auditioned and accepted female musicians: the West Point Band hired its first woman in 1975. Hollywood studio orchestras regularly employed more women, especially in the string sections (a pattern common to the symphony orchestras).

The fight for complete integration is continuing. A Jazz Times panel meeting in New York in September 1984 concluded, " ... Women in jazz [and other freelance fields] continue to show only slow and difficult progress...."[139] The panel's suggestions for women who want to "make it" included, becoming record producers and contractors for club dates and developing an "old girl" network.

Marylou Perhacs of the Women's Caucus of Local 802, writing in the International Musician,[140] itemizes some changes she thinks would improve the marketplace for women. She speaks about the sometimes condescending, intimidating, and insulting attitudes displayed by male peers and the practice of locals and the International in using phrases such as "Dear Brother," "Fraternally," and "sidemen" (instead of side musicians). She objects (and rightly so) to the practice of having women submit 8x10 glossies with résumés for playing jobs, having to answer contractors' questions about age, figure, and marital status when booking a club date, and the instances of explicit sexual suggestions to "solidify" a contract. At least one of these issues has been rectified. The AFM 1987 Convention voted to eliminate use of specific sexist language in all Federation publications.

An evaluation of how women musicians fare in the late 1980s would have to conclude that far more progress has been made within the classical establishment and recording fields than in many other job markets for freelancers. It may not be "a man's world" completely, but much affirmative action is needed to allow equal access for women.

When is a musician too old to perform well? A few years ago symphony orchestra management would answer quickly: sixty-five years of age. And some managers would have added, "or younger." There are (or were) good reasons why management preferred the dismissal of older players. Replacements were usually less costly, and the young players might well be more tractable it they owed their positions to the current conductor. It was this sort of fatuous thinking that caused the breakup of one of the finest woodwind sections in the symphonic world. When oboist Marcel Tabuteau and flutist William Kincaid were retired at the mandatory age of 65 from the Philadelphia Orchestra, they were in the prime of their performance lives. Ironically, Eugene Ormandy, then the conductor of the Philadelphia Orchestra, continued his profession past the age of 80 and, of course, would have argued that he had lost none of his talents.

The Philadelphia Orchestra did not extend its mandatory retirement age until 1975, and then only to 67. However, the Age Discrimination in Employment Act as amended in 1978 and 1986 eliminated mandatory retirement completely in the orchestra world.

As early as 1972, ICSOM passed a resolution urging

strict compliance with AFM bylaws that prohibit mandatory retirement based upon age and not ability to perform.[141] But as all orchestra players know, there are more subtle methods used by conductors to force retirement of older players. More and more frequent conferences with the conductor after rehearsals when missed notes or cues are discussed in great detail are usually very effective, and no written law is broken (only its spirit).

In 1978, Lloyd Haldeman, manager of the Dallas Symphony Orchestra, viewed retirement at 70 with some disapproval. He suggested that a musician must play in time and in tune and older performers might not be able to do so.[142] This statement was probably greeted with disbelief by some of our premier soloists who demanded (and received) huge fees for appearances with the Dallas Orchestra when they were far beyond the early retirement age Haldeman defended.

If more generous pensions or rotation systems were available to symphony players, some might prefer to retire earlier; those that remain on duty might be better able to withstand the mental and physical stress of long orchestral years.

For anyone who has had the privilege of listening to the great Dixieland bands that perform regularly in New Orleans' Preservation Hall, the specter of a performer who is unmusical simply because he or she is "older" is unbelievable. It would seem readily apparent that aging diminishes performing skills only in individual cases and that no true generalizations can or should be made. If unfortunate stereotypes of old age were replaced by the reality of many older players making music at the prime of their performance skills, freelance musicians in the recording studios, Broadway, the club date, and steady engagement fields would have longer productive professional lives.

With long-serving officials such as International Presidents Weber, Petrillo, Kenin, and Emerson (who began his presidency in his seventy-fifth year), it is obvious that age discrimination within the Federation is (and has been) of no consequence.

SUPPLY AND DEMAND

It seems the American Federation of Musicians and the profession itself has always had to contend with an oversupply of musicians. A notice in the *American Musician* in 1898 signed, "By order, Board of Directors, Local #6, San Francisco," said, "... There are now too many musicians in San Francisco, more than enough to fill all the 'jobs.' What we need is work, not musicians. Stay away from San Francisco. You'll find it cheaper in the end."[143]

Petrillo warned repeatedly of the lack of jobs in the profession, saying in 1951, "... A musical career offers no security."[144] He also urged parents to stop music lessons for their children "until the Government guarantees that musicians could earn a living."[145] Petrillo viewed with great suspicion and apprehension the entire field of music education and engaged in a longstanding feud with music educators as president of Local 10 in Chicago and later as International President. He thought (mistakenly) that music education at either the secondary or university level merely turned out more and more professional performers. But he disregarded, or was ignorant of, the goal most music educators consider primary, that of developing an appreciation and understanding of music.

Herman Kenin saw the problem in a different light. He said, "...The union's concern—and the public's—must be for 'sand lot' players from the colleges, the dance bands, the night clubs and the bandstands who must fill the symphonic chairs of tomorrow."[146] This analysis was probably correct in 1964, before the Ford Foundation grants made symphonic performance financially respectable. But most Federation leaders currently believe that Kenin's "tomorrow" has come and gone.

The symphonic field today offers some telling examples. Gilda Greenberg's finding reported above is worth a second consideration. She found that in the 1980–1981 season over 1,100 musicians applied for 47 full-time positions in our major orchestras. The supply-demand ratio is increasing. Bernard Holland, writing in *The New York Times*, describes the situation during the 1984–1985 season. His examples include 240 candidates for a second violin position and 159 for a viola position in the Chicago Symphony, and 108 candidates for the tuba position in the Pittsburgh Symphony.[147] Those who are members of major orchestra auditioning committees know that it is unusual these days to have fewer than one hundred qualified musicians applying for each position.[148]

The various freelance fields are at least as crowded. In 1983, the Labor Institute for Human Enrichment (in conjunction with the Department of Professional Employees, (AFL-CIO) released a report developed by a team of independent economists. It provided an analysis of work habits and employment realities in the performing arts.

Of interest here are the findings that "... musicians were ... likely to have had seven or more employers in 1980" and that "... two out of three ... musicians worked part-time at jobs outside their profession."[149] The report concluded that these figures were probably optimistic, since they dealt only with union members. For non-union performers, all the problems were compounded.

Nor is this a recent phenomenon. A study developed in 1956 by the Research Company of America (sponsored by the AFM) concluded, "What has been happening in the last twenty-five years is that the number of musicians has been increasing while the number of jobs has been decreasing."[150] All indications point to the truth of that statement today. The continued and expanded use of recorded music along with the heightened fidelity of the compact discs, the increasing use of the synthesizer to displace live musicians in recording and TV/movie soundtracks, and the employment of amplification and "music-machines" (i.e., drum and bass computerized equipment) in order to use fewer performers are all factors in today's declining job market. To repeat the San Francisco local's appeal from 1898: there are too many musicians and not enough work.

What is the response to this overcrowded profession from the conservatories and schools of music across the continent? "... A survey by the National Association of Schools of Music of its 500 member colleges and conservatories showed that in the fall of 1983 there were 23,873 students enrolled in Bachelor of Music programs ... [and] 9,997 Master of Music candidates in performance categories."[151] The survey continued by demonstrating that a great many students did not complete their degree program.

One of the important points this survey makes is the huge amount of energy and time that is expended attracting incoming music majors from the high schools around the country without the candid career guidance these students deserve. Music administrators and music faculty recruiters tour the country and scour their immediate geographic area for students to fill the required chairs in their orchestras, bands and choruses and the classrooms in music theory and history. String players and tenors are at a premium, and the proficient double reed performer is not far behind. Scholarships and grants-in-aid are the bribe.

Talent is cheap. Those with even a small amount of talent are exploited by the greed and insensitivity of others. As one recruiter bluntly stated, "... If you want a circus, then you've got to have animals."[152]

The exploitation of these music students is prevalent in all parts of the country. It is the rare university administrator (or university music administrator) who is willing to overcome ego considerations and seek realistic answers to questions such as: What music programs are consistent with the goals and resources of the institution? What are the needs of the music profession and the applicants for the music programs? Does the institution have the faculty, student body, and location to offer quality performance programs? How many average (or even better than average) music performers does the country really need?

At the very least, potential music performance majors preparing to enter a university or conservatory should be told the unvarnished truth about the music performance business. Then, if students are still convinced that performance is the career they want, the school should do all it can to help enable successful careers. This may include advising the student to choose another institution where the new player will have outstanding professional instruction on the instrument, in a city with strong components of professional music easily heard, and surrounded by other talented students who will offer a taste of the competition yet to come. With very few exceptions, music departments and schools of music that are limited in any of these resources should recognize the futility (and untruthfulness) of offering performance degrees. They should put their resources to work on an essential goal: the musical education of the general college student and/or the development of music education majors who are taught that they need not create more professional performers as they build an understanding of music.

One argument often heard is that music performance majors in college and universities do have career choices: they can become music education majors or theorists or musicologists. But these are only good career choices if the potential performer is interested in music theory, music history, or a public school teaching position. If the young player is not interested, it is a bad choice which may produce nothing but career frustration. College teaching as an alternative to unavailable performing opportunities is an equally disheartening endeavor. In 1987, James S. Newton wrote in *The New York Times*, "... Colleges and other sources all report that ... there is a glut of teachers of conventional musical instruments...."[153]

Another argument presented to defend the recruitment of young performers is that a music major receives a solid college education and is equipped after four years to make his or her way in the world outside the music profession. After all, no one expects all French majors to make a living speaking French or all philosophy majors to get rich philosophizing.

The fallacy here is that in most music programs, because the curriculum is filled with courses in music, the student rarely has the opportunity even to become acquainted with the core of courses usually associated with a liberal arts education. In other words, unless the music performance graduate continues in music, he or she is for all practical purposes not college educated.

A few enlightened universities and conservatories have faced the reality of the music business. The Hartt School of Music (in 1982) began encouraging students to take enough computer courses to enable them to enter most competitive training programs offered by large companies.[154] In 1985, New York University held its first job seminar for music majors. The experts represented a variety of music-oriented fields: video producers, music directors, soundtrack experts, music magazine publishers, record company officials, entertainment lawyers, booking agents, recording engineers, sales promotion experts, and songwriters.[155] Again, these are valid options for the performer only if he or she is attracted to them. Otherwise, musical frustration is probable.

Dr. Robert Freeman, Director of the Eastman School of Music, has said there is "... [a] vast oversupply of professional musicians."[156] In recent years, some students at the Eastman School have been graduating with double majors such as music and mathematics, music and chemistry, or music and physics.[157] The Juilliard School is also changing with the times. In the 1985–1986 school year, "...a new liberal arts program, based on great books and a Socratic manner of teaching"[158] was introduced along with courses in the business of music.

Other institutions seem not to have grasped the job situation in its entirety. Shirley Fleming, in her article, "Survival," in the July 1982 issue of *Musical America*, [159] describes a seminar for music majors in which a participant speaks about how to get beyond playing for the bar mitzvahs. A multitude of freelance players in our major cities would be happy to play for a bar mitzvah!

The most recent figures representing music majors in the 500 member institutions of the National Association of Schools of Music (NASM) indicate that possibly there is still worse to come in the unbalanced ratio of supply and demand in the music performance fields. Writing in *The Instrumentalist* in October 1986, Dean Bernard J. Dobroski of the School of Music, University of Oregon, quotes data from a survey by the Higher Education Arts Data Services: there were over 50,000 students enrolled in undergraduate degree programs in music in the 1985–1986 school year; almost 10,000 undergraduate music degrees were awarded between July 1, 1984 and June 30, 1985; and almost 10,000 students were enrolled in music degree programs at the master's level. Dobroski concludes, "These numbers are staggering, particularly when one considers the reality of the marketplace. The supply of music graduates surely must exceed the demand."[160]

Obviously, only a few of these 500 institutions have carefully, honestly, and unselfishly analyzed the positive and negative aspects of their own institution and the best interests of the students they attract. Just because the student "loves" music or has achieved success in the high school music program is not sufficient reason to become a music major. The young performers must be told truthfully about the music business and given honest advice before the freshman year.

The NASM institutions are not the only ones involved with the supply and demand equation. Music vocational schools and even high schools also affect the job market. It is not enough to use the argument that "we don't create musicians, they come to us and we prepare them for better jobs." High school music teachers as well as the vast numbers of private music teachers also must be completely honest with their students.

An encouraging development which helps disprove the notion that performance skills must be taught to build enjoyment of music was noted in 1986 by Paul R. Klehman, vice-president of the Music Educators National Conference. He said, "... I think that the expansion of general music [courses for students who, for whatever reasons, do not participate in performing groups] into the high school represents the most important trend of the late 1980's in our profession...."[161]

It is certainly true that "there's always room at the top" in any profession. But those very very talented individuals will always gravitate to music. What is needed is professional counselling at all levels for those who may not be so extremely talented and therefore have alternative career options.

Chapter VIII
What the Future Holds

TRIALS AND TROUBLES

THROUGHOUT ITS LONG HISTORY, THE American Federation of Musicians has been beset by a series of continuing problems. The wonder is not that these difficulties occurred, but rather that the Federation survived at all. The end of these distressful conditions is not yet in sight.

From its earliest days, the AFM fought the inroads on the job market caused by foreign imported musicians and military bands. These battles still continue. As recently as the summer of 1969, the Zagreb Philharmonic Orchestra was imported as an orchestra "in residence" at Temple University in Philadelphia; the London Symphony performed for several seasons in the 1960s at the Daytona Beach (Florida) Festival.[1] In the 1970s and 1980s, the Federation continues to be concerned with North American tours of famous European orchestras and the importation of small groups (and individuals) from Mexico and the Caribbean Islands that divide a shrinking job market.

The competition from military bands also continues today. But with active AFM members in the armed services of both the United States and Canada, the Federation seems to view this situation as another aspect of union musicians contending for a share of the market.

Of much more consequence are the continuing inroads on the job market by musical organizations in the public schools and universities. The university bands that play for professional football games and the high school and college "big bands" that perform for private social affairs are only two common examples.

A far more serious threat comes from the unorganized musician and the casual amateur. Nor is this competition unique to the lifetime of the AFM. It is fair to say that amateur performers have been prevalent on the North American continent since there was a distinction between amateur and professional. Musical talent is widespread in our society, and it gives great satisfaction to perform. In fact, it's so much fun to play, amateurs apparently don't really care how much (or if) they are paid—a fact which has increased the difficulties faced by professionals who need to earn a living wage.

Adding to the competition of amateurs is the non-union player, a small army of men and women who regularly moonlight and make a portion of their living as performers. Rarely are these musicians in the top professional ranks, but they regularly undercut AFM performers in some freelance fields.

The members of beginning rock bands who learn their trade in garages imitating better known contemporaries by playing along with recordings by the hour are seldom union members. In addition, there are many performers in all communities who play steady dates in bars, clubs, and restaurants without regard for AFM minimum wages. This regular supplemental income (even below minimum rates) is welcomed by the non-union player who can afford this luxury because he or she probably holds a full-time job in another field. The revenue from these cash dates usually becomes part of the underground economy—and the Federation musician and the IRS are the steady losers.

Of even more concern to the Federation is the increasing pressure by its own members on union contracts and basic trade union principles. Of course the huge oversupply of qualified musicians is one of the driving forces that tempt AFM members to accept "dark" dates for single gigs and steady engagements as well as calls to the recording studios. The provisions of Taft-Hartley that force musicians to be classified as independent contractors is still another strong inducement to work without the Federation sponsored fringe benefits (i.e., health, welfare, pension, and reuse plans) in return for a paycheck with no work dues or tax deductions.

Although today's exaggerated oversupply of musicians and the problems associated with current labor law are factors in this problem's magnitude, it is not a new problem. Abram Loft, in a review of an earlier history of the AFM, wrote in 1953, "... As the student of music guild history will recall, spectacular achievements have been made by musicians in times past through unified action under determined and perceptive leadership. In every case, however, the gains have been cancelled through defections on the part of the performers [and] apathy and indifference on the part of the general public...."[2] These "defections on the part of the performer" are at least as prevalent today as they have been in the past.

Automation is a unique problem for the AFM. Not that other unions have not been confronted by automation. But in music, the "music machines" that shrink the job market and put musicians out of work are made by the musicians themselves. "... The musician, because he creates directly what the [music machine] reproduces, is eliminating himself."[3]

North American musicians have been replaced by "music machines" since at least the 1850s, when the first steam calliopes took the place of brass bands on the

Mississippi river boats. Before the end of the century (with the perfection of the perforated cardboard roll), the player piano began appearing in bars, cafes, and brothels, as well as in the homes of the middle classes. The player piano is still in use in bars and restaurants in both the United States and Canada.

Another form of music automation had its beginnings in the nineteenth century: the jukebox. In 1892, *The Musical Courier* reported the incorporation of the Michigan Automatic Music Company which was to distribute "Batdorf automatic orchestras" (made by the National Automatic Orchestra Company of New York) throughout Michigan: "... The orchestra is encased in a handsome cabinet, and the machinery is started by dropping a nickel in a slot at the top of the box.... The Company have a good thing and are bound to reap a big income from their automatic orchestras."[4]

That financial prediction was certainly true for the jukebox industry of the twentieth century. With improvements in recording techniques (and the added impetus of the Depression of the 1930s), jukeboxes have become common in all sorts of public establishments all over the continent with the resultant replacement of much live music. And until copyright law revision in 1976, jukebox manufacturers did not pay royalties to either composers or publishers.

Perhaps the most traumatic displacement of live musicians occurred in the late 1920s with the advent of the sound motion picture. Within a very short time span, over 20,000 performers in theater orchestras lost their jobs and the music business has never been quite the same.

The growth of the recording industry, beginning in the 1930s, was the next major disruption for live performance. Among other things, it caused the dismantling of staff orchestras and the elimination of live musicians in the radio industry. Today it is a distinct rarity to hear live music on radio or television. Ultimately, this unlimited use of recordings (both plate and tape) has produced the radio disc jockeys, who also advertise and compete with live musicians for other job markets. After all, " ... they can play anything that's on record."[5] The DJs advertise " ... entertainment for all parties and promotions ... " and " ... the finest Disc Jockey ... for every occasion. Every era of music...."[6] The identical words might be used to describe the competition—live performers who actually make the music.

The "disco boom" of the 1970s may have begun to subside in the 1980s,[7] but not before these establishments created the ultimate in automation, complete with tapes, amplification, lighting, special effects, music videos, decorations, costumed characters, and, obviously, no live musicians.

With the development in the 1980s of CDs (compact discs) and D.A.T. (digital audio tape), the recording industry has vastly increased the fidelity of its product and, with D.A.T., has created the means to reproduce indefinitely tapes with the same fidelity as the original. Paradoxically, the state of the art has now produced the same desire for duplicate tape royalty in the industry as has always been evident among musical performers for performance royalty.

A further proof of the pervasiveness of music reproduction is the use of tapes to replace the traditional organist at major league baseball parks. Even "Take Me Out to the Ballgame" and "Charge!" are no longer the sacred domain of live music.[8]

Another aspect of automation is the drum machine that reproduces any rhythmic pattern fed to its computer. This device eliminates live drummers on the job and is prevalent in the recording studio. *Overture* reports,

"... Almost all current pop records use drum machines rather than live drummers."9

The most recent form of automation, and perhaps the one most feared by the AFM and the professional musician, is the synthesizer. These music machines produce sound either through electronic synthesis or the reproduction of natural sounds. In other words, they can create completely new sound possibilities or they can reproduce exactly the sounds of older instruments. It is this latter technique, called "sampling," which poses the great threat for the acoustical instrument performer, the profession, and the Federation.

The threat has already become a reality. John Glasel, member of the IEB and president of Local 802 in New York, was quoted in *The New York Times*,

> ... We've already lost work in film scores, jingles and TV shows. The worst-case scenario is that these machines will get better and better and easier to use, and the public will accept these sounds, and most of our music will be produced in studios by one musician. That will change music as an ensemble art; it will become a completely solitary act.10

Many "sound designers" who use the synthesizer are Federation members11 and do not view the situation with alarm. They make the valid argument that there will always be the enjoyment of watching live musicians make music as well as the "other" enjoyment of only listening. They also argue that there is and will be music for both synthesizer and acoustical instruments. All this may be true, but it is also true that jobs for the top of the profession in the recording studios have already been affected; the great probability is that the synthesizer will get better and better and easier to use and that it will affect all of the profession in the near future.

The same *New York Times* article quoted above also reported a conversation with Joseph W. Polisi, president of the Juilliard School of Music. Polisi related, "A producer in Los Angeles asked me, 'If I can do a recording date with four musicians instead of twenty, why not?' Mr. Polisi said, 'I didn't have an answer to that one.' "[12] The economics of the music market will assure the continued and expanded use of the synthesizer.

Another problem area for the AFM is legislation which has hampered its growth and effectiveness and is related to past and present difficulties. In earlier years, court interpretations of the Alien Contract Labor Law of 1885 allowed unlimited importation of foreign musicians and musical organizations because of the "exception for artists." Not until the dark days of the Depression (1932) was the Federation able to persuade Congress to make adequate modifications. As we have seen, these modifications have not been totally successful.

Competition from U.S. military bands and service personnel, which began in the nineteenth century, continued until a Department of Defense directive in 1961 eliminated the conflict "officially." Of course, individual service musicians continued playing civilian engagements, and the major service bands continued their slightly modified schedules. So, in default, in 1978, the Federation's Convention voted to allow U.S. service personnel to become AFM members. Canadian military personnel had been eligible for AFM membership since 1961.

Then came the Congressional inquiries of the Federation during the Petrillo administration. The AFM was the first union so investigated (in 1943) and the "Anti-Petrillo Law" (the Lea Act) soon followed in 1946. Although the Federation was able finally to influence the repeal of this law in 1980, its provisions and much more became part of the Labor Management Relations Act of 1947, the Taft-Hartley legislation.

Taft-Hartley was not immediately applied to the entertainment business. Although the record clearly shows Petrillo was well aware of its potential danger to the Federation, it must be assumed that this lag in application is the reason why the AFM did not push for inclusion when the Act was amended in the 1950s. The amendments gave special consideration to the construction and apparel industries whose employment patterns are similar to the music business.

Difficulties for the AFM began in the 1960s when the courts and the National Labor Relations Board made Taft-Hartley applicable to entertainment industries. According to these interpretations, the Federation could not act as the representative of musicians who play in hotels and lounges because these establishments were not their employers. Instead, the performers were either the employees of the band leader or were independent contractors. This was a drastic blow to the Federation, whose premise has always been that the purchaser of the music was the employer. Now, the AFM could neither take action against the hotel or lounge (Taft-Hartley outlawed secondary boycotts) nor represent the musicians who performed in these rooms. The ruling has certainly affected union membership. After all, who wants to pay Federation dues if the organization cannot be your representative?

The Landrum-Griffin Act of 1965 has caused only minor disruption for the AFM; most procedures of the Federation have been ruled in compliance. But the continued exclusion of performance royalty from the 1976 revisions of copyright law was another grievous blow. In this case, the Federation has been unable to achieve its objective either as a right of law or consistently through contract negotiations with industries.

None of these toils and troubles have been lightened by the pressures in the mid-1980s for a union-free environment. The growth of militant anti-union employer groups and the deteriorating image of organized labor in the United States and Canada have not been helpful to the Federation. This is true despite the fact that the AFM generally can count on support from both sides of the aisle.

Of further concern to the Federation are recent indications of home-rule ambitions of Canadian members. This should be no surprise. All international unions with Canadian members are being faced with similar nationalistic pressures. In response to these desires, the 1987 Convention decided that, beginning with the 1989 Convention, the Vice President from Canada will be elected by Canadian locals only and that he or she shall be empowered to decide all appeals that deal solely with Canadian members and matters. Another unsurprising problem is the continued controversy within the Federation about who pays the bills. With the decrease in AFM employment, fewer full-time performers are paying a greater percentage of the revenue supplied by work dues. ICSOM members are in the forefront of this dispute; the opposition comes from the part-timers and some union officials who worry about where other funds can be obtained.

AFM ATTEMPTS IN PROBLEM SOLVING

The Federation has always fought for more job opportunities for its members. But good intentions alone do not win battles. The record shows that AFM attempts to influence legislative change have been singularly unsuccessful. It took thirty-six years (1896–1932) to effect change in the Alien Contract Law; it took sixty-five years (1896–1961) to gain a modification in Department of Defense attitudes concerning U.S. military bands and service musicians; it took fifty-one years (1914–1965) to convince the Congress to abolish the cabaret tax; and it took thirty-four years (1946–1980) to gain repeal of the Lea Act. Efforts to achieve performance royalty via copyright law revision and modification of the Taft-Hartley Act have so far failed completely.

This lack of success can be at least partially explained by a common phenomenon—lack of money. Ever since the Kenin administration began TEMPO, the fund supported by voluntary contributions to "reward friends," it has been totally inadequate. While other such funds and PACs (Political Action Committees) are contributing many thousands of dollars to individual politicians, TEMPO usually rewards its friends with $100 or perhaps $125 (although there have been a very few contributions in the $500 to $1,000 range). No substantial legislative gains can realistically be expected unless this fund is greatly enhanced.

Another factor in the Federation's inability to effect change in Taft-Hartley is the composition of the Congress and the attitude of the executive branch of the federal government. Thomas R. Donahue, secretary-treasurer of the ALF-CIO, speaking at a conference in 1985, said, " ... The labor movement cannot possibly change the [Taft-Hartley] act until a Democratic President is elected and Democrats have substantial control of both houses of Congress, and this ... could not come until at least the end of the decade."[13] According to an interview published in *The New York Times* in 1986, Lane Kirkland, president of the AFL-CIO, is only slightly less pessimistic. He said in response to a question concerning the likelihood of Taft-Hartley change, " ... In order to have a realistic chance of restoring the balance to the labor laws, we'd have to find 60 votes in the Senate. And I don't think the 60 votes are there ... That's not to say that it may not be possible to effect limited, specific changes where it might be possible to get enough votes."[14] Kirkland holds open the door of possibility to the AFM, whose support on many issues is drawn from both Democrats and Republicans.

The Federation has had somewhat more success in dealing with problems caused by automation. The Music Performance Trust Funds, although now under heavy attack by the recording industry, was (and is) an important, innovative plan to distribute some of the profits from music duplication to the public in the form of free live music. The MPTF pays the musicians scale wages for their services. In this area, the AFM, under Petrillo's leadership, led the way in introducing other trade unions to approaches to automation in their industries. After the MPTF, came the 1945 "welfare and retirement fund" of John L. Lewis' coal miners,[15] the 1960 "mechanization and modernization" agreement of Henry Bridges' longshoremen,[16] and others.

Another important AFM innovation was the entire concept of reuse payments begun under the Kenin administration. This gave a contractual share of the profits to the performers who made possible the music duplication, an interest denied to them under copyright law. These reuse fees also are being fought by the recording industries.

A sign of the times is Los Angeles Local 47's offer to pay half the cost of a retraining seminar for drummers interested in learning to use computerized drum machines.[17] Another development is a recent Federation-wide effort to report disc jockey activities to ASCAP and BMI. At the very least, these people would then be forced to pay performance fees to composers and publishers.[18]

In the long continuing effort to gain and keep membership, the Federation is losing ground, as are almost all unions today. But it is not for lack of effort. The AFM-EP Fund, which assures the possibility of freelance musicians obtaining a pension probably not available to them in any other way, the long list of services offered to members by many locals, the attempts by the International to woo back the traveling lounge musicians, the democratic procedures now in force for participation in and ratification of contracts (a right not won as early in other trade unions[19]), the support for the National Endowment for the Arts and state, provincial, and local arts councils, actions by recent administrations to offer more support to the locals and "to organize the unorganized," and even the Young Sounds plan and other efforts to attract young players are all examples of AFM attempts to gain and keep members.

Services available to AFM members are fine, but jobs are what is needed. The Federation has no control over supply and demand ratios. The shrinking job market coupled with the more and more and more well trained musicians entering the market from colleges, conservatories, trade schools, high schools, and private teachers cause professional performers to be pessimistic. Even President Fuentealba has said, "... More kids are studying music then ever before, but when they graduate, where will they work?"[20]

OTHER AVENUES TO EXPLORE

No history of the American Federation of Musicians can be divorced from the history of musical performance or the art of music in the United States and Canada. It is the live performance of music that has made this long history possible. And it is the business of the AFM to continue to nurture the living performer.

That the Federation has not always done a perfect job of nurturing is no secret. But it is difficult to imagine the diminished condition of both performer and the music profession without its assistance. Certainly there would have been no MPTF, no reuse payment plan, no Congress of Strings, and no AFM-EP Fund.

Its history illustrates that despite past errors and the horrendous problems faced now and in the foreseeable future, the Federation will persevere. It will continue to change with the times. It will continue to fight legislative battles. It will continue to adapt to the challenges of automation. It will continue to represent thousands of performing musicians in all the professions within the profession. It will continue to attract thousands of new musicians in generations to come and will protect their professional futures. The question is only in which directions talented, determined leadership will proceed.

There have been many suggestions from AFM members and others for the preservation of the strength and well being of the Federation. One category of proposals envisions a union of no more than 50,000 members concentrated in a few large cities, a series of enclaves with a special "traveling card" between the fortresses. These considerations are essentially negative and reactionary. Today in hundreds of North American cities and towns there are symphony orchestras and recording studios, to say nothing of the freelance possibilities everywhere. It would make more sense to build the Federation around the nucleus of the city orchestras rather than this drastic retreat.

John Trembath, Chairman of the Organization of Canadian Symphony Musicians, voices a different viewpoint. He advocates a proliferation of "guilds" within the AFM. These guilds, based upon common work, experience, and interest, would be united on a regional basis.[21] Presumably, OCSM, ISCOM, and RMA are examples of the common interest groups which would revitalize the Federation and serve all interests. This proposal will certainly be opposed by the many AFM members who believe in the trade union principle of structure "within-a-single-tent" with room for democratic diversity.

Others propose Federation-wide union sponsored plans such as instrument insurance and booking agent functions. These projects would serve the double purpose of binding professional musicians to the AFM and creating other sources of income to alleviate pressure on the controversial work dues.

Another group of suggestions is based upon the continuation of projects in support of live performance: MPTF engagements for example. A bold campaign would seek partnership with the National Endowment for the Arts and with state, provincial, and local arts councils to make a concerted effort to inform the public of the difference between canned and professional live music, and the value of the latter.

A small beginning has already been made in this direction. After an eight-year lobbying effort by Las Vegas Local 369 and its president, Mark Tully Massagli (who is also International Vice President), the legislature of the state of Nevada committed $150,000 to be used between July 1, 1985, and June 30, 1987 (and continued with somewhat reduced funding through June 1989), as a very real supplement to the MPTF allocation to Nevada.[22]

As a continent-wide commitment for the AFM, this is not such a farfetched idea. When consideration is given to the hundreds of thousands of dollars the Federation has already spent to support the Congress of Strings in order to, in Herman Kenin's words, "... preserve our musical heritage,"[23] the chances for success are reasonable. The new project could start with seminars for public school and university faculties, or by providing live music in class-rooms and lecture halls, or as supplements to the MPTF, or in any one of several other ways.

There are two way to appreciate and enjoy music: by hearing it and by hearing and seeing it made. The task of the Federation is to create and preserve an equitable balance so that music can continue to be a living art.

Chapter Notes

CHAPTER I

1. Gilbert Chase, *America's Music*, 2d ed., New York: McGraw-Hill, 1966, p. 107.

2. *International Musician*, Official Periodical of the American Federation of Musicians, (January 1946), 1.

3. Thomas Jefferson, *The Writings of Thomas Jefferson*, collected and edited by Paul Leicester Ford. New York: G. P. Putnams Sons, 1892–99, vol. II, p. 159.

4. *The U.S. Department of Labor Bicentennial History of the American Worker*, Richard B. Morris, ed., p. 309.

5. Edward Pessen, "Builders of the Young Republic," in *The U.S. Department of Labor Bicentennial History of the American Worker*, Richard B. Morris, ed., p. 62.

6. Ibid., pp. 60–61.

7. For a detailed early history of the New York Philharmonic, see: John Erskine, *The Philharmonic-Symphony Society of New York: Its First Hundred Years*, New York: Macmillan, 1943.

8. Robert D. Leiter, *The Musicians and Petrillo*, New York: Bookman Associates, 1953, p. 13.

9. Robert A. Gerson, *Music in Philadelphia*, Theodore Presser, 1940, p. 56, and Abram Loft, *Musicians' Guild and Union: A Consideration of the Evolutions of Protective Organization Among Musicians*, unpublished Ph.D. dissertation, Columbia University, 1950, p. 282.

10. Both 1860 and 1863 are given as the founding date of the Aschenbroedel Club. John R. Commons, "Types of American Labor Unions—The Musicians of St. Louis and New York," *Quarterly Journal of Economics* (May 1906) 424, gives 1860, while Robert D. Leiter, p. 13, lists 1863. All sources agree that the club was chartered under the laws of New York State in 1864.

11. *Labor Unions*, Gary M. Fink, ed., Westport, Conn.: Greenwood Press, 1977, p. 241.

12. Commons, p. 424, says "the term 'Aschenbroedel' is not the equivalent of 'Cinderella.' It got its name from a musical leader in New York (Asche) and a suffix of "broedel" signifying the rollicking character of the club." All other sources equate Aschenbroedel with Cinderella.

13. Vern Countryman, "The Organized Musicians," *University of Chicago Law Review*, Part I (Autumn, 1948) and Part II, (Winter 1949). Part I, p. 57.

14. H. W. Schwartz, *Bands of America*, New York: Doubleday and Company, 1957, p. 86.

15. Countryman, Part I, p. 57.

16. Loft, p. 285.

17. *International Musician* (December 1951) 8.

18. "Constitution and Price List of the Cincinnati Musicians' Protective Union. Founded June 15, 1881. Amended 1883 and 1885. Printed in 1886."

19. *Overtones*, The Cincinnati Musicians' Association (Fall 1984) 1.

20. *American Musician*, Cincinnati, Ohio (May 1899) 10.

21. *American Musician*, (May 1898) 2.

22. Guy A. Scola, "The History of the American Federation of Musicians of the United States and Canada 1896 through 1980," unpublished research, n.d., p. 2.

23. Commons, p. 419, Scola, p. 2, and Currier *American Musician* (May 1898) 2, all disagree on the number of cities represented. The list given here is Currier's. After all, he was there.

24. *American Musician*, (July 1898) 9.

25. Both Commons and Countryman agree on 101 locals. Leiter says there were only 79 (p. 14).

26. *Musical Courier*, (September 14, 1892) 10.

27. *American Musician*, (May 1898) 2.

28. Countryman, Part I, p. 58.

29. *International Musician*, (January 1946) 1.

30. *International Musician*, (May 1955) 7.

31. *International Musician*, (January 1946) 15.

32. *American Musician*, (May 1898) 3.

33. *The New York Times*, (May 1, 1966) II: 13.

34. *Musical Courier*, (July 6, 1892) 14.

35. *International Musician*, (January 1946) 15.

36. Ibid.

37. Scola, p. 8. Leiter, p. 16, lists twenty-six unions. Owen Miller, writing in *American Musician* (May 1898, p.3) says there were twenty-six unions that responded either by delegate or letter.

38. *American Musician*, (May 1898) 3.

39. *International Musician*, (February 1946) 1.

40. Leiter, p. 19, 20, and Scola, p. 12.

41. There is also evidence that locals of the NLM attempted to expel individual members who joined an AFM local. See Countryman, Part I, p. 59. *American Musician* (May 1898, p. 3) reports the NLM 1897 Convention's efforts to exclude its members who were also members of the AFM.

42. *The New York Times*, (May 1, 1966) II: 13.

43. *American Musician*, (October 1897) 13.

44. *Crescendo*, Toronto Musicians Association, (June 1973) 12.

45. Commons, p. 421.

CHAPTER II

1. *American Musician*, (May 1898) 11.

2. *American Musician*, (February 1897) 1.

3. Leiter, p. 21.

4. *American Musician*, (May 1897) 1.

5. *American Musician*, (June 1897) 1.

6. Ibid., p. 2.

7. *American Musician*, (August 1897) 1.

8. *American Musician*, (October 1897) 1.

9. He temporarily retired for one year (1914) because of poor health and was replaced by Frank Carothers. Scola, p. 12.

10. Joseph Weber died in 1950. The memorial article in the *International Musician*, (January 1951, p. 7) contains more detail.

11. Interviews March 21, 1984 and January 21, 1986. As noted in the preface, since the great majority of those interviewed desired anonymity, I have identified no one except International President Emeritus James C. Petrillo and then International President Victor W. Fuentealba who specifically agreed to be quoted.

12. John H. Mueller, *The American Symphony Orchestra*, Bloomington, Indiana: Indiana University Press, 1951, p. 342.

13. John Tasker Howard, *Our American Music*, New York: Crowell, 1946, p. 30.

14. *Musical Courier*, (March 15, 1893) 7.

15. *Musical Courier*, (December 20, 1893) 60.

16. Mueller, p. 344.

17. *Musical Courier*, (December 20, 1893) 50.

18. *Musical Courier*, (May 30, 1906) 24.

19. Schwartz, p. 187.

20. *Musical Courier*, (September 14, 1892) 10.

21. *Musical Courier*, (August 4, 1927) 25.

22. Mueller, p. 343.

23. *Bylaws of the AFM*, Art. II, Section 11.

24. Actors Equity was equally concerned with foreign competition.

25. *American Musician*, (August 1897) 8. *American Musician* (June 1898) 9, also reports a police band in Montreal accepting civilian musical engagements.

26. Leiter, p. 37.

27. This association of AFM locals within the states of Ohio, Kentucky, and West Virginia is now known as the Tri-State Musicians' Association.

28. *American Musician*, (August 1897) 3.

29. *American Musician*, (October 1897) 3.

30. *International Musician*, (October 1946) 13.

31. *International Musician*, (August 1903) 6. Provisions were made to allow participation of AFM members for certain ceremonial affairs of state.

32. These provisions are contained in the National Defense Act and the Navy Appropriation Act of 1916.

33. *The New York Times*, (June 21, 1953) VI:12.

34. *Department of Defense Directive*, No. 5500.7, Sec. XIVB (July 15, 1961).

35. *AFM Bylaws*, Article 12.

36. *International Musician*, (February 1946) 13.

37. Ibid.

38. *International Musician*, (August 1963) 5.

39. Ibid.

40. Interview, December 23, 1983.

41. *AFM Bylaws*, Article XI, Section 10.

42. *AFM Bylaws*, Article XI, Section 1.
43. *International Musician*, (June 1904) 1.
44. Commons, (1906) p. 421.
45. John R. Commons, *Labor and Administration*, New York: MacMillan, 1913, p. 300.
46. Commons, (1906) p. 422.
47. Commons, (1913) p. 319.
48. Commons, (1906) p. 440.
49. Allen Lincoln Langley, "The Musician: Artist and Laborer," *The Nation*, (September 7, 1921) 262.
50. Countryman, Part I, p. 67.
51. Scala, op. cit., p. 19. Estimates from other sources range from 18,000 to 25,000.
52. Actors and Actors Equity face some similar problems.
53. The mechanical (i.e., "player") piano has been used since the late nineteenth century. A musician performs on a specially prepared piano and produces a punched paper or cardboard roll of the performance. The roll can then be inserted in similarly prepared pianos and the piano "plays" the music as the roll is moved through the mechanism.
54. *International Musician*, (October 1927) 23.
55. *International Musician*, (February 1929) 1.
56. Countryman, Part II, p. 245.
57. *International Musician*, (July 1969) 3.
58. Mueller, p. 17.
59. Allen E. Koenig, ed., *Broadcasting and Bargaining*, Madison, Wisconsin: University of Wisconsin Press, 1970, p. 10.
60. *How Collective Bargaining Works*, "Chicago Service Trades" by C. Lawrence Christenson, New York: Twentieth-Century Fund, 1942, p. 864.
61. Dick Netzer, *The Subsidized Muse*, Cambridge: Cambridge University Press, 1978, p. 55.
62. Fink, ed., *Labor Unions*, p. 242.

CHAPTER III

1. Wellington Roe, *Juggernaut*, New York: J. B. Lippincott Co., 1948, p. 206. Leiter, p. 45, reports Petrillo joined the AFM because he was defeated for re-election as president of the AMU.

2. *International Musician*, (November 1984) 1.

3. *The New York Times*, (June 21, 1953) II:12; *The New York Times*, (June 14, 1956) 26.

4. Leiter, p. 45.

5. Interview, February 29, 1984.

6. Roe, p. 207. Leiter, p. 47, says the ransom was $100,000.

7. Leiter, p. 47.

8. Dan E. Moldea, *Dark Victory: Ronald Reagan, MCA, and the Mob*, New York: Viking, 1986, p. 18.

9. Westbrook Pegler, "Thieves with Union Cards," *Colliers*, (January 9, 1943) 30.

10. Interviews, January 24, 1984 and March 21, 1984. Also, Roe, p. 208.

11. Interview with Mr. Petrillo, January 24, 1984.

12. C. Lawrence Christenson, "Chicago Service Trades," in *How Collective Bargaining Works*, New York: Twentieth Century Fund, 1942, p. 849.

13. Interview, February 22, 1984.

14. Christenson, pp. 849, 850. A quotation from an employer of musicians.

15. Interview, February 14, 1985.

16. *International Musician*, (November 1929) 9.

17. Countryman, part II, pp. 252–261.

18. *International Musician*, (June 1940) 7.

19. Leiter, p. 49.

20. *International Musician*, (May 1950) 9.

21. *International Musician*, (June 1938) 3.

22. Max Kaplan, "The Musician in America: A Study of His Social Roles," unpublished Ph.D. dissertation, Ann Arbor, Michigan: University Microfilms, 1951, p. 214.

23. *International Musician*, (March 1941) 1.

24. *The New York Times*, (August 14, 1940) 21.

25. *The New York Times*, (March 1, 1941) 7.

26. M. A. DeWolfe Howe, *The Boston Symphony Orchestra, 1881–1931*, Boston: Houghton Mifflin, 1931, p. 16.

27. Mueller, p. 78.

28. A detailed account of the early years of the Boston Symphony Orchestra can be found in both M. A. DeWolfe Howe's, *The Boston Symphony Orchestra: 1881–1931*, and Robert R. Craven, "Boston Symphony Orchestra," in Robert R. Craven,

ed., *Symphony Orchestras of the United States*, New York: Greenwood Press, 1986.

29. Mueller, p. 92.

30. Leiter, p. 123.

31. Leiter, pp. 124, 125.

32. Both Hugo Leichtentritt, *Serge Koussevitsky: The Boston Symphony Orchestra and the New American Music*, Cambridge, Mass.: Harvard University Press, 1946, and Moses Smith, *Koussevitsky*, New York: Allen, Towne and Heath, 1947, are important sources of information for the Koussevitsky years with the Boston Symphony Orchestra.

33. Leiter, p. 126.

34. Mueller, p. 94.

35. *International Musician*, (June 1911) 5.

36. AFM Bylaws Article I, Section 1 (1956). See Countryman, part I, p. 60.

37. Roe, p. 210.

38. *The New York Times*, (June 13, 1957) 36.

39. *The New York Times*, (June 6, 1958) 13. Although Petrillo supported this deletion, he favored its retention in 1954 and 1956. See *International Musician*, August 1954 p. 51 and August 1956, p. 29.

40. *International Musician*, (February 1951) 27.

41. *International Musician*, (October 1955) 8. Also, interviews of February 14, 1985 and January 26, 1986.

42. *The New York Times*, (July 29, 1942) 15.

43. The international headquarters of the AFM in New York at one time displayed more than 300 cartoons opposed to Petrillo and/or the Federation—all published between 1942 and 1949.

44. Mary Austin, "Petrillo's War," *Journal of Popular Culture*, (Summer 1978) 15.

45. Scola, p. 35.

46. Leiter, p. 136.

47. Countryman, part II, p. 270.

48. Ibid.

49. *International Musician*, (October 1955) 31.

50. Leiter, pp. 137–138.

51. RCA and Columbia were joined by NBC Transcriptions.

52. Scola, p. 37.

53. Scola, p. 39.
54. *The New York Times*, (October 5, 1944) 1.
55. Ibid.
56. *The New York Times*, (October 11, 1944) 1.
57. *The New York Times*, (October 5, 1944) 14.
58. *International Musician*, (October 1943) 1.
59. Scola, p. 41.
60. *The New York Times*, (April 21, 1944) 1.
61. Leiter, p. 157.
62. Anders S. Lunde, "The American Federation of Musicians and the Recording Ban," *Public Opinion Quarterly*, (Spring 1948) 49.
63. Joseph E. Maddy's U.S. Senate Committee testimony of March 20, 1944. Reprinted in *Music Educators Journal*, (April 1944) p. 16.
64. Leiter, p. 150.
65. Leiter, p. 151.
66. Maddy, p. 16.
67. Lunde, p. 55.
68. *International Musician*, (January 1944) 10.
69. Signed into law April 16, 1946.
70. Leon E. Lunden, "Unions, Legislation, and the Courts," *Monthly Labor Review*, (October 1965) 1177–1178.
71. *The New York Times*, (June 24, 1947) 5.
72. Interview with Mr. Petrillo, January 24, 1984.
73. Maddy, p. 16.
74. *Treasurer's Report, 1965 Convention*, pp. 166–167.
75. *International Musician*, (January 1981) 1.
76. *International Musician*, (November 1947) 6.
77. *International Musician*, (October 1955) 8.
78. Ibid., p. 6.
79. Countryman, part II, p. 283.
80. Interview of February 14, 1985, and Countryman, part II, p. 286. Mr. Diamond had worked for Decca during the first recording ban. This time, he was a legal advisor to the AFM.
81. *Trustee's Regulations, Music Performance Trust Funds*, New York: MPTF, n.d.
82. *The New York Times*, (December 14, 1948) 1.
83. Interview with Mr. Petrillo, January 24, 1984.
84. *International Musician*, (April 1951) 6.

85. Scola, p. 51.
86. *International Musician*, (October 1955) 31.
87. Lunde, p. 45.
88. Ibid., p. 51.
89. Interview of March 21, 1984.
90. Interview of February 14, 1985.
91. Thomas Kennedy, *Automation Funds and Displaced Workers*, Boston: Harvard University Press, 1962.
92. Ibid., pp. 57, 58.
93. *International Musician*, (October 1955) 31.
94. "A Guide to Creative Programming," *Music Performance Trust Funds*, n.d.
95. Kennedy, p. 353.
96. Interview, May 13, 1986.
97. *Variety* (June 6, 1951) 41.
98. *Downbeat*, (May 21, 1952) 3.
99. *Variety*, (February 24, 1954) 43.
100. *Variety*, (November 23, 1955) 45.
101. *Downbeat*, (November 30, 1955) 5.
102. Scola, p. 52.
103. Scola, p. 54.
104. *International Musician*, (March 1956) 12.
105. Interview, February 14, 1985.
106. *The New York Times*, (February 28, 1956) 12.
107. Scola, p. 55.
108. *Los Angeles Times*, (March 1, 1956) 1.
109. Mildred Norton, "Musicians' Battle," *Saturday Review*, (March 17, 1956) 29.
110. *Los Angeles Times*, (April 2, 1956) "The Letter Page."
111. These observations are from personal acquaintance. Also see *Downbeat*, (May 16, 1956) p. 39. Cecil Read died on January 7, 1987.
112. *The New York Times*, (June 13, 1956) 46.
113. Ibid. Also see *International Musician*, (August 1956) 28.
114. *Variety*, (August 1, 1956) 45.
115. Robert A. Gorman, "The Recording Musician and Union Power: A Case Study of the American Federation of Musicians," *Performance Rights in Sound Recordings*, Subcommittee on Courts, Civil Liberties, and the Administration of Justice and

the Committee on the Judiciary House of Representatives, Ninety-fifth Congress, Second Session, June 1978, p. 1126. Although not previously published, this study was first made available in February 1978 as: Gorman, Robert A. "The Recording Musician and Union Power: A Case Study of the American Federation of Musicians." All references here are to this original.

116. *The New York Times*, (December 19, 1956) 55.

117. Ibid.

118. *The New York Times*, (May 24, 1957) 14.

119. *Downbeat*, (October 17, 1957) 7.

120. Gorman, p. 149.

121. Scola, p. 68.

122. Gorman, p. 150.

123. *International Musician*, (August 1958) 45.

124. Scola, p. 69.

125. *Downbeat*, (October 16, 1958) 6.

126. *International Musician*, (May 1958) 6.

127. *The New York Times*, (May 15, 1958) 1.

128. Interview, February 14, 1985.

129. Interview with Mr. Petrillo, January 24, 1984.

130. *The New York Times*, (June 4, 1958) 18.

131. *The New York Times*, (June 5, 1958) 25.

132. Ibid.

133. *Variety*, (October 17, 1962) 56.

134. *The New York Times*, (November 14, 1962) 44.

135. *The New York Times*, (November 17, 1962) 17.

136. Ibid.

137. *The New York Times*, (December 6, 1962) 1, and *Variety*, (December 12, 1962) 45.

138. *Downbeat*, (January 17, 1963) 11.

139. *Variety*, (March 27, 1963) 55.

140. *The New York Times*, (October 25, 1984) 45.

141. Scola, p. 113.

142. *Variety*, (June 6, 1951) 41.

143. Scola, p. 114.

144. "Lester Petrillo Memorial Trust Fund for Disabled Musicians. Statements of Revenues, Expenditures and Changes in Fund Balance." Years ended December 31, 1983, 1984.

145. *International Musician*, (October 1969) 5.

146. *Variety*, (June 6, 1951) 41. Also *International Musician*, (October 1955) 31.

CHAPTER IV

1. According to an article in the *American Labor*, (June, 1970) "Herman David Kenin; Pragmatist With a Soul," the description comes from "a long-time friend."
2. Ibid., p. 20.
3. *The New York Times*, (July 22, 1970) 41.
4. *American Labor*, p. 21.
5. Ibid.
6. *The New York Times*, (June 5, 1958) 25.
7. *International Musician*, (October 1958) 8. A reprint of Kenin's speech before the New York State Conference of Musicians on September 21, 1958 in Newburgh, New York.
8. *International Musician*, (October 1958) 8.
9. The first announcement of this project was in the *International Musician*, (September 1948) p. 8.
10. *The New York Times*, (July 22, 1958) 23.
11. Gorman, p. 159.
12. Gorman, p. 160.
13. Interview, March 20, 1984.
14. *International Musician*, (November 1958) 9. The AFM list of objections to this contract did *not* mention the exclusion of the MPTF.
15. *International Musician*, (February 1959) 9.
16. *International Musician*, April 1959, p. 7.
17. Ibid.
18. *International Musician*, (December 1959) 3, 14.
19. Gorman, p. 180.
20. Gorman, p. 189.
21. *International Musician*, (July 1961) 7.
22. *International Musician*, (September 1961) 36.
23. *The New York Times*, (September, 11, 1961) 25; Gorman, p. 191, 192; *International Musician*, (October 1961) 9.
24. *The New York Times*, (September 11, 1961) 25, gives an MGA membership of 850; Gorman, p. 193, says the membership was roughly 1,000.
25. Interview, February 14, 1985.
26. Interview, December 26, 1984.
27. Gorman, p. 176.
28. *The New York Times*, (June 30, 1963) 9.
29. Ibid.

30. Gorman, p. 200.

31. *The New York Times*, (August 8, 1981) 27.

32. *Variety*, (April 13, 1983) 73.

33. *Variety*, (March 21, 1984) 135.

34. Interview, March 21, 1984.

35. Interview, March 22, 1984.

36. Interview, November 19, 1985.

37. *International Musician*, (February 1987) 3.

38. *Overture*, (February 1987) 2.

39. Ibid., p. 1.

40. *Variety*, (January 28, 1987) 65.

41. Ibid.

42. *Daily Variety*, (January 15, 1987) 32.

43. Letter from John Glasel, president of Local 802, to delegates to the 1987 Convention, May 27, 1987, p. 2.

44. *Variety*, (January 28, 1987) 65.

45. Allen Dodds Frank, "And the Beat Goes On," *Forbes*, (May 18, 1987) 40.

46. Martin Paulson, "Save the Trust Funds! Bargaining Away a Valuable Resource," *Billboard*, (January 10, 1987) 9.

47. Ibid.

48. Interviews, February 14, 1985; March 21, 1984; March 22, 1984.

49. Interview, November 19, 1985.

50. *International Musician*, (February 1959) 9.

51. *American Federation of Musicians' and Employers' Pension Welfare Fund*, New York: American Federation of Musicians' and Employers' Pension Welfare Fund, n.d.

52. *International Musician*, (April 1959) 6.

53. *International Musician*, (June 1960) 8.

54. *International Musician*, (June 1969) 12.

55. *AFM and EPW Fund*, p. 46.

56. Interview, January 12, 1984.

57. *Overtones*, p. 4.

58. *International Musician*, (November 1982) 4.

59. Interview, February 7, 1986.

60. *International Musician*, (November 1965) 5.

61. *Allegro*, New York: Local 802 AFM, (November 1985) 18. On the other hand, jingle residuals are based strictly on the use of music recorded on the dates played by each individual musician.

62. *Allegro*, (October 1968) 3.
63. *Allegro*, (July 1974) 3.
64. *Allegro*, (July 1978) 1.
65. *Allegro*, (November 1985) 18.
66. Scola, p. 90.
67. *International Musician*, (July 1961) 7.
68. "Congress of Strings," *American Labor*, (June 1968) 17.
69. *International Musician*, (October 1958) 12.
70. *International Musician*, (January 1959) 8.
71. Ibid.
72. *AFM Congress of Strings Yearbook, 1959–1983*, New York: American Federation of Musicians, n.d., p. 7.
73. Ibid., p. 18.
74. *International Musician*, (December 1978) 4.
75. *AFM Congress of Strings Yearbook*, op. cit., p. 3.
76. Interviews, March 20, 1984 and January 21, 1986.
77. Lauren W. Lavine, "Structural Changes in Interdependent Relationships Within the Symphony Orchestra in America; A Study of Interaction Between Orchestra and Management," Unpublished Master's Thesis, Arts Administration Program, Columbia University, 1983, p. 34.
78. *Senza Sordino*, Publication of International Conference of Symphony and Opera Musicians, (November 1982) 1.
79. *Senza Sordino*, (April 1986) 3.
80. Interview, January 19, 1986.
81. Interviews, February 2, 1984; February 9, 1984; March 20, 1984.
82. Leon Emanual Lunden, "Major Symphony Orchestra Labor Relations," Unpublished Ph.D. Dissertation, University of Wisconsin, 1967, p. 131.
83. *International Musician*, (August 1960) 32.
84. *International Musician*, (September 1960) 9.
85. *International Musician*, (November 1960) 43.
86. *Variety*, (January 1, 1964) 38.
87. *International Musician*, (September 1962) 39.
88. Henry Shaw, "The International Conference of Symphony and Opera Musicians," in *The Professional Symphony Orchestra in the United States*, George Seltzer, ed., Metuchen, NJ: Scarecrow Press, 1975, p. 375.
89. *International Musician*, (January 1963) 45.

90. Lunden, p. 141.
91. *Senza Sordino*, (April 1, 1977) 1.
92. Interview, February 22, 1984.
93. Interview, February 22, 1984.
94. Interview, February 22, 1984.
95. *Senza Sordino*, (April 1977) 1.
96. *Senza Sordino*, (September–October 1965) 2.
97. *International Musician*, (December 1965) 3.
98. Ibid.
99. *Senza Sordino*, (April 1986) 3.
100. *Senza Sordino*, (October 1982) 1.
101. *Senza Sordino*, (April 1986) 3.
102. *Senza Sordino*, (April 1976) 2.
103. *International Musician*, (December 1984) 6.
104. *Senza Sordino*, (June 1987) 2.
105. Interview, February 22, 1984.
106. Interview, March 20, 1984.
107. Interview, June 17, 1984.
108. *Senza Sordino*, (October 1980) 1.
109. *Senza Sordino*, (October 1985) 1.
110. Interview, February 14, 1985.
111. *Senza Sordino*, (April 1987) 3.
112. *Allegro*, (July/August 1987) 7.
113. Gunther Schuller, "The Trouble with Orchestras," *Symphony News*, American Symphony Orchestra League, (December 1979) 18.
114. Interview, May 19, 1984.
115. Interview, January 21, 1985.
116. H. W. Benson, *Democratic Rights for Union Members*, New York: Association for Union Democracy, 1979, p. 223.
117. Clyde W. Summers, "Admission Policies of Labor Unions," *The Quarterly Journal of Economics*, (November 1946) 68, 69.
118. Donald Spivey, *Union and the Black Musician: The Narrative of William Everett Samuels and Chicago Local 208*, Lanham, Md.: University Press of America, 1984, p. 10.
119. William P. Steeper, "Civil Rights in the American Federation of Musicians," *International Musician*, (December 1954) p. S 24.
120. "Charter restored to Local 455, Uniontown, Pa. (colored)," *International Musician*, (December 1949) 39.

121. *International Musician*, (April 1958) 45.
122. Streeper, p. S 24.
123. *The New York Times*, (January 11, 1953) 43.
124. *Downbeat*, (June 15, 1951) 1.
125. *Variety*, (December 19, 1956) 46.
126. *Downbeat*, (January 23, 1957) 11.
127. *International Musician*, (November 1957) 42, 43.
128. Ibid., p. 43.
129. Interview, March 13, 1984.
130. *The New York Times*, (June 14, 1957) 22.
131. Barbash, p. 331.
132. *The New York Times*, (March 21, 1958) 45.
133. *Variety*, (November 4, 1959) 59, and *Variety*, (December 2, 1959) 57.
134. *The New York Times*, (February 18, 1960) 15.
135. *The New York Times*, (April 22, 1960) 20.
136. *Variety*, (October 10, 1962) 49.
137. *International Musician*, (August 1962) 35.
138. See *Variety*, (March 27, 1963) 53; *Downbeat*, (April 25, 1963) 15; *Variety*, (July 31, 1963) 95; *Variety*, (August 28, 1963) 1; *Variety*, (October 14, 1963) 45; *Variety*, (August 12, 1964) 45; *The New York Times*, (August 15, 1964) 13.
139. *International Musician*, (January 1965) 7.
140. Ibid.
141. Ibid.
142. *The New York Times*, (April 23, 1966) 16.
143. Ibid.
144. Merger Agreement between Locals 11 and 637 dated March 22, 1967.
145. Changed to December 1, 1970. Minutes, Executive Board Meeting, Local 101–473, December 16, 1970.
146. Order of Merger of Dayton Musicians Association Local 101, A F of M with Dayton Musicians Protective Union Local 473, A F of M, dated September 1, 1970.
147. *Variety*, (July 8, 1968) 47.
148. Ibid.
149. Interview, March 13, 1984.
150. *International Musician*, (September 1971) 6.
151. Interview, March 13, 1984.
152. *International Musician*, (April 1976) 20.
153. Bylaws of the AFM, Article 26, Section 2 (Revised

September 15, 1985). In 1977 this addition was to Article 5 of the bylaws then in force.

154. *International Musician,* (November 1978) 4.

155. Whitney Balliett, "John Hammond and Dick Wellstood," *The New Yorker,* (August 31, 1987) 90.

156. *Overture,* Periodical of Local 47, Los Angeles, (May 1985) 6.

157. *The New York Times,* (April 22, 1956) II: 9.

158. *The New York Times,* (November 18, 1958) 39.

159. Ibid.

160. *The New York Times,* (November 19, 1958) 29.

161. *The New York Times,* (February 13, 1963) 6.

162. *The New York Times,* (August 2, 1963) 17.

163. *Musical America,* (July 1964) 9.

164. *The New York Times,* (May 7, 1965) 35.

165. *The New York Times,* (June 25, 1967) II:13.

166. *The New York Times,* (November 26, 1967) II:17.

167. Herbert Russcol, "Can the Negro Overcome the Classical Music Establishment," *High Fidelity,* (August 1968) 43.

168. Russcol, p. 44.

169. Ibid., p. 45.

170. *The New York Times,* (October 31, 1968) 54.

171. *The New York Times,* (November 12, 1986) B1.

172. *The New York Times,* (June 10, 1969) 50.

173. *The New York Times,* (November 17, 1970) 53.

174. Ibid.

175. Donal Henahan, "An About Face on Black Musicians at the Philharmonic," *The New York Times,* (June 11, 1972) II:15.

176. *The New York Times,* (June 6, 1975) 10.

177. *Music Assistance Fund Brochure,* New York: Music Assistance Fund, n.d.

178. *Senza Sordino,* (October 1976) 1.

179. *Senza Sordino,* (February 1978) 4.

180. *Senza Sordino,* (April 1978) 3.

181. *Symphony News,* (April 1979) 16.

182. Luther Lincoln Henderson, *The Role of the New York Philharmonic's Director of Educational Activities: A New Dimension for the Conductor,* Unpublished DMA Treatise, University of Texas at Austin, 1980, pp. 96, 97.

183. *The New York Times,* (March 4, 1987) B1.

184. *Variety*, (May 13, 1970) 53.
185. *Variety*, (May 20, 1970) 47.
186. *Variety*, (April 12, 1972) 43.
187. *International Musician*, (October 1958) 9.
188. *International Musician*, (February 1964) 6.
189. Lunden, p. 1179.
190. *1985 Annual Report, 20th Anniversary, National Endowment of the Arts.*Washington, U. S. Government Printing Office, 1986, p. 220.
191. *The National Endowment for the Arts Composer/Libretlist Program at the American Music Center,* New York: American Music Center, n. d., pp. v, fi.
192. *1985 Annual Report, 20th Anniversary, National Endowment of the Arts,* pp. 238–241.
193. Barbara W. Tuchman, "Generalship," *Parameters,* (Spring 1972) pp. 10, 11.
194. *International Musician*, (November 1965) 3.
195. *Performing Arts: Problems and Prospects,* Rockefeller Panel Report, New York: McGraw-Hill, 1965, p. 57.
196. Lunden, p. 1178.
197. *The New York Times*, (April 26, 1959) 55.
198. *International Musician*, (September 1959) 38.
199. *International Musician*, (July 1963) 12.
200. *International Musician*, (September 1950) 8.
201. *International Musician*, (August 1954) p. S7.
202. *International Musician*, (November 1955) 15.
203. *Variety*, (December 19, 1962) 55.
204. *Downbeat*, (August 1, 1963) 14.
205. Ibid.
206. *Vairiety*, (December 11, 1963) 43.
207. *The New York Times*, (December 8, 1964) 40.
208. *Variety*, (December 9, 1964) 47.
209. Lunden, p. 1181.
210. *Variety*, (June 14, 1967) 47.
211. *Allegro*, (February 1986) 1.
212. Scola, p. 126.
213. *Variety*, (December 8, 1982) 1.
214. *Variety*, (January 16, 1983) 70.
215. *Variety*, (May 4, 1983) 525.
216. *Variety*, (February 19, 1985) 8.
217. *Variety*, (May 4, 1983) 525.

218. *International Musician,* (September 1984) 3.
219. *Allegro,* (November 1984) 14.
220. *International Musician,* (November 1977) 1.
221. Scola, p. 115.
222. *International Musician,* (August 1962) 36.
223. *International Musician,* (March 1986) 18, 19; and *Allegro,* (May 1986) 2.

CHAPTER V

1. *International Musician,* (August 1970) 6.
2. *The New York Times,* (July 31, 1970) 45; *Billboard,* (August 8, 1970) 3.
3. *International Musician,* (August 1970) 6.
4. *International Musician,* (August 1971) 3.
5. *International Musician,* (September 1971) 16.
6. *International Musician,* (January 1970) 3.
7. Ibid.
8. *International Musician,* (August 1972) 21.
9. Ibid.
10. *Variety,* (June 29, 1977) 51.
11. *International Musician,* (September 1975) 3.
12. Information contained in a letter from William R. Lee, General Licensing Project Manager, ASCAP, July 1, 1987.
13. *The New York Times,* (January 13, 1978) B2; also *Billboard,* (January 21, 1978) 146.
14. *The New York Times,* (January 13, 1978) B2. Of course, these strikes were locally authorized, but the permissive attitude at the national level was helpful.
15. *International Musician,* (March 1977) 3.
16. *Variety,* (January 18, 1978) 69.
17. *International Musician,* (February 1978) 5.
18. *Billboard,* (January 28, 1978) 114.
19. *International Musician,* (August 1978) 1; *1978 Official Proceedings, Eighty-first Annual Convention,* AFM, p. 13.
20. Minutes, AFM Convention, June 1978.
21. Minutes, AFM Convention, June 1978.
22. Interview, March 21, 1984.
23. *International Musician,* (April 1979) 3.
24. *Variety,* (June 27, 1979) 63.
25. *Variety,* (July 4, 1979) 55.

26. *International Musician*, (August 1979) 1.
27. Interview, March 21, 1984.
28. *Variety*, (Arpil 23, 1980) 73.
29. *Billboard*, (June 21, 1980) 6.
30. *Variety*, (June 25, 1980) 69.
31. Ibid., p. 77.
32. *Variety*, (July 1, 1981) 61.
33. Ibid., p. 62.
34. Ibid.
35. *International Musician*, (December 1982) 14.
36. *International Musician*, (February 1983) 24.
37. *Variety*, (June 29, 1983) 53.
38. *Variety*, (July 6, 1983) 60.
39. Ibid., p. 62.
40. *International Musician*, (October 1983) 127.
41. *International Musician*, (December 1984) 10.
42. *International Musician*, (January 1985) 4.
43. *International Musician*, (March 1985) 14.
44. *International Musician*, (January 1985) 3.
45. Interview, March 20, 1984.
46. Interview, January 24, 1984.
47. *Overture*, (April 1985) 9.
48. Interview, June 27, 1985.
49. Interview, October 9, 1986.
50. *International Musician*, (July 1987) 3.
51. Letter to local officers from President Fuentealba, January 6, 1983.
52. *International Musician*, (August 1986) 12. This is in drastic contrast to earlier days when the IEB regularly denied local requests to lower fees. See *International Musician*, (December 1959) 42.
53. Letter from John Glasel to delegates to the 1987 AFM Convention, May 27, 1987, p. 2. Also *Allegro*, (July/August 1987) 6.
54. *Daily Variety*, (January 15, 1987) 1.
55. *Daily Variety*, (April 28, 1987) 1.
56. Ibid., p. 19.
57. *Variety*, (June 10, 1987) 71.
58. Letter from Emerson to Fuentealba, June 3, 1987.
59. Letter from Emerson to all convention delegates, June 17, 1987.

60. *Election Brochure, AFM Convention 1987*, p. 2.

61. Letter to delegates, 1987 AFM Convention from the Committee to ReElect President Vic Fuentealba, June 16, 1987.

62. *Variety*, (June 24, 1987) 81.

63. Ibid.

64. *Las Vegas Sun*, (June 19, 1987) 3B.

65. *International Musician*, (July 1987) 16.

66. *Election Brochure, AFM Convention 1987*, p. 3.

67. *International Musician*, (April 1985) 1; and *International Musician*, (August 1985) 1.

CHAPTER VI

1. Fink, ed. *Labor Unions*. p. 242.

2. *International Musician*, (August 1951) 28.

3. *International Musician*, (July 1960) 7.

4. *International Musician*, (August 1970) 3.

5. Information from President's Office, AFM, March 2, 1984.

6. Ibid.

7. *International Musician*, (March 1985) 14.

8. Interview, March 21, 1986.

9. Countryman, Part I, p. 59.

10. In the over ninety-year history of the AFM there have been only eight presidents. Miller served four years before becoming International Secretary; Weber served thirty-nine years; Cruthers served only one year while Weber recovered his health; Petrillo was president for eighteen years; both Kenin and Davis, after terms of twelve and seven years respectively, died in office; Fuentealba served nine years before the election of J. Martin Emerson in 1987.

11. Bylaws of the AFM (revised September 15, 1985) Article 26, Section 2. This section also authorizes additional black delegates based upon the vote of black membership in locals merged to comply with Civil Rights policy.

12. Bylaws of the AFM (revised September 15, 1985) Article 27, Section 4.

13. *Variety*, (July 1, 1981) 61.

14. *International Musician*, (August 1970) 9.

15. *Daily Variety*, (April 10, 1985) 1.

16. Interview, March 21, 1984.
17. Bylaws of the AFM (revised September 15, 1985) Article 3, Section 7-D.
18. *International Musician*, (June 1986) 1.
19. *International Musician*, (February 1959) 11.
20. The information about IEB members was supplied by the staff of the *International Musician*.
21. Bylaws of the AFM (revised September 15, 1985) Article 4, Section 1.
22. Interview, September 23, 1986.
23. *Billboard*, (May 1, 1954) 18.
24. *Allegro*, (July/August 1987) 13.
25. This information was obtained from the International Secretary-Treasurer's Office in a letter of March 27, 1984.
26. Interview, March 21, 1984.
27. *The New York Times*, (January 4, 1983) C12.
28. Interview, January 21, 1986.
29. Interview, July 23, 1984.
30. Interview, February 8, 1984.
31. Reported in many interviews with many musicians in various sections of the U. S. and Canada.
32. Interview, March 21, 1984.
33. Interviews, January 24, 1984; February 8, 1984; January 21, 1986; October 17, 1986.
34. Scola, p. 129.
35. *International Musician*, (February 1972) 1.
36. *International Musician*, (October 1986) 4.
37. *International Musician*, (December 1986) 1.

CHAPTER VII

1. It was not until 1979 that vocalists also were welcomed by the Federation. Before then, a singer with a band applied for AFM membership as a tambourine or cocktail drum player, a real farce.
2. John E. DeMelglio, *Vaudeville U.S.A.*, Bowling Green, Ohio: Popular Press, 1973, p. 11.
3. Interview, March 21, 1984.
4. H. W. Schwartz, p. 16.
5. Ibid.

6. Gilbert Chase, p. 624.

7. *Musical Courier*, (March 15, 1893) 8.

8. *Musical Courier*, (July 13, 1892) 2.

9. *International Musician*, (September 1978) 11.

10. *International Musician*, (April 1977) 5.

11. *International Musician*, (August 1967) 7.

12. *International Musician*, (December 1950) 19.

13. *International Musician*, (December 1981) 10.

14. *International Musician*, (May 1977) 26.

15. *The New York Times*, (May 14, 1985) A:18.

16. Ibid.

17. *The New Republic*, (January 20, 1982) 14.

18. Ibid.

19. Ibid.

20. *International Musician*, (May 1985) 1.

21. *Wall Street Journal*, (May 27, 1986) 1.

22. *Senza Sordino*, (May 1981) 3. And by now, the upper limit is over $50,000.

23. Craven, p. xx.

24. *Symphony News*, American Symphony Orchestra League, Vienna, Virginia, (August/September 1983) 19.

25. *Orchestra Classification Procedures*, American Symphony Orchestra League, May 1987.

26. *International Musician*, (July 1968) 10.

27. *Senza Sordino*, (April 1985) 4.

28. *The New York Times*, (May 1, 1985) C:22.

29. *International Musician*, (April 1950) 46.

30. *International Musician*, (June 1954) 47.

31. *Keynote*, Detroit Federation of Musicians, (January 1954) 7.

32. *Intermezzo*, Chicago Federation of Musicians, (September 1985) 12.

33. *The New York Times*, (March 16, 1986) sec. 2, p. 1.

34. *The New York Times*, (May 18, 1969) sec. 2, p. 19.

35. *The New York Times*, (August 5, 1965) 166.

36. *International Musician*, (March 1986) 5.

37. *The New York Times*, (December 22, 1986) H:24.

38. Interview, June 23, 1986.

39. *The New York Times*, (April 13, 1986) sec. 2, p. 1.

40. *Senza Sordino*, (April 1980) 2.

41. *The Organization, Administration and Presentation of*

Symphony Orchestra Youth Concert Activities for Music Education Purposes in Selected Cities, Part I, Summary by Thomas H. Hill and Helen M. Thompson, Office of Education, Bureau of Research, Washington, D.C.: Government Printing Office, 1968, p. 1.

42. *Symphony Magazine*, (February/March 1984) 25.
43. Letter to the author from the League's Director of Education, March 19, 1984.
44. *Senza Sordino*, (March 1974) 1.
45. Interview, October 9, 1986.
46. *The New York Times*, (October 2, 1983) 19.
47. *The New York Times*, (December 22, 1985) H:24.
48. *The New York Times*, (August 19, 1984) 9. This article states that a busy jingle player in New York can make $80,000 to $100,000 (or more) annually. For such players, incorporation makes much sense. See *Overture*, (March 1985) 4.
49. *The New York Times*, (April 13, 1986) sec. 2, p. 25.
50. *The New York Times*, (September 11, 1961) 25.
51. The RMA was simply an informal coalition of recording musicians until the 1987 Convention granted conference status.
52. *Variety*, (February 2, 1983) 107.
53. *Variety*, (March 30, 1983) 1.
54. *International Musician*, (January 1983) 3.
55. *Allegro*, (January 1985) 19.
56. The Jack Gale articles appeared in *Allegro*, issues of: May 1985, p. 10; June 1985, p. 18; July–August 1985, p. 15; and September 1985, p. 10.
57. *The New York Times*, (November 16, 1986) H:19.
58. *Cincinnati Enquirer*, (November 30, 1986) I:4.
59. *Allegro*, (May 1985) 8.
60. *Allegro*, (July/August 1987) 1.
61. Ibid.
62. A comment from a long-time friend.
63. *Allegro*, (July/August 1987) 1.
64. *International Musician*, (January 1980) 13.
65. Mona Coxson, *Some Straight Talk About the Music Business*, Toronto: C. M. Books, 1984, p. 31.
66. *International Musician*, (May 1976) 18.
67. *Cincinnati Enquirer*, (January 12, 1986) F:6.
68. *The New York Times*, (May 17, 1979) C:14.

69. Interview, February 2, 1984.

70. Interview, November 23, 1985.

71. *Chicago Scene*, Chicago Educational Television Association, (November 1986) 14.

72. Interview, February 8, 1984.

73. Interview, February 10, 1984.

74. James W. Deering, *Making Money Making Music (No Matter Where You Live)*, Cincinnati: Writers Digest Books, 1982, p. 77.

75. *International Musician*, (March 1976) 7.

76. *Wall Street Journal*, (October 13, 1986) 5.

77. Information supplied by Actor's Equity Association, 1985.

78. *The New York Times*, (December 21, 1975) 1.

79. *The New York Times*, (August 2, 1980) 30.

80. *Wall Street Journal*, (January 16, 1981) 10.

81. *The New York Times*, (January 16, 1981) p. C:9.

82. *The New York Times*, (July 10, 1980) C:12

83. *The New York Times*, (September 26, 1980) A:34.

84. *The New York Times*, (October 26, 1980) 1.

85. *The New York Times*, (October 29, 1980) 1.

86. *The New York Times*, (December 11, 1983) 115.

87. Donal Henaham, "What Price Peace at the Metropolitan," *The New York Times*, (December 7, 1980) Z:1.

88. *The New York Times*, (April 2, 1984) A:14.

89. *The New York Times*, (April 4, 1984) A:14.

90. *The New York Times*, (April 8, 1984) L:24.

91. *The New York Times*, (April 28, 1984) L:6.

92. *The New York Times*, (April 30, 1984) A:10.

93. *The New York Times*, (May 22, 1984) A:14.

94. *The New York Times*, (May 26, 1984) 6.

95. *The New York Times*, (June 7, 1984) A:20.

96. *The New York Times*, (June 8, 1984) A:14.

97. Ibid.

98. *The New York Times*, (June 16, 1984) 28.

99. *International Musician*, (December 1984) 20, 21.

100. *Allegro*, (January 1984) 12, 13.

101. *International Musician*, (November 1986) 3.

102. Interview, November 10, 1986.

103. *Crescendo*, (June 1973) 11.

104. *Crescendo*, (June 1973) 12.

105. William P. Steeper, "Civil Rights in the American Federation of Musicians," *International Musician*, (December 1954) S:24.

106. *International Musician*, (July 1951) 11.

107. *International Musician*, (January 1959) 39.

108. Ibid.

109. *Music Educators Journal*, (April 1984) 32.

110. *Music Journal*, (March 1974) 33.

111. *International Musician*, (January 1959) 39.

112. *International Musician*, (December 1970) 8.

113. *International Musician*, (April 1974) 10.

114. *Overture*, (June 1985) 2.

115. *International Musician*, (April 1965) 18.

116. *International Musician*, (August 1963) 12.

117. *The New York Times*, (February 22, 1981) II:19.

118. Susan Starr, "The Prejudice Against Women," *Music Journal*, (March 1974) 14.

119. *International Musician*, (March 1986) 22.

120. *The New York Times*, (October 20, 1946) X:7.

121. Ibid.

122. *International Musician*, (October 1948) 30.

123. *Stereo Review*, (September 1978) 76.

124. *The New York Times*, (October 10, 1970) II:33.

125. *International Musician*, (May 1953) 24.

126. *International Musician*, (April 1982) 15.

127. Letter from the ASOL, September 6, 1984.

128. Report from Houston Symphony Orchestra, September 25, 1984.

129. *Cincinnati Enquirer*, (October 29, 1985) D:1.

130. *Senza Sordino*, (April 1982) 2.

131. *Senza Sordino*, (April 1982) 1.

132. Lewis Porter, "She Wiped All the Men," *Music Educators Journal*, (September 1984) 44.

133. *Overture*, (April 1985) 4.

134. *International Musician*, (April 1953) 46.

135. *International Musician*, (April 1956) 62.

136. *International Musician*, (July 1953) 36.

137. *International Musician*, (April 1951) 15.

138. *International Musician*, (December 1970) 8.

139. *Allegro*, (March 1985) 7.

140. *International Musician*, (October 1983) 5.

141. *Senza Sordino*, (October 1972) 4.

142. *Senza Sordino*, (June 1978) 4.

143. *American Musician*, (July 1, 1898) 5.

144. *International Musician*, (July 1951) 7.

145. *The New York Times*, (June 5, 1951) 29.

146. Herman Kenin, "Conserving America's Cultural Resources," *The American Federalist*, reprinted in *Senza Sordino* in 1964 and in April 1977, p. 4.

147. Bernard Holland, "What Will All These Musicians Do?" *The New York Times*, (June 16, 1985) sec. 2, p. 1.

148. Interview, November 12, 1986.

149. *The Washington Post*, (May 24, 1983) B:7.

150. *The New York Times*, (January 1, 1956) sec. II, p. 7.

151. *The New York Times*, (January 8, 1986) C:14.

152. Interview, September 6, 1984.

153. James S. Newton, "What's New in Music Technology," *The New York Times*, (March 1, 1987) F:19.

154. *The New York Times*, (October 10, 1982) CN:17.

155. *The New York Times*, (May 28, 1985) D:15.

156. *Newsweek*, (January 5, 1987) 55.

157. *The New York Times*, (May 28, 1985) D:15.

158. *The New York Times*, (October 27, 1985) sec. 2, p. 21.

159. *Musical America*, (July 1982) 31.

160. *The Instrumentalist*, Chicago: The Instrumentalist Co., (October 1986) 82.

161. *Music Educators Journal*, (April 1987) 33.

CHAPTER VIII

1. *International Musician*, (April 1970) 3.

2. Abram Loft, Book Review, *The Musicians and Petrillo* by Robert Leiter, *Notes*, Music Library Association, (December 1953) 102.

3. James C. Petrillo, "Man, Machine, Music and Musicians," *International Musician*, (April 1955) 16.

4. *Musical Courier*, (August 31, 1892) 19.

5. *Cincinnati Enquirer*, (January 3, 1985) C:1.

6. *The New York Times*, (October 26, 1986) magazine section, p. 67.

7. *The New York Times*, (August 22, 1982) sec. 2, p. 1.

8. *Cincinnati Enquirer*, (March 6, 1986) B:2.
9. *Overture*, (January 1986) 9.
10. John Rockwell, "Electronics Is Challenging Traditions of Music," *The New York Times*, (August 7, 1986) C:19.
11. For example, over 25 percent of new members in local 47 (Los Angeles), were synthesizer players, as reported in the September 1986 issue of *Overture*, pp. 22, 23.
12. Rockwell, p. 19.
13. *The New York Times*, (September 22, 1985) sec. 1, p. 21.
14. *The New York Times*, (December 14, 1986) Y:19.
15. Saul Alinsky, *John L. Lewis: An Unauthorized Biography*, New York: G. P. Putnam's Sons, 1949, p. 330.
16. *The New York Times*, (December 1, 1985) sec. 1, p. 14.
17. *Overture*, (January 1986) 9.
18. *Intermezzo*, (June 1985) 1.
19. *The New York Times*, (July 13, 1985) L:27.
20. *The New York Times*, (August 22, 1982) L:1.
21. *OCSM Newsletter*, (March 1987) 16.
22. Information from President Mark Tully Massagli, Local 369, Las Vegas, Nevada, in letters of January 21, 1987 and June 30, 1987.
23. *AFM Congress of Strings Yearbook*, p. 3.

Bibliography

PERIODICALS IN PRINT

AFL-CIO American Federationist. AFL–CIO, Washington, D.C.

Allegro. Local 802 (New York) American Federation of Musicians. Official Publication

American Labor. American Labor Education Center, Washington, D.C.

Billboard

Business Week

Crescendo. Local 149 (Toronto) American Federation of Musicians. Official Publication

Daily Variety

Downbeat

Intermezzo. Local 10-208 (Chicago) American Federation of Musicians. Official Publication

International Musician. American Federation of Musicians. Official Publication

Monthly Labor Review. U.S. Bureau of Labor Statistics. Washington, D.C.

Music Educators Journal

Music Journal

The New York Times

New Yorker

Overtones. Local 1 (Cincinnati) American Federation of Musicians. Official Publication

Overture. Local 47 (Los Angeles) American Federation of Musicians. Official Publication

Senza Sordino. International Conference of Symphony and Opera Musicians, a Conference within the American Federation of Musicians. Offical Publication

Symphony News. American Symphony Orchestra League. Official Publication

Variety

Wall Street Journal

The Washington Post

BOOKS

Adams, Joey with Henry Tobias. *The Borscht Belt.* New York: Avon Books, 1966.

Albertson, Chris. *Bessie.* New York: Stein & Day, 1972.

Alinsky, Saul. *John L. Lewis: An Unauthorized Biography.* New York: G.P. Putnam's Sons, 1949.

American Federation of Musicians. *AFM Congress of Strings Yearbook. 1959–1983.* New York: American Federation of Musicians, N.D.

_____. *Constitution By-Laws and Policy of the American Federation of Musicians of the United States and Canada.* American Federation of Musicians, N.D.

_____. *Diminuendo.* New York: American Federation of Musicians, N.D.

_____. *Eventful Decade: Cartoonists' Version of James C. Petrillo and the AFM over the Last 10 Years.* New York: American Federation of Musicians, N.D.

_____. *Official Proceedings of Annual Conventions.* N.D.

_____. *The Record on Records.* New York: American Federation of Musicians, N.D.

_____. *Wage Scales and Conditions in the Symphony Orchestra.* Annual Editions for Major Orchestras and Regional Orchestras. American Federation of Musicians, N.D.

American Federation of Musicians' and Employers' Pension Welfare Fund. *American Federation of Musicians' and Employers' Pension Welfare Fund.* N.D.

American Federation of Television and Radio Artists. *Articles of Agreement and Constitution, Revised 1980.* New York: N.D.

American Guild of Musical Artists. *Agreement Constitution and By-Laws.* New York: May 1980.

American Symphony Orchestra League. *Orchestra Education Programs.* A.S.O.L., 1984.

_____. *Principles of Orchestra Management.* 2nd Edition. A.S.O.L., 1983.

_____. *Resource Guide.* Vienna, Va.: A.S.O.L., 1975.

Arian, Edward. *Bach, Beethoven, and Bureaucracy.* University: University of Alabama Press, 1971.

Aronowitz, Stanley. *Working Class Hero: A New Strategy for Labor.* New York: Pilgrim Press, 1983.

Associated Actors and Artistes of America. *Constitution of the Associated Actors and Artistes of America.* New York: N.D.

Atkinson, Brooks. *Broadway.* New York: Macmillan, 1974.

Austin, William W. *Music in the Twentieth Century.* New York: W.W. Norton, 1966.

Bailey, Pearl. *The Raw Pearl.* New York: Pocket Books, 1969.

Balliett, Whitney. *American Musicians: 50 Portraits in Jazz.* London: Oxford University Press, 1986.

Bane, Michael. *Who's Who in Rock.* New York: Everest House, 1981.

Barbash, Jack, ed. *Unions and Union Leadership.* New York: Harper & Brothers, 1959.

Baskerville, David. *Music Business Handbook and Career Guide,* fourth edition. Los Angeles, Denver: Sherwood Co., 1985.

Baumol, William J. and William G. Bowen, *Performing Arts: The Economics Dilemma.* New York: Twentieth-Century Fund, 1966.

Becker, Howard S. *Outsiders: Studies in the Sociology of Deviance.* New York: Macmillan, 1963.

Bekker, Paul. *The Orchestra.* New York: W.W. Norton, 1936.

Bennett, H. Stith. *On Becoming a Rock Musician.* Amhurst: University of Massachusetts Press, 1980.

Benson, H.W. *Democratic Rights for Union Members.* New York: Association for Union Democracy, 1979.

Bergreen, Laurence. *Look Now, Pay Later: The Rise of Network Broadcasting.* Garden City, N.Y.: Doubleday & Company, 1980.

Bernheim, Alfred L. *The Business of the Theatre: An Economic History of the American Theatre, 1750–1932.* New York: B. Blom, 1964.

Blesh, Rudi and Harriet Janis. *They All Played Ragtime: The Story of American Music,* revised edition. New York: Music Sales Corp., Oak Publications, 1966.

——————. *They All Played Ragtime: The True Story of an American Music.* New York: Alfred A. Knopf, 1959.

Block, Adrienne Fried and Carol Neuls-Bates. *Women in American Music: A Bibliography of Music and Literature.* Westport, Conn.: Greenwood Press, 1979.

Bouton, Jim. *Ball Four.* New York: Dell Publishing, 1970.

Branch, Harold and Irving Dwier. *The Club Date Handbook.* Plainview, N.Y.: Harold Branch Publishing, 1968.

Browning, Norma Lee. *Joe Maddy of Interlochen.* Chicago: Henry Regnery Co., 1963.

Carpenter, Paul S. *Music: An Art and a Business.* Norman: University of Oklahoma Press, 1950.

Chapple, Steve and Reebee Garofalo. *Rock 'n' Roll is Here to Pay: The History and Politics of the Music Industry.* Chicago: Nelson-Hall, 1977.

Chase, Gilbert. *America's Music: From the Pilgrims to the Present,* revised second edition. New York: McGraw-Hill, 1966.

Chasins, Abram. *Leopold Stokowski.* New York: Hawthorn, 1979.

Chilton, John. *Who's Who in Jazz: Storyville to Swing Street.* Philadelphia: Chilton Book Company, 1972.

Coe, Linda and Stephan Benedict, compilers. *Arts Management: An Annotated Bibliography.* Washington: National Endowment for the Arts, Cultural Resources Development Project, 1978.

Commons, John R. *Labor and Administration.* New York: Macmillan Co., 1913.

Condon, Eddie. *We Called It Music.* Narration by Thomas Sugrue. New York: Holt, 1947.

Coryell, Julie and Laura Friedman. *Jazz-Rock Fusion: The People, the Music.* New York: Delacorte Press, 1978.

Coxson, Mona. *Some Straight Talk About the Music Business.* Toronto: CM Books, 1984.

Craven, Robert R., ed. *Symphony Orchestras of the United States.* Westport, Conn.: Greenwood Press, 1986.

Csida, Joseph and June Bundy Csida. *American Entertainment: A Unique History of Popular Show Business.* New York: Watson-Guptill Publications (Billboard), 1978.

Cumming, Robert, ed. *They Talk about Music,* Vols. I & II. Rockville Centre, N.Y.: Belwin/Mills Publishing Corp., 1971.

Dagnal, Cynthia. *Starting Your Own Rock Band.* Chicago: Contemporary Books, 1983.

Dahl, Linda. *Stormy Weather: The Music and Lives of a Century of Jazzwomen.* New York: Pantheon Books, 1984.

Damrosch, Walter. *My Musical Life.* New York: Scribners, 1926.

Davidson, John and Cort Casady. *The Singing Entertainer.* Sherman Oaks, Calif.: Alfred Publishing Company, 1979.

Deering, James W. *Making Money Making Music (No Matter Where You Live).* Cincinnati: Writers Digest Books, 1982.

Dexter, Dave, Jr. *The Jazz Story: From the Nineties to the Sixties.* Englewood Cliffs, N.J.: Prentice-Hall, 1964.

Dickson, Harry Ellis. *Gentlemen, More Dolce Please!* Boston: Beacon Press, 1969.

DiMelglio, John E. *Vaudeville U.S.A.* Bowling Green, Ohio: Bowling Green University Popular Press, 1973.

Dochinger, Beth. "The Movement Towards Participation of Symphony Musicians: AFM vs. ICSOM." Unpublished Arts Administration Research Report. University of Cincinnati, 1984.

Dubinsky, David and A.H. Raskin. *David Dubinsky: A Life with Labor.* New York: Simon & Schuster, 1977.

Dworkin, James B. *Owners Versus Players: Baseball and Collective Bargaining.* Boston: Auburn House, 1981.

Ellington, Duke. *Music is my Mistress.* Garden City, N.Y.: Doubleday, 1973.

Epstein, Helen. *Music Talks: Conversations with Musicians.* New York: McGraw-Hill, 1987.

Epstein, Lavily Keir, ed. *Women in Professions.* Lexington, Mass.: Lexington Books, 1975.

Erskine, John. *The Philharmonic-Symphony Society of New York: Its First Hundred Years.* New York: Macmillan, 1943.

Estey, Marten. *The Unions: Structure, Development, and Management,* second edition. New York: Harcourt Brace Jovanovich, Inc., 1976.

Etzkorn, K. Peter, ed. *Music and Society.* New York: Wiley, 1973.

Faulkner, Robert R. *Hollywood Studio Musicians: Their Work and Careers in the Recording Industry.* Chicago & New York: Aldine-Atherton, 1971.

_____. *Music on Demand.* New Brunswick, N.J.: Transaction, 1983.

Ferman, Louis A., ed. *The Future of American Unionism.* Vol. 473, May 1984. The Annals of the American Academy of Political and Social Science. Beverly Hills, Calif.: Sage Publications, 1984.

Fink, Gary M., ed. *Labor Unions.* Westport, Conn.: Greenwood Press, 1977.

Ford Foundation. *The Finances of the Performing Arts,* Vols. I & II. New York: 1974.

Fox, Dan, ed. *How to Make Money Playing Rock Guitar.* New York: G. Schirmer, 1976.

Freeman, Richard B. and James L. Medoff. *What Do Unions Do?* New York: Basic Books, 1984.

Frey, Eugene Victor. "Jullien in America." Unpublished MM thesis, University of Cincinnati, 1956.

Furlong, William Barry. *Season with Solti: A Year in the Life of the Chicago Symphony.* New York: Macmillan, 1974.

Gans, Herbert. *Popular Culture and High Culture.* New York: Basic Books, 1974.

Gaventa, John. *Power and Powerlessness.* Oxford: Clarendon Press, 1980.

Gelatt, Roland. *The Fabulous Phonograph: From Edison to Stereo.* New York: Appleton-Century-Crofts, 1966.

Gerson, Robert A. *Music in Philadelphia.* Philadelphia: Theodore Presser, 1940.

Gibson, James R. *How to Make More in Music: A Freelance Guide.* Atlanta: Workbooks Press, 1984.

Gifford, Courtney D., ed. *Directory of U.S. Labor Organizations, 1982–83*. Washington, D.C.: Bureau of National Affairs, 1982.

Gilbert, Douglas. *American Vaudeville, Its Life and Times*. New York: Whittlesey House, 1940.

Ginzberg, Eli and Hyman Berman. *The American Worker in the Twentieth Century: A History Through Autobiographies*. New York: Free Press of Glencoe, 1963.

Goldin, Milton. *The Music Merchants*. New York: Macmillan, 1969.

Gompers, Samuel. *Seventy Years of Life and Labor*. New York: E.P. Dutton & Co., 1925.

Goodman, Benny and Irving Kolodin. *The Kingdom of Swing*. Harrisburg, Pa.: Stackpole Sons, 1939.

Gorman, Robert A. *The Recording Musician and Union Power: A Case Study of the American Federation of Musicians*. Performance Rights in Sound Recordings. Subcommittee on Courts, Civil Liberties, and the Administration of Justice of the Committee on the Judiciary, House of Representatives, Ninety-Fifth Congress, Second Session, Washington, D.C.: U.S. Government Printing Office, 1978.

Goulden, Joseph C. *The Money Givers*. New York: Random House, 1971.

Grant, Margaret S. and Herman S. Hettinger. *America's Symphony Orchestras*. New York: Norton, 1940.

Green, Abel and Joe Laurie, Jr. *Show Biz: From Vaude to Video*. New York: Henry Holt and Company, 1951.

Hair, Roy. *Making it in The Music Business*. New York: American Federation of Musicians, 1985.

Handy, D. Antoinette. *Black Women in American Bands and Orchestras*. Metuchen, N.J.: Scarecrow Press, 1981.

Harding, Alfred. *The Revolt of the Actors.* New York: William Morrow & Co., 1929.

Hart, Philip. *Orpheus in the New World.* New York: Norton, 1973.

Hazen, Margaret Hindle and Robert M. Hazen. *The Music Men: An Illustrated History of Brass Bands in America, 1800–1920.* Washington, D.C.: Smithsonian Institution Press, 1987.

Henderson, Luther Lincoln. "The Role of the New York Philharmonic's Director of Educational Activities: A New Dimension for the Conductor." Unpublished DMA Dissertation, University of Texas, Austin. Ann Arbor: University Microfilms International, 1980.

Hill, Thomas H. and Helen M. Thompson, eds. *The Organization, Administration and Presentation of Symphony Orchestra Youth Concert Activities for Music Education Purposes in Selected Cities.* Washington, D.C.: Office of Education, Bureau of Research, 1968.

Hirsch, S. Carl. *This is Automation.* New York: Viking Press, 1964.

Hixon, Don L. and Don Hennessee. *Women in Music: A Bio-bibliography.* Metuchen, N.J.: Scarecrow Press, 1975.

Holmes, Lowell D. and John W. Thomson. *Jazz Greats: Getting Better with Age.* New York: Holmes & Meier, 1986.

Howard, Donald S. *The WPA and Federal Relief Policy.* New York: Russell Sage Foundation, 1943.

Howard, John Tasker. *Our American Music.* New York: Crowell, 1946.

Howe, M.A. DeWolf. *The Boston Symphony Orchestra 1881–1931.* Boston: Houghton Mifflin, 1931.

Hughes, Charles W. *The Human Side of Music.* New York: Philosophical Library, 1948.

Hurok, Solomon. *Impresario.* New York: Random House, 1960.

Hutchinson, John. *The Imperfect Union: A History of Corruption in American Trade Unions.* New York: Dutton, 1970.

Jones, LeRoi. *Blues People: Negro Music in White America.* New York: William Morrow, 1963.

Kaplan, Max. "The Musician in America: A Study of His Social Roles." Unpublished Ph.D. dissertation, University of Illinois. Ann Arbor, Michigan: University Microfilms, 1951.

Keil, Charles. *Urban Blues.* Chicago: University of Chicago Press, 1966.

Kennedy, Thomas. *Automation Funds and Displaced Workers.* Boston: Harvard University Press, 1962.

Koenig, Allen E., ed. *Broadcasting and Bargaining: Labor Relations in Radio and Television.* Madison: University of Wisconsin Press, 1970.

Krehbiel, Henry Edward. *The Philharmonic Society of New York.* New York and London: Novello, Ewer and Co., 1892.

Kupferberg, Herbert. *Those Fabulous Philadelphians.* New York: Scribner's, 1969.

Labor Institute for Human Enrichment. *Employment in the Performing Arts: Reality and Myth.* Washington, D.C.: Labor Institute for Human Enrichment in cooperation with the AFL-CIO Department for Professional Employees, N.D.

Lavine, Lauren W. "Structural Changes in Interdependent Relationships within the Symphony Orchestra in America: A Study of Interaction between Orchestra and Management." Unpublished Master's Thesis, Arts Administration Program, Columbia University, New York, 1983.

LeBlond, Richard Emmett, Jr. "Professionalization and Bureaucratization of the Performance of Serious Music in the United States." Unpublished Ph.D. dissertation. University of Michigan, Ann Arbor, Michigan: University Microfilms, 1968.

Leichtenstritt, Hugo. *Serge Koussevitzky: The Boston Symphony Orchestra and the New American Music.* Cambridge, Mass.: Harvard University Press, 1946.

Leiter, Robert D. *The Musicians and Petrillo.* New York: Bookman Associates, 1953.

Leonard, Neil. *Jazz and the White Americans: The Acceptance of a New Art Form.* Chicago: University of Chicago Press, 1962.

Levant, Oscar. *A Smattering of Ignorance.* New York: Doubleday, Dorman, 1940.

Lewiton, Mina. *John Philip Sousa, The March King.* New York: Didier, 1944.

Loft, Abram. "Musicians' Guild and Union: A Consideration of the Evolutions of Protective Organization among Musicians." Unpublished Ph.D. Dissertation. Columbia University, New York, 1950.

Lovell, Hugh and Tasile Carter. *Collective Bargaining in the Motion Picture Industry.* Berkeley: Institute of Industrial Relations, University of California–Berkeley, 1955.

Lull, James. *Popular Music and Communication.* Newbury Park, Calif.: Sage Publications, 1987.

Lunden, Leon Emanuel. "Major Symphony Orchestra Labor Relations." Unpublished Ph.D. dissertation, University of Wisconsin. Ann Arbor: University Microfilms International, 1967.

MacLeod, Bruce Alan. "Music for All Occasions: The Club Date Business of Metropolitan New York City." Unpublished Ph.D. dissertation, Wesleyan University. Ann Arbor: University Microfilms International, 1979.

Madeira, L.C., compiler. *Annals of Music in Philadelphia and History of the Musical Fund Society from its Organization in 1820 to the Year 1858.* Edited by Philip H. Geopp. Philadelphia: J.B. Lippincott Company, 1896.

Malone, Bill C. *Country Music, U.S.A.* Austin: University of Texas Press, 1968.

Marsh, Robert C. *The Cleveland Orchestra.* Cleveland: World, 1967.

May, Earl Chapin. *The Circus from Rome to Ringling.* New York: Dover, 1963.

McCarthy, Albert J. *Big Band Jazz.* New York: G.P. Putnam's Sons, 1974.

—————. *The Dance Band Era.* London: Hamlyn Publishing Group, 1971.

—————. *Louis Armstrong.* New York: A.S. Barnes and Co., 1961.

McDonald, William F. *Federal Relief Administration and the Arts.* Columbus: Ohio State University Press, 1969.

Mellers, Wilfrid. *Music and Society.* New York: Roy Publishers, 1950.

Midwest Research Institute. *An Evaluation of the Performing Arts: The Symphony.* Kansas City, 1969.

Miernyk, William H. *Trade Unions in the Age of Affluence.* New York: Random House, 1962.

Miller, Russell and Roger Boar. *The Incredible Music Machine.* London: Quartet Books Ltd., 1982.

Moldea, Dan E. *Dark Victory: Ronald Reagan, MCA and the Mob.* New York: Viking, 1986.

Montgomery, David. *Workers' Control in America.* New York: Cambridge University Press, 1979.

Morison, Bradley and Kay Fliehr. *In Search of an Audience.* New York: Pitman, 1968.

Morris, Richard B., ed. *The United States Department of Labor Bicentennial History of the American Worker.* Washington: U.S. Department of Labor, 1977.

Moskow, Michael H. *Labor Relations in the Performing Arts: A Preliminary Survey.* New York: Associated Councils of the Arts, 1969.

Mueller, John H. *The American Symphony Orchestra.* Bloomington: Indiana University Press, 1951.

Mueller, Kate Hevner. *Twenty-Seven Major American Symphony Orchestras.* Bloomington: Indiana University Press, 1973.

Music Assistance Fund. *Music Assistance Fund Brochure.* New York: N.D.

Music Performance Trust Funds. *A Guide to Creative Programming.* N.D.

——————. *Music Live and Free.* New York: N.D.

——————. *Trustee's Regulations. Revised 1978.* New York: N.D.

Musselman, Joseph A. *Music in the Cultured Generation.* Evanston, Ill.: Northwestern University Press, 1971.

Nanry, Charles. "The Occupational Subculture of the Jazz Musician: Myth and Reality." Unpublished Ph.D. dissertation, Rutgers University, 1970.

National Committee for Cultural Resources. *National Report on the Arts.* New York: NCCR, 1975.

The National Committee for Symphony Orchestra Support. *Funding the Arts: An Economic, Educational and Cultural Priority.* March 1975.

National Endowment for the Arts. *Artists Compared by Age, Sex and Earnings in 1970 & 1976.* Washington, D.C.: January 1980.

_____. *Artists Employment and Unemployment: 1971–1980.* Washington, D.C.: January 1982.

_____. *Economic Aspects of the Peforming Arts: A Portrait in Figures.* Washington, D.C.: May 1971.

_____. *1985 Annual Report, 20th Anniversary.* Washington, D.C.: U.S. Government Printing Office.

National Music League. *The Future of Concerts and the Young Concert Musician.* New York: 1969.

National Research Center of the Arts. *Americans and the Arts.* New York: Associated Councils of the Arts, 1974.

Netzer, Richard. *The Subsidized Muse: Public Support for the Arts in the United States.* Cambridge, Mass.: Cambridge University Press, 1978.

Northrup, Herbert R. *Organized Labor and the Negro.* New York: Harper & Brothers, 1944.

Otis, Philo A. *The Chicago Symphony Orchestra: Its Organization, Growth and Development.* Chicago: Clayton F. Summy, 1924.

Placksin, Sally. *American Women in Jazz: 1900 to the Present.* New York: Seaview Books, 1982.

Raynor, Henry. *The Orchestra.* New York: Scribners, 1978.

_____. *A Social History of Music.* New York: Schocken, 1972.

Read, Oliver and Walter L. Welch. *From Tin Foil to Stereo: Evolution of the Phonograph,* second edition. Indianapolis: Howard W. Sams & Co., 1976.

Reische, Diane L., ed. *The Performing Arts in America.* New York: H.W. Wilson Co., 1973.

Reiss, Alvin H. *The Arts Management Handbook.* New York: Laws-Arts Publishers, 1970.

Rich, Allen. *Careers and Opportunities in Music.* New York: Dutton, 1964.

Rockefeller Brothers Fund. *The Performing Arts: Problems and Prospects.* A Rockefeller Panel Report. New York: McGraw-Hill, 1965.

Roe, Wellington. *Juggernaut: American Labor in Action.* Philadelphia and New York: J.B. Lippincott, 1948.

Ross, Murray. *Stars and Strikes.* New York: Columbia University Press, 1941.

Ross, Steven Joseph. *Workers on the Edge.* New York: Columbia University Press, 1985.

Russcol, Herbert and Margalit Banai. *Philharmonic.* New York: Coward McCann and Geoghegan, 1970.

Russell, Charles Edward. *The American Orchestra and Theodore Thomas.* Garden City, N.Y.: Doubleday, Page, 1927.

Ruttenberg, Friedman, Kilgallon, Gutchess & Associates. "Working and not Working in the Performing Arts: A Survey of Employment, Underemployment and Unemployment among Performing Artists in 1980." Unpublished research prepared for the Labor Institute for Human Enrichment, Inc. in cooperation with the Department for Professional Employees, AFL-CIO, N.D.

Ryan, John. *The Production of Culture in the Music Industry: The ASCAP-BMI Controversy.* Lanham, Md.: University Press of America, 1985.

Schlesinger, Janet. *Challenge to the Urban Orchestra—The Case of the Pittsburgh Symphony.* N.P., 1971.

Schwartz, Alvin. *The Unions: What They Are; How They Came to Be: How They Affect Each of Us.* New York: Viking Press, 1972.

Schwartz, H.W. *Bands of America.* Garden City, N.Y.: Doubleday & Co., 1957.

Schwartz, Nancy Lynn (completed by Sheila Schwartz). *The Hollywood Writers' Wars*. New York: Knopf, 1981.

Scola, Guy A. "The History of the American Federation of Musicians of the United States and Canada, 1896 through 1980." Unpublished research, N.D.

Screen Actors Guild. *Constitution and By-Laws, 1933–1983*. February 1983.

_____. *The Story of the Screen Actors Guild*. Los Angeles: 1982.

Seligson, Sureva. *Economic Aspects of the Performing Arts: A Portrait in Figures*. Washington, D.C.: Government Printing Office, 1971.

Seltzer, George, ed. *The Professional Symphony Orchestra in the United States*. Metuchen, N.J.: Scarecrow Press, 1975.

Shanet, Howard. *Philharmonic: A History of New York's Orchestra*. New York: Doubleday, 1975.

Sharp, Erica. *How to Get an Orchestra Job—And Keep It*. Encinitas, Calif.: Encinitas Press, 1985.

Shaw, Arnold. *The Jazz Age*. New York: Oxford University Press, 1987.

_____. *The Rockin' '50s*. New York: Hawthorn Books, 1974.

Shemel, Sidney and M. William Krasilovsky. *This Business of Music*. New York: Billboard Publishing Co., 1977.

Siegel, Alan H. *Breakin' into the Music Business*. Port Chester, N.Y.: Cherry Lane Publishing Company, 1986.

Silbermann, Alphons. *The Sociology of Music*. Translated by Corbet Stewart. London: Routledge and Kegan Paul, 1963.

Simon, George T. *The Big Bands*. New York: Macmillan Publishing Company, 1967.

Smith, Moses. *Koussevitsky.* New York: Allen, Towne and Heath, 1947.

Snyder, Carl Dean. *White-Collar Workers and the UAW.* Urbana: University of Illinois Press, 1973.

Sousa, John Philip. *Marching Along; Recollections of Men, Women and Music.* Boston: Hale, Cushman & Flint, 1928.

Spero, Sterling D. and Abram L. Harris. *The Black Worker: A Study of the Negro and the Labor Movement.* New York: Columbia University Press, 1931.

Spivey, Donald. *Union and the Black Musician: The Narrative of William Everett Samuels and Chicago Local 208.* Lanham, Md.: University Press of America, 1984.

Staudohar, Paul D. *The Sports Industry and Collective Bargaining.* New York: ILR Press, 1986.

Stoddard, Hope. *Subsidy Makes Sense.* Newark, N.J.: American Federation of Musicians, N.D.

Sultan, Paul E. *The Disenchanted Unionist.* New York: Harper & Row, 1963.

Swododa, Henry, ed. *The American Symphony Orchestra.* New York: Basic Books, 1967.

Taft, Philip. *Organized Labor in American History.* New York: Harper & Row, 1964.

Taubman, Howard. *The Music Profession.* New York: Scribners, 1939.

Thomas, J.C. *Chasin the Trane: The Music and Mystique of John Coltrane.* New York: DeCapo Press, 1976.

Thompson, Helen M. *Report of Study on Governing Boards of Symphony Orchestras.* Charleston, W.Va.: American Symphony Orchestra League, 1958.

Thomson, Virgil. *The State of Music.* New York: Morrow, 1939.

Toll, Robert C. *Blacking Up: The Minstrel Show in Nineteenth Century America.* New York: Oxford University Press, 1974.

Toobin, Jerome. *Agitato: A Trek through the Musical Jungle.* New York: Viking Press, 1975.

Troy, Leo and Neil Sheflin. *Union Sourcebook.* West Orange, N.J.: Irdis, 1985.

Twentieth-Century Fund. *How Collective Bargaining Works.* New York: 1942.

Ulanov, Berry. *A History of Jazz in America.* New York: DeCapo Press, 1972.

United States Bureau of Labor Statistics. *A Brief History of the American Labor Movement,* Third Edition, Bulletin #1000. Washington, D.C.: U.S. Government Printing Office, 1964.

Wacholtz, Larry E. *Inside Country Music.* Marshall, Wash.: Thumbs Up Publishing Company, 1984.

Weissman, Dick. *The Music Business: Career Opportunities and Self-Defense.* New York: Crown, 1979.

Williams, Raymond. *Culture and Society.* Garden City, N.Y.: Doubleday Anchor Books, 1960.

Willis, Thomas. *The Chicago Symphony Orchestra.* Chicago: Rand McNally, 1974.

Zeidman, Irving. *The American Burlesque Show.* New York: Hawthorn Books, 1967.

Zieger, Robert H. *American Workers, American Unions, 1920–1985.* Baltimore: Johns Hopkins University Press, 1987.

ARTICLES

Aarons, Max. "Strike! Strike! Strike!" *International Musician,* March 1976.

Acker, Robert. "Club Dates and the Free-Lance Guitarist." *International Musician,* November 1982.

Allen, Sanford. "Why Hasn't the Negro Found a Place in the Symphony." *The New York Times,* June 25, 1967.

American Labor Staff. "Congress of Strings." *American Labor,* June 1968.

——————. "Herman David Kenin; Pragmatist with a Soul." *American Labor,* June 1970.

——————. "There's No Business Like—." *American Labor,* September 1968.

American Symphony Orchestra League. "Women in American Symphony Orchestras." *Symphony News,* April 1976.

Anderson, A. Donald. "A Computer for Tin Pan Alley." *New York Times,* July 3, 1988.

——————. "What's New in Electronic Music." *New York Times,* November 22, 1987.

Apone, Carl. "Symphonies Vie for Top Orchestras' String Players." *Pittsburgh Press,* April 25, 1971.

Arian, Edward. "Some Problems of Collective Bargaining in Symphony Orchestras." *Labor Law Review,* November 1974.

Austin, Mary. "Petrillo's War." *Journal of Popular Culture.* Summer 1978.

Bagley, C.L. "Indianapolis in Federation History." *International Musician,* May 1940.

Balliett, Whitney. "Art Tatum." *New Yorker,* September 9, 1985.

——————. "Black and White." *New Yorker,* July 21, 1986.

——————. "Coleman Hawkins." *New Yorker,* October 28, 1985.

——————. "Joe Wilder." *New Yorker,* January 6, 1986.

——————. "John Hammond and Dick Wellstood." *New Yorker,* August 31, 1987.

——————. "Little Jazz." *New Yorker,* December 16, 1985.

——————. "Scoop." *New Yorker,* November 10, 1986.

——————. "Still There." *New Yorker,* August 5, 1985.

Baumol, Hilda and William Baumol. "In Culture, the Cost Disease Is Contagious." *The New York Times,* June 3, 1984.

Beatty, Jerome. "Hard-Boiled Maestro." *American Magazine,* October 1940.

Bedell, Douglas H. "When Is a Musician Too Old." *Philadelphia Bulletin,* September 26, 1961.

Bellamy, Ralph. "The Union with a Difference." *American Federationist,* June 1963.

Berger, Joseph. "Excellence and Equality: A Conflict?" *The New York Times,* March 4, 1987.

Bergman, Bruce. "Getting Ahead in Club Date Rock Guitaring." *International Musician,* January, February 1980.

Bernhardt, Clyde E.B. and Sheldon Harris. "The Memoirs of a Jazzman." *The New York Times,* June 1, 1986.

Berry, Jason. "The Cradle of Jazz Still Swings." *New Orleans Guest Informant,* 1984–1985 edition.

Blau, Judith R. "High Culture as Mass Culture." *Culture and Society,* May/June 1986.

Blitz, Rudolph C. "Women in the Professions, 1870–1970." *Monthly Labor Review,* May 1974.

Bloom, Steven M. "American Labor at the Crossroads." *American Demographics,* September 1985.

Brustein, Robert. "Can the Show Go On?" *The New York Times,* July 10, 1977.

_____. "The Coming Crisis for the Arts: Who's Going to Foot the Bill?" *The New York Times,* September 15, 1974.

Bundy, June. "Petrillo Retires, and Everybody Weeps; Kenin Gets Post." *Billboard,* June 9, 1958.

Burns, Don. "The Distaff'd Composers." *Music Journal,* March 1974.

Burrell, Melanie. "The Professional Problems of Orchestra Women." *Senza Sordino,* April 1982.

Business Week Staff. "Coping with Automation." *Business Week,* June 9, 1956.

_____. "Most Union Honchos Escaped the Squeeze that Pinched the Rank and File." *Business Week,* June 25, 1984.

_____. "Rank-and-File Austerity Filter Upward." *Business Week,* May 10, 1982.

Calta, Louis. "Dissidents Stir Musicians' Union." *The New York Times,* February 25, 1964.

Campbell, Mary. "Few Blacks in Classical Orchestras." *Rocky Mountain News,* January 18, 1970.

Cerulli, Dom. "Marian McPartland." *International Musician,* December 1959.

Chamot, Dennis. "Professional Employees Turn to Unions." *Harvard Business Review,* May/June 1976.

Chancellor, John. "Melodic Lines and Bottom Lines." *Symphony News,* August/September 1983.

Clarke, George A. "A Pension Plan for Musicians: The American Federation of Musicians' and Employers' Pension Welfare Fund." *International Musician,* June 1960.

Clendinen, Dudley. "At 100, the Boston Pops Still Packs Them In." *The New York Times,* May 1, 1985.

Cohen, Joe. "N.Y. State Joins U.S. Congress in Battle to Declare Performers Are Employees and Not Indies." *Variety,* May 23, 1984.

Collins, Julia. "Music Copyists: Dwindling Breed, But a Hardy One." *The New York Times,* May 15, 1988.

Commons, John R. "Types of American Labor Unions—The Musicians of St. Louis and New York." *Quarterly Journal of Economics,* May 1906.

Conroy, Frank. "Lester Lanin: The Beat Goes On for the Ageless Leader of America's Name-brand Dance Band." *People Weekly,* December 21, 1987.

Cooklis, Ray. "Knowing the Score." *Cincinnati Enquirer,* October 29, 1985.

Cooper, Wendy. "Labor's New Drive to Learn about the Bottom Line." *The New York Times,* July 24, 1983.

Cory, Ed. "Angry Musicians: Hollywood Local Aims to Hike Its Own Take, Clip Petrillo's Power." *Wall Street Journal,* June 11, 1956.

Coughlan, Robert. "Petrillo." *Life,* August 3, 1942.

Countryman, Vern. "The Organized Musicians." *University of Chicago Law Review,* Part I: Autumn 1948, and Part II: Winter 1949.

Cox, Meg. "More Work Leaves Less Time for Arts, Harris Survey Says." *Wall Street Journal,* March 16, 1988.

——————. "Stock-Music Houses Offer Grunts, Slurps, Rattles, Pseudo-Beatles and Beethoven." *Wall Street Journal,* February 5, 1985.

Cox, Patrick. "Unions Won't Change, Don't Deserve a Future." *USA Today,* August 30, 1985.

Crouch, Beth. "Earning a Living in the Lively Arts." *Catalyst,* September 1975.

Crutchfield, Will. "Why Today's Orchestras Are Adrift." *The New York Times,* December 22, 1985.

Cummings, Judith. "Blacks Gain on Broadway; Lag in 2 Other Arts." *The New York Times,* June 6, 1975.

Cummings, Michael. "The Father of the American Concert Band." *International Musician,* March 1970.

Current, Gloster B. "Celebration of Black Composers—Black Music at the Philharmonic." *Crisis,* January 1978.

Davis, Peter G. "Met Opera and Its Unions to Resume Talks Today." *The New York Times,* October 4, 1980.

_____. "Opera–Union Talks Unsuccessful." *The New York Times,* October 5, 1980.

_____. "Reform Sought in Way Orchestras Audition." *The New York Times,* May 7, 1981.

_____. "Why Conductors Are Treated like Gods." *The New York Times,* May 7, 1978.

Dawson, John B. "Musical Medicine." *Senza Sordino,* April 1976.

Delatiner, Barbara. "40 Years of Music, Unless it Rains." *The New York Times,* July 7, 1985.

_____. "Philharmonic's Approach Pays Off." *The New York Times,* October 2, 1983.

Dennis, Bruce. "He Was Always Good at Arithmetic." *Saturday Evening Post,* October 12, 1940.

Dibacco, Thomas V. "Labor Has a White-Collar Future." *USA Today,* August 30, 1985.

Dinardo, Robert. "Musicians vs. Tape—A Survival Battle." *The New York Times,* August 22, 1982.

Dixon, Lucille. "Is it 'Artistic Judgement' or Is it Discrimination?" *The New York Times,* August 1, 1971.

Dobroski, Bernard J. "Choosing a Music School." *Instrumentalist,* October 1986.

Dreher, Ted. "Performing-fee Societies." *International Musician,* September 1976.

Dullea, Georgia. "Municipal Music: A Symphony Marks Its 15th Year." *The New York Times,* November 12, 1986.

Durso, Joseph. "Of Batting Averages and Bottom Lines." *The New York Times,* April 7, 1985.

Dyer, Richard. "What's behind the BSO Dispute." *Boston Globe,* October 12, 1986.

Early, Steve. "Revival Is Possible—And Necessary." *The New York Times,* January 20, 1985.

Eckert, Thor, Jr. "Boorishness Pervades World's Orchestras." *Houston Post,* September 2, 1984.

Emge, Charles. "Little Personal Venom in Read and teGroen Fight." *Downbeat,* May 16, 1956.

——————. "Move Grows to Scrap L.A.'s Jim Crow Union." *Downbeat,* June 15, 1951.

End, Jack. "Some Make it, Some Don't." *International Musician,* March 1974.

Epstein, Helen, "The Philharmonic—A Troubled Giant Facing Change." *The New York Times,* December 19, 1976.

——————. "The View from the Second Horn." *The New York Times,* January 20, 1974.

Ericson, Raymond. "The Fight for the Integrated Orchestra." *The New York Times,* October 20, 1974.

——————. "Pioneer and Paragon of Women Flutists Visits to Aid Mannes." *The New York Times,* January 12, 1979.

Fantel, Hans. "Barriers to DAT Recorders Are Breaking Down." *The New York Times,* April 24, 1988.

——————. "Newcomers Seek Admission to the Family of Instruments." *The New York Times,* August 19, 1984.

Ferretti, Fred. "Silent Opera: Restaurants Sing Blues." *The New York Times,* October 22, 1980.

Flaim, Paul O. "New Data on Union Members and Their Earnings." *Employment and Earnings,* January 1985.

Fleming, Shirley. "Survival." *Musical America,* July 1982.

Foeller, Ken. "What Does the Union Do for Me?" *International Musician,* June 1976.

Forrester, Joel. "Nightclub Nightmares: A Musician's View." *Downbeat,* May 1987.

Fosburgh, Lacey. "2 Musicians' Jobs Stir Coast Conflict." *The New York Times,* June 12, 1974.

——————. "Two Musicians Reinstated for a Year in Coast Dispute." *The New York Times,* August 2, 1974.

Fowler, Elizabeth M. "Finding a Niche in Music." *The New York Times,* May 28, 1985.

Frank, Allan Dodds. "And the Beat Goes on." *Forbes,* May 18, 1987.

Fraser, C. Gerald. "Strike Threat at Met Part of U.S. Trend." *The New York Times,* December 21, 1975.

Freedman, Audrey. "There's No Recovery in Sight for Unions." *The New York Times,* January 20, 1985.

Freedman, Geraldine. "Women in Jazz." *Allegro,* March 1985.

Freedman, Guy. "The Heifetz of Negotiators." *Music Journal,* January 1976.

Freeman, Ira Henry. "Petrillo Will Retire; Led Union 18 Years." *The New York Times,* May 15, 1958.

Friedwald, Will. "Ghost Bands—Very Much Alive." *The New York Times,* February 7, 1988.

Fuentealba, Victor W. "AFM's 'Young Sounds' Program Is Revitalized." *International Musician,* September 1978.

——————. "Musicians Aren't a Typing Pool." *International Musician,* July 1978.

Gale, Jack. "Contract Enforcement." *Allegro,* September 1985.

——————. "Modern Recording Techniques." *Allegro,* December 1985.

——————. "Non-Union Dates." *Allegro,* May 1985.

——————. "The Phonograph Industry." *Allegro,* November 1986.

——————. "Runaway Productions." *Allegro,* July–August 1985.

——————. "Synthesizer Use." *Allegro,* June 1985.

Gargan, Edward A. "Past Is Swinging at Club for 'Colored Musicians.'" *The New York Times,* August 7, 1985.

Garvey, Edward R. "From Chattel to Employee: The Athlete's

Quest for Freedom and Dignity." *The Annals of the American Academy of Political and Social Science,* September 1979.

Gent, George. "Movie Unions are Accused of Job Discrimination." *The New York Times,* August 28, 1968.

Ginell, Richard S. "High Tech Threatens to Take Music Away from the Musicians." *Overture,* October 1986.

Glasel, John. "The Jazz Musician and the Union." *Allegro,* November 1984.

—————. "Wither Synthesizers?" *Allegro,* June 1987.

Glueck, Grace. "A Federal Benefactor of the Arts Comes of Age." *The New York Times,* November 10, 1985.

Godbout, Oscar. "Coast Musicians Sue Union Again." *The New York Times,* May 1, 1957.

—————. "Local Votes Out Petrillo Slate." *The New York Times,* December 19, 1956.

Goldberg, Joe. "Making Music by the Byte." *The New York Times,* August 7, 1988.

Greenberg, Gilda M. "Women in Major Symphonies: Why a Minority?" *International Musician,* April 1982.

Greenhouse, Steven. "Reshaping Labor to Woo the Young." *The New York Times,* September 1, 1985.

Griffin, Nancy. "The Minority Orchestral Training Program." *Senza Sordino,* February 1978.

—————. "More on Orchestral Assistance Programs." *Senza Sordino,* April 1978.

Guthrie, Ned. "How We Won the Lea Act Repeal." *International Musician,* January 1981.

Halprin, Diana, "Now or Never." *Allegro,* September 1984.

_____. "Union Standards Endangered." *Allegro,* November 1984.

Hammond, John. "Symphony of the New World." *International Musician,* August 1968.

Haney, F. Paul. "Sonny Osborne Reflects on Music, Life." *International Musician,* September 1984.

Hannusch, Jeff. "Booking the Bands." *New Orleans Magazine,* November 1985.

Harmetz, Aljean. "Musicians in Hollywood Go on Strike." *The New York Times,* August 2, 1980.

_____. "2 Unions Agree to Let Actors Work." *The New York Times,* October 3, 1980.,

Harper, Timothy. "Music Without Musicians." *San Francisco Chronicle,* March 20, 1988.

Harrington, Richard. "Performers on the Job." *Washington Post,* May 24, 1983.

Harris, Roy. "Report on the International String Congress." *International Musician,* September 1959.

Heckscher, August. "The Danger of Amateurism in the Arts." *International Musician,* June 1963.

Helyar, John. "Background Music: Life in the Rear Row of a Major Orchestra Isn't All Sweet Melody." *Wall Street Journal,* January 28, 1981.

Henahan, Donal. "About That Timpanist Who Got Drummed Out." *The New York Times,* September 7, 1975.

_____. "An About Face on Black Musicians at the Philharmonic." *The New York Times,* June 11, 1972.

_____. "The Aging Musician and His Rights." *The New York Times,* June 11, 1978.

_____. "Are Conductors Necessary?" *The New York Times,* April 17, 1983.

_____. "Basking in the Twilight Glow of an Old Master." *The New York Times,* April 20, 1986.

_____. "Concert: Met Orchestra in Mahler's 'Resurrection' " *The New York Times,* December 11, 1980.

_____. "Dark Metropolitan Opera? Trepidation and Sadness." *The New York Times,* October 3, 1980.

_____. "Hiring and Salary Policy of Philharmonic Listed." *The New York Times,* August 2, 1969.

_____. "Labor Trouble at the Met in Perspective." *The New York Times,* October 12, 1980.

_____. "Only Black in Philharmonic Is Resigning After 15 Years." *The New York Times,* August 29, 1977.

_____. "Opera's Own Drama Played Behind Scenes." *The New York Times,* July 14, 1983.

_____. "The Philadelphia Gets First Black." *The New York Times,* November 16, 1969.

_____. "Philharmonic, City in Antibias Pact." *The New York Times,* May 30, 1971.

_____. "Philharmonic Plans Workshop, Its First, To Train Minorities." *The New York Times,* August 27, 1971.

_____. "Philharmonic's Hiring Policy Defended." *The New York Times,* July 31, 1969.

_____. "Philharmonicsville (pop. 106)." *The New York Times,* September 28, 1969.

_____. "Remember When Toscanini Forgot." *The New York Times,* May 29, 1988.

_____. "Rights Unit Bars Philharmonic from Filling 2 Disputed Chairs." *The New York Times*, November 27, 1969.

_____. "The San Francisco Musicians' Revolt Is Shaking the Conductor's Podium." *The New York Times*, June 16, 1974.

_____. "A Tough New Role for Beverly." *The New York Times*, September 23, 1979.

_____. "What Price Peace at the Metropolitan." *The New York Times*, December 7, 1980.

_____. "Which Runs an Orchestra: the Conductor? the Men? the Dollar?" *The New York Times*, May 18, 1969.

_____. "Will 'Cultural Apartheid' Poison the Arts in America?" *The New York Times*, August 28, 1977.

_____. "Women Are Breaking the Symphonic Barriers." *The New York Times*, January 23, 1983.

Hentoff, Nat. "Anti-Petrillo Rumblings Heard in New York 802." *Downbeat*, May 16, 1956.

_____. "A Honky-Tonk Crooner." *Wall Street Journal*, November 5, 1986.

_____. "The Sweethearts of Rhythm.": *Overture*, April 1985.

Hershenson, Roberta. "Portrait of an Oboe Player: A Deepening Commitment." *The New York Times*, January 19, 1986.

Hickman, C. Sharpless. "Los Angeles' Local Forty-Seven: A Model Union." *Music Journal*, May 1954.

Hinely, Mary Brown. "The Uphill Climb of Women in American Music: Performers and Teachers." *Music Educators Journal*, April 1984.

Hinton-Braaten, Kathleen. "Symphony Auditions—The Tough Way to Get a Job." *International Musician*, July 1980.

Holden, Stephen. "Whitney Houston—Pop's New Queen." *The New York Times,* May 25, 1986.

Holland, Bernard. "The Fair, New World of Orchestra Auditions." *The New York Times,* January 11, 1981.

————————. "It Takes More than Talent to Build a Musical Career." *The New York Times,* February 19, 1984.

————————. "Met Opera Contract May Have Long-Term Effect." *The New York Times,* December 11, 1983.

————————. "Violist, 20, Attains Philharmonic Post." *The New York Times,* February 12, 1986.

————————. "What Will All These Musicians Do." *The New York Times,* June 16, 1985.

————————. "Youth Revitalizes the Symphony Orchestra." *The New York Times,* April 13, 1986.

Hughes, Allen. "New Faces for Tonight's Philharmonic." *The New York Times,* November 11, 1971.

————————. "Singers' Union Joins Met Musicians' Pickets." *The New York Times,* September 3, 1980.

Hunter, Charlayne. "Harlem a Symphony for Orchestra." *The New York Times,* November 16, 1971.

James, George. "New York City's Own Music Man Recollects Ice Cream with Sousa." *The New York Times,* June 20, 1987.

Janson, Donald. "AFM Shelves Bid for Integration." *The New York Times,* June 14, 1957.

————————. "Negro Violinist Wins an Apology." *The New York Times,* February 13, 1963.

————————. "Petrillo Pleads for Cut in Power." *The New York Times,* June 13, 1957.

―――――――――. "Petrillo Reports Union in Harmony." *The New York Times*, June 11, 1957.

Johnson, Ron D. "The World's Greatest Jazzband." *Mississippi Rag*, December 1973.

Johnston, Laurie. "At the Met, 'Civilization' Takes Leave of Absence." *The New York Times*, September 26, 1980.

Joyce, Fay S. "Opera Strike Mediator See Solution 'In Time.' " *The New York Times*, July 11, 1983.

Kaiser, Henry. "Report on California Trust Fund Cases." *International Musician*, May 1957.

Kart, Larry. "Juggernaut's Jazz True to Big Bands." *Chicago Tribune*, November 22, 1986.

Kella, John J. "Medical and Social Concerns of Musicians." *Allegro*, April 1988.

Keller, Bill. "Unions' Economic Troubles Are Spurring Merger Trend." *The New York Times*, May 13, 1984.

Kenin, Herman D. "Conserving America's Cultural Resources." *Senza Sordino*, April 1977.

―――――――――. "The Growth of the AFM–EPW Fund." *International Musician*, March 1967.

―――――――――. "Musicians' World-Wide Rights in Mechanicals." *International Musician*, May 1950.

Kerner, Leighton. "The End of the Met?" *Village Voice*, October 8–14, 1980.

Kihss, Peter. "Orchestras Here Accused of Bias." *The New York Times*, November 18, 1958.

Kilpatrick, James J. "Hard Times for the Unions." *Cincinnati Enquirer*, May 19, 1985.

King, Marshall. "Getting Your Foot in the Door." *International Musician,* January 1983.

King, Peter B. "Musicians' Union Beats Drum for Taft–Hartley Amendment." *Pittsburgh Press,* July 7, 1985.

—————. "Musicians' Union Fights for Jobs as Synthesizers Tune Them Out." *Pittsburgh Press,* July 7, 1985.

Kiraly, Philippa. "Youth Concerts Come of Age." *Symphony Magazine,* February/March 1984.

Kirk, Cynthia. "AFM Convention Delegates Save Work Levy, Reject One-Time Tax; Union Will Remain in AFL–CIO." *Variety,* July 1, 1981.

—————. "Battle Lines Drawn between Large, Small Locals on Work Levy." *Variety,* April 29, 1981.

—————. "Fuentealba Warns of Bankruptcy unless AFM Can Trim Deficit." *Variety,* June 27, 1979.

—————. "Musicians' Union Returns to Solvency." *Variety,* June 29, 1983.

—————. "Travelling Musicians' Woes Addressed at AFM Convention, National Work Levy Retained." *Variety,* July 6, 1983.

Kirk, Russell. "Musicians' Union Plays Off Key." *Boston Herald,* May 30, 1963.

Kirkland, Lane. "New Solidarity Spirit is Bolstering Unions." *USA Today,* August 30, 1985.

Kleiman, Dena. "A Few Good Musicians." *The New York Times,* May 14, 1985.

Klemesrud, Judy. "Is Women's Lib Coming to the Philharmonic?" *The New York Times,* April 11, 1971.

——————. "Mehta's Mystique: Baton in Hand, Foot in Mouth?" *The New York Times,* October 18, 1970.

Kolodin, Irving. "Zubin Mehta." *Stereo Review,* September 1978.

Koplewitz, Laura A. "Musicians' Union Debates Freeze." *Alternative Media,* Spring 1983.

Korall, Burt. "Exploring the Versatility of Grady Tate." *International Musician,* July 1984.

——————. "Point of View: Ruby Braff." *International Musician,* June 1985.

Kotlowitz, Alex. "Labor's Ultimate Weapon, the Strike, Is Mostly Failing." *Wall Street Journal,* October 13, 1986.

Kuchwara, Michael. "Musicals Hit Sour Note on Broadway." *Cincinnati Enquirer,* November 30, 1986.

Langley, Allen Lincoln. "The Musician: Artist and Laborer." *The Nation,* September 7, 1921.

Lastrucci, Carlo L. "The Professional Dance Musician." *Journal of Musicology,* Winter 1941.

Lehmann, Phyllis. "Women in Orchestras: The Promise and the Problems." *Symphony News,* December 1982.

Leinsdorf, Erich. "One Conductor's Prescription for Musical Survival." *The New York Times,* March 16, 1986.

Leonard, Arthur S. "Collective Bargaining in Major Orchestras." *Industrial and Labor Relations Forum,* Winter 1975.

Levey, Stanley. "Eisenhower Gets Petrillo Praise." *The New York Times,* June 14, 1956.

——————. "Foe of Petrillo Ousted for Year." *The New York Times,* June 13, 1956.

——————. "Music Union Acts to Check Revolts." *The New York Times,* June 15, 1956.

Levine, Ed. "TV Rocks with Music." *The New York Times,* May 8, 1983.

Lewis, Ephraim. "BW/Harris Poll: Confidence in Unions is Crumbling." *Business Week,* July 8, 1985.

Lewis, Peter H. "Harmony of Art and Science Lifts a Music Industry Barrier." *The New York Times,* March 4, 1987.

Lindsey, Robert. "Las Vegas Strikers Seek Union Boycott." *The New York Times,* April 8, 1984.

Lloyd, Leslie. "Schools Note Growing List of Endangered Instruments." *Cincinnati Enquirer,* June 19, 1988.

Loft, Abram. "Book Review: The Musicians and Petrillo." *Notes,* December 1953.

Lunde, Anders S. "The American Federation of Musicians and the Recording Ban." *Public Opinion Quarterly,* Spring 1948.

Lunden, Leon E. "Bargaining in Major Symphony Orchestras." *Monthly Labor Review,* July 1969.

_____. "Unions, Legislation, and the Courts." *Monthly Labor Review,* October 1965.

Lynes, Russell. "The Case against Government Aid to the Arts." *The New York Times,* March 25, 1962.

Maddy, Joseph. "Statement on the Interlochen Case before the Senate Committee." *Music Educators Journal,* April 1944.

Markey, Morris. "What Petrillo's Victory Means to You." *Liberty,* May 19, 1945.

Matthews, William. "Jingle Music: A Tough Trade." *The New York Times,* August 19, 1984.

McCarthy, Eugene. "Musical Wars." *The New Republic,* January 20, 1982.

McDonough, John. "Heeeere's the Band... But How Much Longer?" *The New York Times,* August 7, 1988.

McNamara, Robert J. "A History of Recording: From Foil to Floppy Discs." *Houston Post,* September 2, 1984.

Miller, Michael W. "High-Tech Alteration of Sights and Sounds Divides the Arts World." *Wall Street Journal,* September 1, 1987.

Millstein, Gilbert. "Mr. Petrillo Talks of Music Etcet." *The New York Times,* June 21, 1953.

Mitgang, Herbert. "Trust Fund Keeps Live Music Alive." *The New York Times,* August 8, 1981.

Molotsky, Irvin. "Carter Asks Opera and Unions to Resume Talks to End Dispute." *The New York Times,* October 3, 1980.

——————. "Smithsonian Musicians vs. Management." *The New York Times,* February 11, 1983.

Morganstern, Joe. "The Blues Man From Boise." *Wall Street Journal,* June 6, 1988.

Musselman, Mary Jane. "Musicians Turn to Other Careers." *The New York Times,* October 10, 1982.

Nelson, Joan. "A Melody for International Women's Year." *International Musician,* July 1975.

Nesbitt, Jim. "Kemp Case Exacerbates Debate over Athletics." *Cincinnati Enquirer,* February 16, 1986.

Newton, James S. "What's New in Music Technology." *The New York Times,* March 1, 1987.

Norton, Mildred. "Musicians' Battle." *Saturday Review,* March 17, 1956.

Nye, William P. "The Social Organization of Time in a Resort Band." *Popular Music and Society,* Vol. 10, No. 4, 1986.

Page, Tim. "Eight Opera Unions Call for Binding Arbitration." *The New York Times,* August 24, 1983.

_____. "An 'Elated' Miss Sills Takes Stock." *The New York Times,* August 31, 1983.

_____. "For Some Gifted Musicians, Freelancing Offers Career." *The New York Times,* January 15, 1984.

_____. "Juilliard's Future Takes Shape." *The New York Times,* October 27, 1985.

_____. "Local President Assails City Opera and Unions." *The New York Times,* August 25, 1983.

Paige, Earl. "The Jukebox Story." *Billboard,* December 27, 1969.

Palmer, Robert. "Nashville Sound: Country Music in Decline." *The New York Times,* September 17, 1985.

Pareles, Jon. "Digital Technology Changing Music." *The New York Times,* October 16, 1986.

_____. "Hearing Jazz at Its Risky Best—in the Clubs." *The New York Times,* June 28, 1987.

_____. "The Legacy of Teddy Wilson's Subtle Approach." *The New York Times,* August 7, 1986.

_____. "Some in Jazz Hope Streets Are Avenue to Success." *The New York Times,* September 26, 1985.

Parmenter, Ross. "Fifty Million: Performance Trust Fund Has Given away that Much in Past 15 Years." *The New York Times,* June 30, 1963.

_____. "Working Part-Time." *The New York Times,* January 1, 1956.

_____. "The World of Music: Petrillo Makes a Decision." *The New York Times,* December 24, 1950.

Parsons, Geoffrey, Jr. and Robert M. Yoder. "Petrillo: Mussolini of Music." *American Mercury,* November 1940.

Pegler, Westbrook. "Thieves with Union Cards." *Collier's,* January 9, 1943.

Per-Lee, Myra. "Reaching out to Minority Musicians." *Symphony News,* April 1979.

Peterson, Iver. "Strike Dims the Glitter of Las Vegas." *The New York Times,* April 22, 1984.

Petrillo, James C. "The Decision of the National War Labor Board and the Canned Music Controversy." *International Musician,* July 1944.

——————. "Man, Machine, Music and Musicians." *International Musician,* April, May, June 1955.

——————. "The Musician's Fight." *International Musician,* October 1955.

Pettigrew, Jim, Jr. "ASCAP: The Business of Performing Rights." *Sky,* December 1986.

Peyser, Joan. "The Negro in Search of an Orchestra." *The New York Times,* November 26, 1967.

Phillips, Harvey E. "American Orchestras Are Back in the Recording Studios." *The New York Times,* September 28, 1975.

Phillips, Karen. "Women Musicians Offer Advice." *Music Journal,* March 1974.

Polisi, Joseph W. "Art, Education and Our Society." *Allegro,* May 1987.

Pollock, Michael A., et al. "Construction Unions Try to Shore up a Crumbling Foundation." *Business Week,* February 4, 1985.

Porter, Bob. "Ghost Bands Keep the Sounds of the Big Band Era Alive." *Cincinnati Enquirer,* January 19, 1986.

Porter, Lewis. "She Wiped All the Men." *Music Educators Journal,* September 1984.

Pryor, Thomas M. "Coast AFM Unit Gets Court Help." *The New York Times,* July 22, 1958.

_____. "New Suit is Filed Against Petrillo." *The New York Times,* November 30, 1956.

Quinn, John C. "Unions Have Future, If They Can Change." *USA Today,* August 30, 1985.

Radel, Cliff. "Royalties Are the Rub in DAT Skirmish." *Cincinnati Enquirer,* March 10, 1987.

_____. "Sounds That Go Round." *Cincinnati Enquirer,* January 3, 1985.

Raskin, A.H. "Labor's Grand Illusions." *The New York Times,* February 10, 1958.

_____. "Musician Rebels Face Suspension." *The New York Times,* May 8, 1956.

_____. "Musicians Scrap Dictational Rule." *The New York Times,* June 6, 1958.

_____. "Petrillo Silent on Election Only." *The New York Times,* June 3, 1958.

_____. "Petrillo Spurns Musicians' Pleas." *The New York Times,* June 4, 1958.

_____. "Petrillo's Choice Heads Musicians." *The New York Times,* June 5, 1958.

_____. "Two Get Backing for Petrillo Post." *The New York Times,* June 1, 1958.

Riccardi, A. Rex. "How to Earn Half a Living, Play in a Symphony Orchestra." *National Music Council,* January 1953.

Rich, Alan. "Symphony in Woe Minor." *Chicago,* December 1977.

Robb, David. "Second-Highest-Paid Labor Leader in Showbiz

Comes from Small Chi Local 110." *Daily Variety,* April 10, 1985.

Rockwell, John. "A.G.M.A. Votes to Wait for Talks by the Met's Chorus." *The New York Times,* November 5, 1980.

_____. "Both Sides in City Opera Strike Pessimistic as They Prepare New Talks." *The New York Times,* July 18, 1983.

_____. "Can the Met Meet the Cost of High Artistic Standards?" *The New York Times,* July 20, 1980.

_____. "City Opera Management Seeks New Contract with Musicians." *The New York Times,* September 1, 1979.

_____. "City Opera Orchestra Votes Today on Contract to End 53-Day Strike." *The New York Times,* August 29, 1983.

_____. "City Opera Proposes Year's Wage Freeze." *The New York Times,* July 29, 1982.

_____. "City Opera Settles Musicians' Dispute." *The New York Times,* October 9, 1979.

_____. "City Opera Strike Seen as Talks Break Down." *The New York Times,* July 6, 1983.

_____. "City Opera Talks Halted; A Strike is Authorized." *The New York Times,* June 23, 1983.

_____. "Electronics Is Challenging Traditions of Music." *The New York Times,* August 7, 1986.

_____. "Gloom at City Opera." *The New York Times,* August 20, 1983.

_____. "Half a Century of Song with the Great 'Ella.'" *The New York Times,* June 15, 1986.

_____. "Hopes Rise for Accord in City Opera Dispute." *The New York Times,* July 7, 1983.

_____. "Impasse at the City Opera." *The New York Times,* July 9, 1983.

_____. "A Lockout at Met Opera Likely as Talks Resume." *The New York Times,* August 30, 1980.

_____. "Many Orchestras in Financial Straits." *The New York Times,* January 19, 1987.

_____. "Met and Orchestra Await Vote on Pact." *The New York Times,* October 27, 1980.

_____. "Met and Orchestra Meet in Daylong Negotiations." *The New York Times,* October 23, 1980.

_____. "Met Cancels '80–81 Opera Season, Blaming Demands of the Orchestra." *The New York Times,* September 30, 1980.

_____. "Met Opens 96th Season with a Few Differences." *The New York Times,* December 11, 1980.

_____. "Met Opera and Orchestra Ratify 4-Year Contract." *The New York Times,* October 28, 1980.

_____. "Met Opera Chorus Meets Today: Vote on Contract Offer Possible." *The New York Times,* November 13, 1980.

_____. "Met Opera Chorus Ratifies Accord; Opening Is Planned about Dec. 8." *The New York Times,* November 14, 1980.

_____. "Met Opera Opens Dec. 10." *The New York Times,* November 18, 1980.

_____. "Met Opera Talks Are at a Standstill; No Sessions Set." *The New York Times,* October 1, 1980.

_____. "Met Opera Unions Focusing on 'Quality of Life' Demands." *The New York Times,* July 10, 1980.

_____. "Music Clubs Resist Perils of Overkill." *The New York Times,* September 4, 1974.

_____. "Opening-Night Strike Set at the City Opera." *The New York Times,* July 2, 1983.

_____. "Opening of Met Sept. 22 'Postponed Indefinitely.'" *The New York Times,* September 10, 1980.

_____. "Opera Board Firm on Strike, But Appears Split Internally." *The New York Times,* August 1, 1983.

_____. "Opera Orchestra's 32-to-21 Vote Ends Strike." *The New York Times,* August 30, 1983.

_____. "Opera Settlement: Weighing the Gains and Losses." *The New York Times,* August 31, 1983.

_____. "Opera Talks Fail, Rehearsals Put Off." *The New York Times,* September 2, 1980.

_____. "The Opera: Who Won?" *The New York Times,* October 29, 1980.

_____. "Orchestra Strike Cancels Opening of City Opera." *The New York Times,* July 8, 1983.

_____. "Parties in City Opera Labor Dispute Meet Today in Hopes of Settlement." *The New York Times,* October 5, 1979.

_____. "Parties in Opera Dispute Gloomy." *The New York Times,* October 7, 1980.

_____. "Philharmonic Pay Offer Rejected by Musicians." *The New York Times,* September 30, 1982.

_____. "State Board Will Study Dispute at City Opera." *The New York Times,* August 16, 1983.

_____. "Tentative Accord Reached at Met; Hope is Voiced for Starting Season." *The New York Times,* October 26, 1980.

_____. "2 Sides in Opera Strike Reveal Their Positions." *The New York Times,* August 12, 1983.

Roddy, Joseph. "A School of Note Scores Big Back Home in Indiana." *Smithsonian,* January 1986.

Rosenbaum, Samuel R. "Recording Industries' Music Performance Trust Funds." *International Musician,* June 1969.

Roth, Morry. "Chi Tooter's Racial Discord; Negro Local 208 Won't Integrate." *Variety,* July 31, 1963.

_____. "Petrillo's End as Chi Tooters' Prexy Stuns Victors as Much Losers." *Variety,* December 12, 1962.

Rothstein, Edward. "City Opera, the Strike Behind It, Warms Up for Sept. 21 Opening." *The New York Times,* September 12, 1983.

_____. "'Friends' Help Baltimore Symphony." *The New York Times,* January 14, 1982.

_____. "Philharmonic Musicians Complain." *The New York Times,* June 30, 1983.

Russcol, Herbert. "Can the Negro Overcome the Classical Music Establishment." *High Fidelity,* August 1968.

Schipper, Henry. "AFM Boots Out Fuentealba." *Variety,* June 24, 1987.

_____. "AFM Local Leaders Plan Attempt to Oust Fuentealba at Union Meet." *Variety,* June 10, 1987.

_____. "AFM Reaches an Unpopular Accord with the Diskeries." *Variety,* January 14, 1987.

_____. "Tuners Want More Democracy." *Daily Variety,* April 28, 1987.

Schonberg, Harold C. "Chowder Parties, Fairs, Funerals." *The New York Times,* May 1, 1966.

_____. "Musicians' Disabilities Provoke Medical Study." *The New York Times*, August 27, 1983.

_____. "The Symphony Orchestra Has Refused to Die." *The New York Times*, May 7, 1978.

Schuller, Gunther. "The Trouble with Orchestras." *Symphony News*, December 1979.

Scott, Mel. "Federal/State Partnership in the Arts." *Public Administration Review*, July/August 1970.

Seitz, Peter. "Orchestra Planners and Players: Harmony or Dissonance?" *Symphony Magazine*, December 1981.

Seligman, Daniel. "Who Needs Unions?" *Fortune*, July 12, 1982.

Serrin, William J. "Class Distinctions Add to Discord Complicating Met Labor Problem." *The New York Times*, October 15, 1980.

_____. "For Harry Bridges, the Heart of Unionism Still Lies with the Rank and File." *The New York Times*, December 1, 1985.

_____. "Labor Conference Focuses on Future." *The New York Times*, September 22, 1985.

_____. "Rebel Unionist: Anthony Mazzocchi." *The New York Times*, May 15, 1983.

_____. "Strike at City Opera Points Up Musicians' Reliance on Union." *The New York Times*, July 12, 1983.

_____. "The Union Movement Looks in the Mirror." *The New York Times*, February 24, 1985.

_____. "U.S. Cites Continued Drop in Union Membership." *The New York Times*, February 8, 1985.

Shaw, Henry. "ICSOM: An Investment to Protect." *Senza Sordino*, April 1977.

_____. "The Musician at 65—Will Fairness Prevail?" *Senza Sordino,* June 1978.

_____. "The Strike Fund." *Senza Sordino,* October 1982.

_____. "Turbulence in Portland." *Senza Sordino,* October 1980.

Sheler, Jeffrey L. "Unions Flex Muscles in Professional Sports." *U.S. News and World Report,* July 20, 1981.

Shepard, Richard F. "Ford Foundation Makes Big Gift to Music." *The New York Times,* July 7, 1966.

_____. "A Lady Beats the Drums." *The New York Times,* May 2, 1965.

Sherman, Robert. "An Orchestra that Mellows with Age." *The New York Times,* November 26, 1976.

Sills, Beverly. "DAT's Menace for U.S. Music." *Cincinnati Enquirer,* July 1, 1987.

Starr, Susan. "The Prejudice against Women." *Music Journal,* March 1974.

Steeper, William P. "Civil Rights in the American Federation of Musicians." *International Musician,* December 1954.

Steif, Bill. "Calif. Atty. General's Merger Order to White & Negro Frisco AFM Locals; 1st Major Ukase under State's FEP." *Variety,* November 4, 1959.

_____. "Calif. Atty. Gen.'s 'Reasonable Time' Stance on White–Negro AFM Merger." *Variety,* December 2, 1959.

Stetson, Damon. "Glasel Puts Down Trumpet, Raises Union Baton." *The New York Times,* January 4, 1983.

_____. "Musicians Vote Out Old Leaders." *The New York Times,* December 9, 1982.

Sullivan, Ronald. "City Opera Suspends Schedule Indefinitely in Musicians' Dispute." *The New York Times,* October 1, 1979.

Summers, Clyde W. "Admission Policies of Labor Unions." *The Quarterly Journal of Economics,* November 1946.

Takiff, Jonathan. "Music Business Hits Troubled Times." *Cincinnati Enquirer,* August 23, 1982.

Taubman, Howard. "An Even Break: Negro Instrumentalists Ask for Chance to Earn Way into Major Ensembles." *The New York Times,* April 22, 1956.

—————. "For Orchestras, a Ray of Hope." *The New York Times,* March 11, 1970.

—————. "Petrillo Quietly Battles Musicians' Segregation." *The New York Times,* April 23, 1966.

Terry, Ken. "AFM Adopts Work Levy of 1%; Fuentealba Re-Elected President." *Variety,* June 25, 1980.

Thomas, Fred W. "A Seat in a Symphony Orchestra." *Symphony News,* April 1972.

Turner, Wallace. "Hilton Pact Aids Suspect Union Fund." *The New York Times,* May 5, 1984.

Tusher, Will. "ITAA Confab to Lay Battle Plans against AFM-Sponsored Proposal." *Variety,* February 27, 1985.

Velie, Lester. "The Union that Fights Its Workers." *Readers' Digest,* December 1956.

Waleson, Heidi. "Female Quartets Not Just Sister Acts." *Wall Street Journal,* April 1, 1987.

Walsh, Michael. "Let's Do the Time Warp Again." *Time,* January 11, 1988.

Warren, Virginia. "They Call the Tune for Society's Dancing Feet." *The New York Times,* September 18, 1966.

Webster, Daniel. "Barriers Crumble in Orchestra World." *Philadelphia Inquirer,* November 23, 1969.

Weinstein, Stanley. "The 'Minority' Musician." *Senza Sordino,* October 1978.

Westby, David L. "The Career Experience of the Symphony Musician." *American String Teacher,* November/December 1960.

Wigler, Stephen. "Fate Deals Margaret Hillis Successful Hand as Conductor." *Cincinnati Enquirer,* December 27, 1985.

Willard, Bill. "Dissidents Waging Drive to Oust AFM Prexy Fuentealba in June." *Variety,* April 23, 1980.

Wilson, John S. "Artie Shaw's Band Is Appearing at Blue Note." *The New York Times,* August 16, 1985.

_____. "Benny Goodman, King of Swing is Dead." *The New York Times,* June 14, 1986.

_____. "Joyce Brown, Conductor of the Broadway Hit, 'Purlie.'" *International Musician,* December 1970.

_____. "The Pop Life." *The New York Times,* March 5, 1986.

_____. "Women in Jazz, Past and Present." *The New York Times,* June 11, 1978.

Windham, Daniel J. "Music Assistance Fund Orchestral Fellowship Update." *Senza Sordino,* December 1983.

_____. "Music Assistance Fund Orchestral Fellowship Update." *Senza Sordino,* February 1985.

_____. "Music Assistance Fund Update." *Senza Sordino,* December 1985.

Winkler, Karen J. "Precipitous Decline of American Unions Fuels

Growing Interest Among Scholars." *The Chronicle of Higher Education,* November 12, 1986.

Wright, Irene. "Music for Mayhem and Murder." *Cincinnati Enquirer,* April 10, 1986.

Young, Steve and Howard Garniss. "Are Music Schools Preparing Performers for Real Life?" *Allegro,* May 1988.

Zaslow, Jeffrey. "'Ghost' Swing Bands Follow the Leader Without the Leader." *Wall Street Journal,* May 27, 1986.

Zheutlin, Carol P. "Interview: Catherine Comet." *Overture, The Magazine of the Baltimore Symphony,* March 15–April 14, 1984.

Zukerman, Eugenia. "Why More Women Aren't Superstars in Music." *The New York Times,* February 22, 1981.

Index

anti-Petrillo law *see* Lea Act
Armco Band   174
Armenra, Dolly Jones   217
Armstrong, Lil Hardin   217
Armstrong, Louis   115
arrangers (orchestrators)   89, 140, 197
Arts and Humanities Bill   124, 125
arts councils   139
ASCAP   32, 238
Aschenbroedel Club   2, 3
Ashby Band   174
Associated Actors and Artistes of America   34, 133
Association for Classical Music   181
auditions   21, 36, 104, 117, 118, 120, 121, 175, 177, 183, 184, 185,
     201, 222
Austin, Mary   41
automation   23, 24, 27, 32, 40, 41, 42, 55, 56, 58, 59, 126, 127,
     140, 150, 178, 193, 194, 195, 197, 199, 201, 202, 203, 222, 223,
     230, 231, 232, 233, 238, 240
Ax, Emanual   178

Balliett, Whitney   115
Baltimore Symphony   118, 215
bandleader   *see* conductor
bands   *see* big bands; brass bands; concert bands; dance bands;
     foreign bands; house bands; industrial bands; military
     bands; municipal bands; school bands; show bands; society
     bands
bargaining   *see* negotiations
Barnum, P.T.   173
Basie, Count   115, 176
bassoon (bassoonist)   1, 201, 215, 223
Batdorf Automatic Orchestras   231
Bayne, William   173
bebop   54
Bechet, Sidney   165
Beecham, Sir Thomas   215
Beissenherz, C.F.   8
Belkin, Boris   178
Benson, H.W.   107